SACRED EARTH RISING WITHIN

*The Making
of a Spiritual Ecologist in
a Creative Cosmos*

K. LAUREN DE BOER

Praise

The trauma as well as the joy and wonder of the author's life journey pour open-heartedly onto the pages of this beautifully-written new book. In prose and in poetry, Lauren weaves a compelling tapestry of his personal journey with that of our society's, keeping readers immersed throughout in both the individual (the microcosm) and the collective (the macrocosm) story. *Sacred Earth Rising Within* is the expanded perspective we sorely need in our times.

> — **Betty-Ann Kissilove**, educator and author of
> *Great Ball of Fire: A Poetic Telling of the Universe Story*

This book is filled with heartbreak and with longing for a world in which we know ourselves as part of a sentient Earth and Universe, and in which healing and meaning can be found in the very nature of existence. I loved this book, for its gorgeous language, landscape descriptions, and poetry—and above all for its potent and timely message: to heal on both a personal and planetary level, we must reclaim our place in the rousing chorus of life.

> — **Mary Reynolds Thompson**, author of *Reclaiming*
> *the Wild Soul* and *The Way of the Wild Soul Woman*

This is a fabulous book, and a creative and original development of the new cosmology. The focus on trauma puts it at the very center of the spiritual concerns of our contemporary society. This book will travel into worlds in which previous works of cosmology have never been seen. The power of the narrative and the force of its reflections on the deep issues kept me going right through from the first to the last page.

It is loaded with quotable passages; they pile up powerfully in so many places. I have to include one to represent a hundred others: "This is the power of a life-enhancing cosmology. It restores a sense of the sacred that has been tragically banished in Western culture due to its roots in the secular imagination. It begins to cut through the chronic emptiness and speaks to our human need for meaning and purpose. It evokes deeper patterns that connect us to the universe."

Sacred Earth Rising Within: The Making of a Spiritual Ecologist in a Creative Cosmos and my own book, *Cosmogenesis: An Unveiling of the Expanding Universe,* are the first two examples of auto-cosmology at this time.

My prediction is that one day there will be thousands, tens of thousands, of such works, and that they will refer back to these two books as the start of the whole adventure. Lauren has given birth to a work that will heal so many struggling souls. A beautiful achievement!

— **Brian Thomas Swimme**, evolutionary philosopher and author of
Cosmogenesis, The Universe Story, Hidden Heart of the Cosmos, and
The Journey of the Universe (also an award-winning documentary),
and other books.

In *Sacred Earth Rising Within* Lauren weaves memoir with a lifelong growing awareness of the relationship between inner life and life as an integral part of Earth and Cosmos.

This is a book that is written with texture and passion. The texture threads together a life of exploring the author's inner and outer world—personal grief and grief for the Earth. The passion is for healing self and self-in-relationship to Earth's beauty and sustainability—all through the lens of cosmogenesis and humanity's role as integral to life. It is an absolutely wonderful read with its poetic language and deep insights.

— **Philip Snow Gang**, dean of The Institute for
Educational Studies (TIES) and author of *Reinventing Education*
and *Education for Right-Action and Love.*

As an elder with decades of teaching experience, I was deeply moved by this candid and thoughtful spiritual memoir. Lauren de Boer's journey resonates with my own roots in the Midwest and respect for the natural world. His honest portrayal of overcoming personal trauma and transitioning from a fall/redemption religious tradition to a creation-centered spirituality grounded in the sacred Earth is vibrant, meaningful, and well-crafted.

This book is a valuable resource for the ongoing creation spirituality movement, highlighting the healing power of creativity, art, and meditation. I am honored that my teachings have been woven so beautifully into Lauren's worldview. I highly recommend this book as a powerful testament to the transformative potential of a life enhancing cosmology.

— **Matthew Fox**, spiritual theologian, and author of 37 books,
among them *Original Blessing, The Coming of the Cosmic Christ,* A
*Spirituality Named Compassion, The Reinvention of Work, The Hidden
Spirituality of Men, Christian Mystics* and *The Pope's War.*

De Boer, drawing on his own life experience, has written an American odyssey. A child of the American Midwest, (Iowa), he discovers that his Dutch ancestor was named Boer, meaning "farmer." In an attempt to reconnect to the land, he reclaims his ancestral name of de Boer (Lauren the Farmer). His resonance with the land is evident throughout as he recounts in detail the names of plants, animals, geographies, and histories of the natures he inhabits throughout his life.

So too, as a preacher's kid, Lauren tells the story of his Calvinist upbringing. This story of special election and protection was shattered by the abduction and rape of his nine-year-old sister when he was seven (the full details of which he would not learn until forty years later). Here begins his lifelong quest to heal from trauma—his family's trauma, the trauma of American history, and the trauma of the separation of humans and nature, especially in Western modernity.

As Odysseus did, de Boer wanders through many landscapes, often blocked from returning home, only to find his home and his wholeness in the creative, evolutionary cosmos through the New Story of the Universe as told by Teilhard de Chardin, Thomas Berry, Brian Thomas Swimme, and others. His story, as told in *Sacred Earth Rising Within,* is the great journey of our time.

— **Herman Greene**, President, Center for Ecozoic Studies;
Thomas Berry Scholar-in-Residence, Earth Law Center.

What a wonderful book Lauren de Boer has gifted us with! *Sacred Earth Rising Within* is so beautifully and soulfully written, both poetic and profound. The interweaving of personal trauma and tragedy and the universal healing available to us in our relationship with Nature is deeply moving. As we find ourselves confronted with more and more challenging times on our home planet, it's increasingly important for many of us—especially those favoring spirituality over traditional religious paths—to find a deep, Earth-embedded spirituality to inspire and support us going forward.

Lauren de Boer, former editor of the pioneering *EarthLight Magazine,* is the guide we need. Here's a small taste of the powerfully-healing insights the author shares with us: "the more I am 'out in nature,' the more I realize that I'm not just in nature. I am nature. I am the biosphere evolving through me and within me. To spend any length of time 'out there,' is to awaken to the reality that we are nature evolving. My inner life is every bit the 'natural world' as the wilderness I trek. That is a deeply healing realization."

Highly recommended!

— **Linda Buzzell**, LMFT, co-editor, *Ecotherapy: Healing with Nature in Mind*; Admin, "Ecopsychology" Facebook group; Adjunct Faculty, Pacifica Graduate Institute, Santa Barbara, California

Lauren de Boer's new book, *Sacred Earth Rising Within,* is a sacred text. It is part of an emerging genre that arises out of the search for spiritual meaning and a solution for the ecological destruction of the planet. It draws from the individual's sensorium and perception of nature, individual purpose, and the revealing of greater meaning. This book is a teaching of how individual trauma and hardship can be transformed into purpose through a renewal of our relationship with nature. It is also a compelling narrative of how the cosmos is alive within us. This is where Lauren's vision meets the new genre of auto-cosmology.

Lauren reminds us of the lost connection. He inspires us to see nature with direct perception, to see what is actually here, and not through the eyes of constructs or rationalized intellectual obscurity. He reminds us of what we have lost and how we need to challenge ourselves to reconnect again.

Sacred Earth Rising Within has far reaching implications for a new way of life and the changing values of a culture that has lost its way. The author leaves us with the question of how we can recover from the violence inflicted on the Earth, especially through the healing of the violence that has been inflicted upon us. This book gives new meaning to the spiritual quest of becoming one with nature.

— **Lee Embrey**, PhD, author of *A Training Ground for Love*

K. Lauren de Boer
TerraVita Books
©2025

Cover design by Arjan van Woensel
Author photo by Robert Capra
Back cover text by Philip Gang

. . . . .

Library of Congress Cataloging-in-Publication Data

Names: de Boer, K. Lauren, author

Title: Sacred Earth Rising Within: the Making of a Spiritual
Ecologist in a Creative Cosmos

Description: First edition
Walnut Creek, Calif.: TerraVita Media, 2025

Identifiers:
LCCN 2025910230
ISBN 979-8-9926118-0-9 (paperback)
ISBN 979-8-9926118-1-6 (e-book)

Subjects: Nature | Cosmology | Memoir | Philosophy

. . . . .

terravitamedia.com

To my dear sister, Kristin,
whose brave heart and bright soul
live within me as surely as stardust.

Previously Published Chapters and Poems

Chapters

"The Land Between Two Rivers," in *Courting the Wild: Love Affairs with the Land*, edited by Jamie K. Reaser and Susan Chernak McElroy Hireath Press, 2008.

"Prairie Heart," in *Parabola Magazine*, Winter 2024-25.

"At Home in the Breath," in *Parabola Magazine*, Spring 2004.

"Practicing the Art of Wonder through Radical Presence," in *Kosmos Quarterly*, July 2021.

"The Healing of a Beautiful World," in *Eco-therapy: Healing with Nature in Mind*, Sierra Club Books, 2009 (original title "Healing and the Great Work").

"Kinglet at the Door," in *What Does God Look Like in an Expanding Universe*, Imago Books, 2006.

"The Mine and the Rainbow," in *Parabola Magazine*, Winter 2023-24..

"The Great Enamorment," an excerpt of which was published under the title "A Magnificent Pedigree" in *Parabola Magazine*, Summer 2022.

"Cosmic Citizen," in *Minding Nature Journal*, Spring 2020, Vol.13, No.2 under the title "Toward a New Cultural Reverie: A Cosmological Basis for the Ecological Citizen."

Poems

"Midwest Reverie" in *Iodine Poetry Journal*, Spring/Summer 2014.

"A Night on the Des Moines River," "How Stories Appear," "Lady of the Grotto," and "The Small Song," in *Where it Comes From: 95 Poems*, K. Lauren de Boer, 2008.

"On the Seam" in *Pudding Magazine*, 2019.

"Awakening" and "My Seal of Memory" in *Volutions: Savant Poetry Anthology*, 2014.

"Earth Says," in *Reclaiming the Wild Soul*, Mary Reynolds Thompson.

"The Good Story," in *Green Fuse*, 1996.

"Discernment," in *EarthShine Poetry Journal*, 2020.

Contents

Foreword

It was fun reading this candid and thoughtful spiritual autobiography created by a former student of mine. As an elder, now 83 years old, with about 50 years of teaching under my belt, I was moved to see how parts of Lauren's story and mine overlap and also how he has taken my work on creation spirituality as well as my educational efforts and woven them into his worldview.

The overlapping parts of our journeys include growing up in the Midwest—he in Indiana and Michigan and Iowa—myself in Wisconsin and Iowa and also summers in Michigan visiting my sisters when they attended a summer camp there run by a great aunt who lived in Chicago. Also, there seems to be an interesting overlap when Lauren mentions a summer destination for his family at the Warren Dunes in southern Michigan. This struck a note for me because that very park seems to have been the place I contracted polio when I was 12 years old and was returning home from a visit with my family with our relatives in Pennsylvania (my mother's side of the family). Lauren does an excellent job of describing the prairie landscape, lakes and forests, plants, animals, fish, insects, and so much of nature and creation that permeated my own childhood summers and family outings in the Midwest.

Of course there were many differences in our growing up as well. He was churched in a conservative Protestant tradition and with his father was a pastor; myself in a Roman Catholic tradition with Dominicans as our parish priests. But we both clearly had nature and Midwest seasons and landscapes and excursions in common. He and his family underwent the trauma of his sister's kidnapping, an event that deeply impacted their story. I had no experience like that. (I did have polio which had an impact on my story but nothing so violent and negative.) And we both had experiences in France that marked our journeys and a deep respect for Henry Adam's study on *Mont-Saint-Michel and Chartres*.

Both of us were ripe for a new science-based creation story when it came along, primarily as articulated by evolutionary philosopher Brian Thomas Swimme and cultural historian Thomas Berry. I can see where my naming of the fall/redemption religion in contrast to the creation spirituality tradition hit home for Lauren, the son of a Calvinist preacher. And I can see where art as meditation hit home as a proper spiritual practice for him since his interest in poetry, writing, music, and more were foundational for his healing and his developing a spiritual path. I admired the journal *EarthLight* he edited for many years. *EarthLight* carried on much in the same vein as our *Creation Spirituality* magazine which we let go in order to pursue a reinvention of Western Liturgy by way of elements of the rave movement.

Beyond these points of overlap in our journeys, I found *Sacred Earth Rising Within* to be an honest and substantive telling of an inspiring spiritual journey. Coming out of woundedness and trauma, the journey is marked by an abiding love of nature in spite of the author's fall/redemption religious upbringing. It culminates in the eventual embrace of a practice of spiritual ecology that compellingly integrates a life-enhancing cosmology. The importance of creativity as a spiritual practice is highlighted, along with a cosmology and cosmogenesis that completes the healing of a family trauma and tragedy. All of this created within the author an ongoing compassion and caring for Earth and her creatures, humans included. This is the creative cosmos at work within and around all of us.

This book is a well-written and meaningful spiritual auto-biography for our times. It powerfully integrates the four paths of creation spirituality: The *Via Positiva* experience of growing up in nature in the Midwest is highlighted along with the emerging new cosmology; the *Via Negativa* of a family tragedy and of our radical severance from the natural world; the healing of the *Via Creativa* and art as meditation all play a major role; and finally, the gifts of service and healing and compassion called the *Via Transformativa* (and this book is an example of that). These paths all merge wonderfully in this book.

Sacred Earth Rising Within constitutes a valuable resource for the ongoing movement of recovering the creation spirituality lineage. It shares one man's journey in an honorable and well-crafted story that will prove to be valuable to many wisdom seekers in our challenging times. I highly recommend it. As one of his teachers along the way, I am honored that the author has taken my teachings to heart and implemented it in so vibrant a story.

—**Matthew Fox**

Author's note

The structure of this book is a weaving of two different styles of writing—personal narrative and more lyrical "landscape interludes." They are meant to convey two aspects of human experience in a kind of dialogue that honors both. The more discursive side of our nature dances with a sensuous connection with nature and our inner landscape; the intelligences of head and heart intertwine. More is said in the Introduction.

Introduction

When I was eleven years old, my father Thomas, a Christian Reformed minister, left the Church. He wouldn't step foot inside another church for over four decades. While he was a figure of authority and leadership in the church community when I was a boy, he was also a humble and sensitive man. That side of him could express itself as warmth, a quite strength, and a kind of earthy wisdom. I both looked up to him and was occasionally the recipient of that warmth. But he was also a fatherless man, a situation that made him alternately distant as a father in his own right, or driven by a dark, unpredictable anger. I say fatherless because my grandfather had been mostly absent from his family due to work on the road as a businessman and some carousing tendencies when he was closer to home. He attempted to compensate for these lapses by showering my father, his two siblings, and my grandmother with material gifts. And then he died suddenly and young, at age 46, when my own father was just coming into manhood.

The events that led up to my father's break with the Church would come to define the trajectory of my family member's lives for decades to come, even as our awareness of its impact remained mostly dimmed by denial and avoidance. Foremost among those events was the kidnapping of my sister, Kristin, at age nine. My family was totally unprepared for this traumatic event and for the subsequent break with the religious community that had given us a center of gravity, a way of understanding the world that had made us feel special and protected. The kidnapping, along with our feelings about it, went mostly unspoken for over thirty years. The event took place in a time when the culture and its mental health professionals were ill-equipped to provide the tools needed to face such a traumatic occurrence. We each developed our individual coping strategies for dealing with the trauma we felt inside. For me, the break with the religious community set me on an early spiritual search that would eventuate in healing, but was marked by rebellion and other compensating behaviors for many years.

Writing this book became something of a balancing act. It began simply enough as an attempt to tell the story of how this early traumatic event in my family caused a rupture that set me on a transformative path toward a new spiritual integration. As I began to tell some of the more difficult emotional aspects of this story, another part of me kept trying to assert itself. My head-centered, rational side wanted to erect a wall of protection. And so the balancing act became a dialogue between the intelligence of my head and that of my heart; between the power of ideas and the poetic sensuousness of experience; between feeling and thought, between the intuitive and rational sides of my nature.

The masculine and feminine principles within me, archetypal energies found within all of us, both wanted to be heard. There is the masculine capacity to discern, to create and take action, and the feminine capacity to be still, to receive, to love, to intuit, and surrender to the sacred essence of nature. They each have their piece of the story. I found that to properly tell this story, I could neither reject nor segregate these two aspects of myself. I had no choice but to hold the tension between them and accept the paradoxes I found there. Once I did, a dynamic equilibrium and a kind of resolution began to manifest. Rather than a dualism, a synergistic relationship emerged.

Listening to the sacred intelligence of the body has become a lost art for many of us in our head-centered Western culture. But finding ways back to that more intuitive way of knowing is to make our way back to a sense of belonging. I see body awareness, which is our intuitive nature, as an integral part of the practice of spiritual ecology. This is our way through to transformation, a new, and yet very old way of being human that will form the basis for a new faith in the human.

When I use the phrase "spiritual ecology," I often think of the word spiritual as describing the animating dynamic we feel in the web of relationships that is ecology. It has to do with our capacity to feel the sensuousness of nature as joy, wonder, terror, exhilaration. The body is the locus of this dynamic. There are two stories in this book where I describe running with another animal in a state of self-abandonment and play. One is with a harbor seal on a beach on the Pacific Ocean and the other with a Rottweiler dog in a cemetery in my home state of Iowa. They correspond to two states within me, one wild, the other partly domesticated. The illusion of duality was dissolved, if only for a brief time, in a process of forgetting that helped me remember something beyond myself. They were both learning as well as healing experiences. They helped bridge a divide. One divide was kinetic, a severance of thought from the body; the other was existential, a mistaken belief that we are separate from the other-than-human world. Connection to the other in both of these experiences was a reconnection to myself, a return to heart-centered knowledge, an undervalued gift of play that energizes the imagination. Imagination and play are two sides of the same coin. They are activated simultaneously in a moment of communion. And communion is the energy needed not only to heal trauma but to create the future.

Spiritual ecology is at its essence non-dual consciousness, a bodily awareness of how integral we are with the web of life. And so, a practice of spiritual ecology has become, for me, a path of healing from trauma. This is true of personal trauma, which I describe in the early chapters, but cultural trauma as well, which unfolds in later chapters. That cultural trauma has its origins in what Thomas Berry called a "radical discontinuity" between the human and the other-than-human. This is "radical" in the sense of "having roots" (from the Latin *radicalis*), a severance so traumatic that we have nearly destroyed the most beautiful place in the universe as we currently know it, our garden planet. Because of this severance, our culture has suppressed our inborn ability to attune to the field of consciousness that we share with all life on Earth. Something is deeply wrong at the heart of my country. Our public education system has suppressed spirit. Our major religions have abandoned their capacity to induce awe and embrace the profound. Our political system has lost touch with what it means to be truly human, and to act humanely toward each other. In other words, our capacity for love and connection is atrophied.

This is a good part of what is preventing our recovery from collective trauma. The despair underlying that trauma in the U.S. alone is everywhere evident. As I complete this book, mass shootings are an almost daily reality. The number of high schoolers contemplating suicide is nearing 20%, and nearly 10% of those have made an attempt. Addiction is rampant; the number of Americans in 2020 with Substance Use Disorder was forty million, up from twenty million in 2018. Twenty-nine percent of U.S. adults have been diagnosed with depression in their lifetime; thirty-one percent suffer from anxiety disorder. Political polarization is worse than any time in the nation's history, and we are experiencing an epidemic of loneliness and alienation. Long-standing antagonisms are surging up into war in the Middle East, Ukraine, Sudan, Syria, and elsewhere.

Another face of this alienation is the lack of a life-giving, cultural cosmology adequate to the challenges of our time, from species extinction and climate change to an increasingly toxic world and an ocean full of plastic. In a very real sense, the personal trauma experienced by my family was a result of similar feelings of alienation and loss of belonging to a community. My sister's kidnapper suffered from this greater sense of alienation in our culture as well, whether or not he was ever aware of it. And whatever the failings of the religious community of which we were a part, the loss of that community was still a traumatic separation for my family.

It doesn't have to be this way. Even the most seemingly solitary life is deeply communal. I've taken great solace and found healing power in solitude throughout the years, especially in the natural world. But I've never felt alone in nature. Solitude attuned me to my inner life, and the more strongly I felt that attunement, the greater was my sense of the sacred within all of nature. I've always been in non-verbal dialogue with the plants, animals, and landscapes that have given me a sense of belonging. This was part of my healing from the rupture of community. In describing my own personal trauma and my family's, as well as our attempts at healing, including the missteps, I am telling the story as well of our larger cultural rupture and the need for healing. The Earth speaks to all of us in healing language if we can only listen.

As Canadian physician and trauma researcher Gabor Mate explains, "Trauma is not the bad things that happen to you, but what happens inside of you as a result. Trauma is the psychic wound that we sustain. And healing is a reconnection with the authentic self." I found that this is true on both a personal and a societal level. The psychic wound we have sustained in our severance from nature can be healed by a connection to our larger ecological Self. I believe that the same spiritual transformation that happened on an individual level with me can be recapitulated on the collective level. But we need to generate a cosmology, a story of our origins and existence that is up to the task of that transformation.

My pathway to healing has been fourfold, all having to do with connection: a sacred connection to nature and to the body; connection to a new story that has given me a sense of purpose; the cultivation of creativity in my life that has helped me process emotional and psychological aspects of trauma and to feel the radiance underlying everything; and connection to various communities over the years that have a positive commitment to the future. This book explores each of these connections in various ways.

There are many pathways toward healing from trauma. Spiritual ecology has been a big part of mine, a road I still travel imperfectly, but with heartfilled intent.

ψ

This book interweaves personal narrative and what I call "landscape interludes." The interludes are lyrical explorations of the outer land-scapes of my life, often in dialogue with my inner landscape. These landscapes correspond, either directly or indirectly, with the events and time periods of my life, as well as the spiritual growth depicted in the regular chapters. They progress from earlier accounts through the eyes of a young boy, growing in complexity throughout the book to reflect the maturation into adolescence, young manhood, and elderhood. The whole book complexifies in this way, mirroring a human life or the universe complexifying, as they unfold. In addition, some chapters end with a short poem I've written on a similar theme. The book ends with a Postlude, an original piece of mythology, a "Cosmic Fable," that began in a dream as I was writing the book.

As part of my reckoning with the past, I share the story of Kristin's kidnapping, a trauma that sent deep emotional and spiritual tendrils into my own life. Kristin's story and her ongoing journey of healing is part of my story; her personal trauma was the family's trauma, her healing my healing and that of my other family members; and our healing is part of society's healing from the rape and plunder of the Earth. But Kristin's story is also unique, not wholly my own story, and only she can fully tell it. By interviewing her and breaking the silence between us, I have attempted to relate her part of my story more authentically.

In telling this story, I present a number of teachers I have encoun-tered along my path. Each gave me food for the journey, nourished me in unique ways, and challenged me to forge my own identity. Their commonality is a dedication to something larger than the small self.

I was guided back to a connection with the web of Life, but also to a cosmology, a way of making sense of the universe that returned me to a feeling of belonging. The right story, a functional cosmology, makes us feel guided and accepted in a larger community. It prevents loneliness, makes us feel a part of the grand theater of the universe.

A good part of my own story involved secrets and silence. When the silence was broken and my family began to see the truth, the wheels of healing began slowly turning. And they are still turning. For too long now, we humans in Western society have engaged in a deadly silence about what is destroying our world. Breaking the silence is the first step out of denial. There have been prophetic voices crying in the wilderness, people out there who have been doing this work of giving voice to the trauma and attempting to heal the rupture. Now it must become central to our path forward as a species. It's an attempt to deal with reality as it is. We can't be afraid of the truth. This is the ascendent archetype of the spiritual ecologist in our time.

Essentially, this book is a chronicle of my lifelong attempt to rekindle and sustain a religious mind. Not religion in the sense of dogma, creed, and God, but in the sense of a religious devotion to life, the cultivation of wonder and reverence, a renewed sense of the sacred, and an embrace of mystery and magnificence in the universe. As such, it is my credo, an affirmation of life and faith. It is something of a hybrid of the rational and the sensual, but mostly this is a book that tells a story that is both highly personal and universal. Or, perhaps it is universal precisely because it is deeply personal. As Teilhard de Chardin wrote in *The Human Phenomenon*: "Are we not experiencing at each instant a universe whose immensity is being gathered up more and more simply within each one of us through the interplay of our sense and our reason?"[1] Teilhard saw personalization in the universe as the internal deepening of consciousness on itself. As human beings, we are an embodiment of that deepening of consciousness in the universe. The more deeply personal we become, the greater our unity with a universe that is always seeking greater depth and complexity.

Finally, this book is not strictly speaking an autobiography in that it doesn't attempt to chronicle all of the events, or even the key events, of a life. There are so many people, landscapes, and events I couldn't include, even if they have been very dear to me. It is instead a kind of spiritual memoir, one narrative strand from the life of one person whose story is both unique and universal. Because it integrates the personal with the cosmological, the narrative and the interludes are an example of Teilhard's interplay of "our sense and our reason" throughout. Brian Thomas Swimme, an advance reader of the manuscript, affirmed that this book falls into the emerging genre, along with his own book, *Cosmogenesis*, that he has identified as "auto-cosmology."

This book is at the very least descriptive of what it means to be human, perhaps a new way of being human in a time of both great destruction and great opportunity. It's a narrative of how a life-giving cosmology can heal and of how the powers and graces of the natural world can sustain cultural and spiritual wholeness. It isn't inevitable, but rather a choice. The better we bring the gifts of science into dialogue with spirit into a meaningful cultural cosmology for our time and the future, the better informed our choices will be.

The title of one of this book's landscape interludes, "The Mine and the Rainbow," came to me as a gift. In fact (although I decided against it), I considered using it as the book's title because it is such an apt image for trauma and recovery. It's not merely a poetic image. It is based on an experience my wife, Diana, and I had in southeastern Arizona some years ago. Our visit there to see hummingbirds also took us to the remains of an open pit copper mine in Bisbee, Arizona. It was during monsoon season, and after getting caught in a fierce storm, we experienced a vivid rainbow arcing over the town and the mine. (The landscape interlude recounts this experience.)

The open pit mine is emblematic of the wounds of trauma, wounds that we are inflicting on the Earth and on each other. And it is also quite literally a wound in the Earth's crust. By extension, it is emblematic of the self-inflicted wound that we too, as Earth's children, have sustained. It is a drawdown and exploitation of the planet's gifts, or in industrial parlance, of "natural resources." But a wound, as many have pointed out, can also contain within it a blessing. The rainbow, long a symbol of promise, is the blessing shining from the wound.

The rainbow is also an image, for me, of the new story of the universe. You could also call that story a life-enhancing cosmology. It is a unifier. It spans space in the way that the universe spans deep time. It includes the entire color spectrum of life. It is a bridge between ancient wisdom and a newly emerging consciousness. It is an image of promise and of a new covenant between the human and the Earth. Contemplating the rainbow calls us beyond dualistic thinking. It also represents the goddess Sophia, the connecting power of the feminine principle, and the embracing curvature of the universe.

Inspired by the rainbow's beauty, we can continue the work of healing ourselves and our world. It's a humbling and harrowing privilege to be alive in our time, when we are presented with the greatest work ever: creating what Thomas Berry called mutually-enhancing relations with all life.

SECTION I
Childhood

Chapter 1

The Dunes

If you wanted to locate my family on any given Tuesday throughout any summer during much of my boyhood, you would need look no further than Warren Dunes State Park on the southeastern tip of Lake Michigan. My family included my three siblings, all four of us appearing with assembly-line regularity into the world, almost exactly nineteen months apart. It was as if my mother, Beatrice, or "Beebee," as my father, Thomas, called her, insisted on a six-month breather in between births from the toll that it took on her body. First came Mark, then Kristin, then myself, and finally, Philip. This last birth prompted my grandfather, Peter, to quip, "So, my dear Beatrice, now I guess you've had your Phil."

We were at Warren Dunes on Tuesdays because that was my father's day off each week. Sundays he preached. Mondays he met with the church elders, and then on Tuesdays he was untethered. We piled into an old burgundy-colored Rambler station wagon in the pre-dawn hours and headed out for the fine sands of Lake Michigan. We would reach Warren Dunes while there was still a chill in the air and the sun was barely above the dunes. Like the ocean, you could see nothing but water all the way to the far horizon.

The first items out of the back of the station wagon were a large picnic basket, a cooler, a vinyl red-checkered table cloth, and the Coleman camp stove. My father would pump up the white gas tank, open the valve until you heard the telltale hollow hiss, and then light both burners with Diamond Blue farmer's matches. The main burner, which always burned more intensely than the secondary one, was for the main course of bacon and fried eggs that my father cooked.

"I have fond memories of the lake in those days," my mother reminisced years later. "It was the only time I got a break from cooking every day." In truth, Lake Michigan meant much more than relief from drudgery and routine. It had been my parents' playground as children and young adults. They grew up near its shores, fished off the piers with my grandpa at Ottawa Beach for perch, swam there each summer as kids, hung out with their high school friends, and watched sunsets with their first teenage crushes.

Soon the smell of coffee and bacon dominated the scene. In the chill dawn air, the laughter of gulls echoed across the sand. Under the branches of aspens, in view of the lake, breakfast never tasted so good. Even so, breakfast was never a drawn-out affair, because the lake, not far off, was already luring us away with its siren songs of fun and discovery.

It was just a short trek from the picnic table across the fine soft sand to the shoreline. On our bare feet, the sand still felt cool from the fingers of night air. As we approached the lake, the fine sand grew coarse and damp. There, adorning the water's edge, was a fine necklace of small pebbles for as far as you'd care to walk. And among the pebbles, exciting treasure. Successive waves washed fossils to the surface like panned gold, and they were easy pickings. If not, a probing toe or pass of the hand through the pebbles brought the prize to the surface. They took many forms—little cylinders with hollow cores, tiny discs with minute eyes in their centers, twisted stems like fusilli pasta, and tiny wagon-wheels. Sometimes, there was a larger flattish rock embedded with congregations of these spirals, fans, circles, stars, barrels, and other shapes. We called them fossilized fish bones, and we collected them all day long as we played on the lake. On the way home, my mother would always give each of us a Hershey's chocolate almond bar to eat in the back seat. Between bites, my siblings and I would take stock in the back seat of the Rambler, sometimes bartering different denominations of fossils, bits of driftwood, and other beach treasures back and forth. Years later, I would discover that what we thought were fish bones were actually three-hundred-million-year-old coral fossils from an ancient inland sea.

By mid-morning, the sun had warmed the sand. The wind picked up some, and the waves began to roll in greater swells. It was a relief to plunge into the frigid water. There was a trick to diving into the body of a wave just at the right moment between crest and crash. Then, underwater, a great stillness and quiet as I swam to the bottom. Crawling along the sandy bottom with my hands, I held my breath as long as I could before shooting back to the surface.

After what seemed like hours swimming, there was the creek to explore just down the way. It flowed summer-long into the lake, but not before creating a shallow lagoon where jet black polliwogs the size of garbanzo beans thrived and swam, their undulating black tails like dark scarves propelling them. Some were showing vestigial legs. On successive Tuesday outings to the lake, polliwogs gave way incrementally to thumbnail-sized frogs and, eventually, a visit to the lagoon yielded herds of them, fleeing before our feet like the parting waters of the Red Sea as we walked the edge of the lagoon.

Lunchtime meant a visit to the concession stand for a burger or a hot dog, but especially the rare treat of a popsicle, fudgesicle, ice cream sandwich, or a push-up made of orange sherbet and cream. These weren't part of our regular fare as kids, just a Warren Dunes treat, which made it that much more special. My parents let down their hair a little on these days, making an effort to indulge our childhood whims a little more than usual.

After lunch, there was the challenge of Tower Hill. For us young kids, this dune was a formidable mountain, the tallest in the park, and just a short walk inland. A long climb up its face of fine sand, now even warmer with the afternoon sun, brought us to a giant aspen tree at the peak, from which hung a massively long rope swing. We would grasp the rough rope, walk it back from the limb, and then, in a flirt with danger, sail out over the chasm of the dune's opposite flank and back to the safety of the soft sand. Then came the giddy race back down the face of the dune, running as fast as our legs could carry us to keep us from tumbling head over heels. These days lasted until the sun, an ever-deepening orange orb on the horizon, was swallowed into the great horizontal mirror of the lake. We usually stayed for the sunset and drove home in the dark.

We seldom visited the lake in winter. But there was a Tuesday in the super-cold winter of 1963 when we were lured to Warren Dunes with news that Lake Michigan had frozen over completely. A rare occurrence, the freeze created some wondrous effects on the lake.

"Dad, what *are* those?" I asked, shielding my eyes from the glare on the ice as we walked, cold wind whipping around our ears, toward the lake. Giant fantastic shapes hulked out on the lake at a distance.

"Pillars," he said.

I thought: *Lot's wife, turned to a pillar of salt for looking back at the city of Sodom.* Biblical imagery is never far off for a preacher's kid.

"Pillars of ice," he elaborated, "frozen waves."

I pictured the waves, ten to fifteen feet high, flash frozen as they attempted to crash onto the beach.

"But how?"

"I'm not sure, son. There must have been a storm one night, and below zero weather. The waves just piled up, stopped in their tracks because of the cold."

This was enough for my seven-year-old imagination to dream of these giant ice monsters for months, heaving up from the deeps of the lake. We walked onto the ice among the mounded waters, circling them, climbing on them, dumbfounded at this eerie winter landscape.

Lake Michigan, my father told us on the drive home, has had more shipwrecks than any other fresh body of water in the world.

"A lot of lives have been lost out on that lake," he said. "It's a dangerous place in a storm."

I shivered, thinking of the lake. Shipwrecks. Frozen wave-monsters towering around us. The crunch and squeak of snow under my winter galoshes. Never quite sure I wouldn't fall through a patch of thin ice. This was not the idyllic warm Tuesdays of summer on Lake Michigan. And out over the still white plain of the great lake, dark clouds had loomed as we left, gathering force with a cold wind from beyond the horizon that would soon sweep into and through our lives.

The Petrified

The summer sands of Warren Dunes
yielded bottle caps and nickels,
and at water's edge, fossilized coral and bones.

One winter the waves stood still and frozen
piled like high-society coiffeur,
as if Lake Michigan were some opera hall

for the lake's roll call of the drowned.
We climbed them like rock towers,
circled them, searching for clues to living,

reconstructing the fabled storms,
where the final breath of shipwrecks
blew icy ripples across the dunes.

Chapter 2
Life in the Bubble

Wednesday mornings found my father back in the harness of ministerial work. There were the sermon to write for the following Sunday, home visits to elderly congregation members and those in spiritual need, a wedding or a funeral now and then, and an occasional radio spot on the Back to God Hour. For me and my two brothers and sister, it was back to the playground of the undeveloped field that abutted the parsonage and the church. Combined with the summertime trips to Lake Michigan, the field would be the seedbed for my love of nature.

At the far end of the wild field was a largely untouched grove of oaks, elms, maples, and ironwoods. This was our ultimate destination on most days. The field also offered a towering giant we called the "sap" tree because it oozed big gobs of just such a substance from its trunk and branches. When you climbed it, the sap painted your bare arms and legs to which a solid coat of dark powdery dirt would stubbornly adhere. Further enticements were a large stretch of open meadow with milkweed, black-eyed susans, coneflowers, and a host of other plants; a small vineyard housing giant yellow garden spiders; and an abandoned apple orchard with prolific but green and wormy apples. The apples rarely ripened fully, and our parents warned us of the horrible stomach ache that would afflict us if we "ate of the trees." But the small green apples did make a ready stockpile of "ammunition" for our imaginary Cowboy & Indian and WWII war games. We dug "foxholes" in the prairie soil and lobbed them at each other, now and then painfully hitting the mark.

This undeveloped land, perhaps twenty acres, sat next to "the projects," a tract home area where immigrant families, mostly from Puerto Rico, had settled. We harvested wild blackberries that grew in profusion in the field, which we would peddle for $.25 a quart in the projects, a fortune for a kid at the time, which we jealously guarded in our sticky, purple-stained fingers. Several quarts would yield enough to buy gum, candy, pop, or, for me, mail-order packets of postal stamps from around the world available through ads found in the back pages of *National Geographic*. I spent hours affixing them into albums with stamp hinges. It was my main geography lesson as a kid. I was as entranced with the names of the countries as I was with their colorful stamps. Places with alluring names like Gabon, Burma, Persia, Toga, Helvetia, Magyar, Congo, Chad, and Malaysia. They all seemed to have more exotic stamps than my own country, whose two-color offerings I mostly found drab and unimaginative. I gazed at the colorful depictions of kings, queens, plants, animals, and landscapes from these fantastic locales, and imagined myself an adventurer and hero.

The field was our summertime haven, a stark contrast to the constricted world of Bethel Brethren Christian Day School. The school used corporal punishment to enforce its rigid rules, and some teachers seemed to take to this system with a certain zeal. There was Miss Stewart, the Spanish teacher, who always carried a four-foot long wooden stick with a black tapered tip. She used it to point to words on the blackboard, but its other purpose was more sinister, rapping students' knuckles or even skulls if they were out of line. Mr. Butt, also the principal, drilled holes in a flat paddle used to spank disobedient kids. The holes made the punishment sting more. My generally inattentive, and occasionally disruptive behavior in the classroom put me on the receiving end on more than one occasion.

By contrast, was the wild field. It invited us into a different world. Our imaginations were enriched by maple, oak, and ironwood trees;

by flickers, meadowlarks, and goldfinches; by daddy long-legs, flying grasshoppers, box turtles, and "squinnies" (a uniquely local name for ground squirrels); by milkweed, swallowtail butterflies, crickets, wild grapes; and a host of plants known only to us by our made-up names for them. There was a neighborhood pond where we caught two-inch-long bluegills. They were stunted in size because there were too many of them for the food supply and were so voracious that they would take a bare hook thrown in at the end of a bamboo pole and a short length of monofilament line. Judy Creek, which flowed through the grove and into the pond, was home to crawfish under its rocks, frogs along its contours, snapping turtles under the shelter of its banks, and chubs darting from one deep hole to the next.

Once, on a visit to a nearby abandoned rock quarry filled with water, I found the fossilized head of a crinoid, an ancient plant. The proprietor of a local rock shop, when I presented him with the fossil, showed me a box of elongated rock tubes and said, "These are the stems. You know, it walked on water, that plant." The only other being I knew at that point in my boyhood imagination who did that was Jesus. He may have been pulling my leg, but his interest was keen enough to offer me a good price for the fossil, which I declined.

We captured and kept painted turtles in a makeshift pond made from a kiddie pool into which we placed rocks and vegetation for them to sun and hide. To feed them, we scoured the undersides of logs and rocks for giant black crickets and chased down grasshoppers with brilliant red, yellow, and blue wings, who fled our pursuits, colorful bright sparks flaring out from their bodies. Larger grasshoppers we called locusts spit brown "tobacco juice" onto our fingers when they were caught. They were as long as our fingers and pale green. And there was a box turtle we kept in an enclosure made of cinder blocks to whom we fed wild berries; and who, when my brother Phil tried to hand-feed a raspberry, bit his finger, uncapping a boiling fountain of blood. We came out one

morning after a period of inattention to find that the turtle had bur-
rowed his way under the cinder blocks and out to freedom. Although
we kept a sharp eye out in the field for weeks afterward, the turtle had
made good his escape and was never seen again.

On Saturday evenings, we were scrubbed clean of the accumulated
bugs, dirt, and tree sap. We gathered around the television, hair still
wet from the bath, to watch The Lawrence Welk Show. It was one
of the very few concessions my parents made to TV watching. TV,
especially to my father, was a potential tool of Satan. An hour or two
a week of carefully curated content was the limit. Then, on Sunday
morning, we were paraded into the church sanctuary and presented to
the congregation as the first family of the church. We filed reluctantly
into the hard, shiny pews where we waited, my brothers' and my hair
gleaming with Suave hair gel, Kristin's curls pulled back with a plastic
barrette, for our father to ascend to the pulpit. My brother Phil and I,
known as "the little guys," because we were the youngest and nearly
inseparable, tried our best to keep still for the duration of the service.
This was mostly accomplished under bribes and inducements from
our mother or grandmother of chewy mints. We too often gave way to
the temptation to fidget and poke at each other. On one occasion, our
transgressions reached such a fever pitch that our father interrupted
his sermon to scold us from the pulpit: "Kurt and Phil, will you please
separate!" (I went by my first name as a boy, not my middle name of
Lauren.) It was as if God himself had spoken and we were duly subdued
for the remainder of the service. It turns out that a dose of public shame
proved that we weren't inseparable after all.

Sunday afternoons saw walks with our mother to the forest of
towering oaks and elms across from our house on McKinley Avenue,
urban older growth trees that had somehow escaped development.
The destination was often the public library on the other side of the
forest, from where we returned with stacks of books. Along the way,

in autumn, we collected leaves from the great trees, which our mother pressed into a book. But the weekdays of summer more often found us outside, reading the primary text of nature, rather than library books.

The field was home to a plentiful population of swallowtail butterflies, both yellow and black, and we chased them down with nets and pinned them to foam boards for our "museum" collections of natural objects. My earliest entrepreneurial urges emerged at this time and I convinced my siblings to charge a quarter for admission to said museum and ten cents for a glass of lemonade. Our patrons, very few, included our parents and motorists with kids we managed to lure in from McKinley Avenue with a crooked sign that read "Museum, 25 cents."

I once found a nest of black swallowtail caterpillars, which I placed in an empty coffee can along with their host plant and poked holes in the lid for oxygen. The timing must have been fortuitous in terms of the life cycle of the butterflies because I forgot about the can until weeks later. When I rediscovered it and anxiously pried off the lid, instead of finding a mass of dead caterpillars, I stood mesmerized by the emergence of a dozen or so black swallowtails who took to the air in a smoky swirl of black, yellow, and blue.

Those weekdays in summer that my brothers and I spent in the "field," my father mostly spent barricaded in his office on the second floor of the brick church building writing sermons. I can only imagine now the internal wrestling match that took place between Calvinist theology and my father's natural sensitivities. Calvinism had little to offer in terms of insights on the human relationship to nature, and even less on the nature of love. My father's more conscious objections, which would emerge later on in his spiritual path, had to have already been festering beneath the surface. As my mother would point out years later, even under the thumb of this theology, "your father preferred to preach more about a loving God than a punishing one."

My father's relationship to the wonders and trials of the natural world seemed as complex, contradictory, and ambivalent as his relationship to the theology he was taught in seminary. Much of his youth was spent playing on Buck Creek in Granville, Michigan, where he and his brother Jim and sister Beth were born and raised. He hung out on the creek with his best friend, Ernie, whom my father characterized in his memoirs years later as a kind of Daniel Boone woodsman figure who knew the woods and creeks like "the back of his hand." In his later years, my father spoke often of the creek and even made an attempt to visit the site with uncle Jim when they were well into their eighties. A video taken by my sister on her own visit to the site years later shows a beautiful tree-lined stretch of the creek flowing along one side of the town cemetery. The water flows strong and clear, glistening in the sun. Deep pools swirl at every bend. I could almost see my father fishing, skinny dipping, playing in the creek with Uncle Jim, their friend Ernie as their guide.

While he loved the Buck Creek of his boyhood and seemed to cherish the memory, there were other incidents that seemed to put him at odds with nature. At times, nature seemed to inconvenience him more often than move him. At other times, he described moments of wonder that overshadowed the irritation. He would tell the story of a time when he was out rabbit hunting in his youth, and he unaccountably but intentionally shot and wounded a Snowy Owl. Approaching the bird on the ground, it held its talons up in defiance to the very end. He had to kill the owl, a lifelong regret that he mentioned over and over. He loved cardinals and wrens and hummingbirds, but was known to shoot at grackles and starlings in the trees at his house with a BB pistol. He marveled at the existence of redwoods, but never went to see them.

I don't recall that many of my father's sermons extolled the wonders of nature, or even spoke to humanity's duty to care for "God's creation." In his later years, I began reading through his sermons, which he had carefully preserved in binders. Early on, when he was fresh out the seminary, his sermons were pretty heavy in theology and points of Calvinist doctrine, more cerebral and distant from day-to-day human experience. But over time, they progressed and become more personal, more about a loving, not a vengeful God. One of his sermons stood out for me because it was based on a 1936 story, "To See It Fall," by Morrow Mayo from *Harpers Magazine*. The tale was of a gigantic sequoia tree nearly four thousand years old, the largest in the grove at over three hundred feet, taller than a twenty-story building and a trunk 42 feet in diameter. A group of men decide to cut the tree down, for no other reason than to see it fall. They work on it every day for twenty-three days until finally, in a windstorm in the middle of the night, the great tree falls. In their slumber, they never witness its fall. From the pulpit, my father read from the story: "Great was the disappointment of the men when they discovered that the tree had fallen while they slept. They had destroyed the oldest, tallest, largest, and without question the mightiest living being on Earth. This tree had stood the test of ages. Since its fifteen-hundredth year it had probably been through ten thousand wind and lightning storms, and perhaps a thousand forest fires and a hundred earthquakes. In twenty-three days six men had destroyed the work of four thousand years — and then been robbed of the thrill of witnessing the climax of their destruction."

What was the point of his sermon? It is difficult to tell from his sermon notes. The fact that the sermon stood out for me was probably more of a tell about about my own life's orientation toward protecting the planet than it was about my father's feelings about the destruction of nature. But

I like to imagine it being about how in the sleep of our more destructive impulses, we are missing the glorious reality of our beautiful planet. The gap in the mountain where that tree had lived and had its being is like the gap in our souls as we destroy the planet. There is wonder at being in the presence of the giant sequoia. Seeing the tree fall is selfish desire for titillation, a shallow grasping after momentary thrills, a numbness to the numinous quality of our Earth. And a presentiment of our own fall from the graces and powers of the natural world.

Chapter 3

Big Star

I can't see anything except watery light filtering from above as I strain to keep from sinking, my arms flailing wildly, my lungs bursting. Then, as I begin to weaken and sink, I feel the sudden grip of a hand under my armpit and my arms go still in submission. Suddenly I'm surging upward quickly, my head breeches the surface, and I inhale deeply once and gasp several times in a row. I'm up on the dock on my side, coughing, and my father is yelling my name.

I was six going-on-seven and hadn't yet gone beyond a dog-paddle in my swimming abilities. Fishing for bluegills off the dock, I had turned my back on the lake, stooped to bait the hook with a worm, and then, excited to catch the first fish of the day, spun around, and… stepped forward into thin air. I hit the water in a tangle of fishline and bamboo pole, and in a state of complete surprise. I don't know how many times I went under, but I do remember the panic. I'm not sure what would have happened had my father not been just down the way, getting the rowboat ready to launch. He had given me life seven years earlier, and that day, may well have saved it.

Our weeklong stay at the cottage at Big Star Lake near Baldwin, Michigan, once each summer, didn't normally start with such drama. But nothing about our vacations at Big Star felt ordinary. We were so poor on a minister's salary that we could never have afforded to lease a cottage. It belonged to our Great Uncle Fritz and Aunt Midge, and their way of supporting my father's work was to give us the place for a week in the summer. It was a special place where the magic of childhood still held sway, perhaps even for my parents.

Over the course of the week, my father took each of us out in an old wooden rowboat equipped with an outboard motor that was always at dockside. Sometimes he took us out two at at time, but more often I was alone with him in the boat. His preferred fishing method at Big Star Lake was trolling. We'd rig up, cast out red and white daredevil lures, and he would run the outboard as slowly as possible, trolling parallel to the shoreline for northern pike and largemouth bass. Big Star is where he taught me how to rig a line, work a bait-casting reel, bait a hook, use a landing net, and, most importantly, how to work a fish.

"Loosen the drag! Let him run! But keep the line tight or the hook'll drop and you'll lose him!" The fish swept sideways in a sudden surge of desperate energy.

"Turn him! Turn him! Don't let him reach those cattails or he's gone!"

The fish dove and the drag on the reel screamed as the line peeled out. Then the pike turned and headed straight back toward the boat.

"Reel! Reel! Take up the slack!"

Two repetitions of this scenario and the fish was tiring, but so was I. As the two-foot-long fish came parallel to the boat, my father dipped the landing net under his hard snout and held up the northern pike twice as long as my seven-year-old arm. I can still see the red and white lure dangling from the mean toothy maw of the fish. A metal leader on the end of the line kept the sharp teeth from severing the line.

After trolling the shoreline, we often dropped anchor near some reeds and snags across the lake from the cottage. That cove seemed to harbor a swarm of life in its waters. Redwing blackbirds and wrens in the cattails. Dragonflies and water bugs. On one outing, two giant green mud turtles, as big around as a manhole cover, cruised lazily by the rowboat. My father attempted to snare one with a landing net, but the turtle easily batted the net away and swam for the depths.

One of my most vivid memories is of my father lifting the perforated basket from the inside of a galvanized metal minnow bucket. The bucket clunked against the side of the boat, water gushed outward through the holes in its side as he tied it to the gunwale, and then dropped it into the brackish water.

"Bait the hook like I taught you the last time," he said. "Do you remember?"

I unlatched the hinged lid and peered down onto the dark backs of a dozen or so wriggling minnows, an inch or two long. As I inserted my hand into the bucket, I felt the soft wet flutter of their bodies against my palm. Pulling up one minnow, I held it firm by the tiny head to immobilize it, then threaded the hook carefully through the meaty body just under the spine back toward the tail. Not severing the spine or piercing an organ would keep the minnow alive and wriggling. Crappies is what we were after, and they would only take live fish.

"You need a slightly larger hook for a crappie than a bluegill. Crappies have large mouths, but they're paper thin. When the bobber goes under, set the hook gently," my father advised. "Gently, or it will tear through the mouth."

Sometimes, even in these rare times of bonding, there is a gaff, a goof, some unintended slip that reminds us that the Trickster is always in the wings. On one of these outings, I moved too eagerly to grab my rod when a fish took the bobber under, and I knocked my father's prized bait-casting rig overboard into the drink. He groaned, hovered over the side of the boat, peering down for a disconsolate moment into the black water, then turned to me. I braced for some kind of scolding, but all he said was, "Don't worry, son. It's late. Reel in. I think it's time to head back."

My father was someone else on these trips to Big Star. There was a different way of connecting, out on the lake together, "in the same boat," quieter moments where things seemed less strained, more forgiving, so that even in small moments of loss, like a prized rod and reel plummeting to the bottom of the lake, there was little need for blame or shame. Of course I felt bad, but he didn't punish me for it. Nor did he ever bring it up again.

There was one ritual we enacted as a family each evening at Big Star. In the smaller guest house in back of the cottage, we gathered around him on one big bed, my mother to one side listening in, as my father read children's tales to us. They were mostly A. A. Milne's *When We Were Very Young* and *House at Pooh Corner* but also Uncle Remus tales and an obscure book called *Sweat and Tears*. These latter were hilarious stories made to seem all the more so because they were written in Yankee Dutch, a hybrid of the two languages that sounded clownish to our young ears. My father's quiet, expressive, baritone voice, entertained, delighted, and comforted us. This was not the father of the pulpit, full of authority and piety and strength, but the father of warmth and play and earthiness. Recast from a distant, unreal simulacrum of minister as God the Father, he became father in the lower case, one who was real, touchable, and present.

When I remember him now, it is often just him and me in the boat, his hand on the tiller, expectant, gazing ahead, heading somewhere together, or perhaps nowhere in particular.

Chapter 4

Tornado

My father, all six-foot, four-inches of him, thick dark shock of hair framing a handsome face, towered in the pulpit each Sunday. To me, his young son, he seemed to be the very God he preached about in the flesh. An unquestionable figure, the leader of the flock, as mythic to me as any storybook character when in the pulpit, and yet day-to-day, he was utterly real. He embodied the certainty, comfort, and solidarity of the Christian Reformed community of believers. My boyhood imagination equated him with strength and protection—everything I knew or needed; and in many respects, feared. Even his occasional flare-ups of dark anger fit the image of a jealous Old Testament Jehovah that was a staple from the Bible readings at nearly every family meal. At age seven, I was not of the maturity to question it, nor did I have a reason to. Which all made his departure from the ministry, his "fall" from grace, such a blow. That fall may well have begun early on with his own misgivings about the theology, but it was accelerated on August 15, 1964.

ψ

It was the day before my older brother Mark's birthday. My maternal grandparents were visiting from Holland, Michigan, to celebrate. Other than that, it was a summer day like many others in South Bend, Indiana. Humid, bright, a nearly cloudless sky. Heat mirages rippling over the far stretches of the field. My sister, Kristin, was nine. Riding her bike, she passed by a section of the field where the giant sap tree stood. She was headed for the housing projects, where we often rode bikes.

When she didn't reappear at lunchtime, my mother grew uneasy. Unease soon grew to alarm. When Kristin still failed to appear hours later, the police arrived. I remember them in their dark blue uniforms, peering with flashlights underneath my bed and in my closet, searching every corner of the parsonage and church to be sure she wasn't simply hiding. Then came the search parties by church people and police in the field. I now roamed the friendly, familiar acres of the wild field in back of the parsonage not as a carefree boy, but as part of a group of anxious searchers. We checked the "foxholes" I'd dug in the field with my siblings in mock war games, using those green, unripe apples from the nearby orchard as "ammo." We peered into the makeshift shed my brothers and I had hammered together with scrap lumber one day. We scoured the grove of trees. We called her name over and over. We combed the neglected apple orchards and vineyards, all the way to the border with the housing project. For a boy of seven, it felt like some mysterious game. It couldn't be real. Kristin would pop out of her hiding place anytime. And yet, I was old enough to be afraid.

The next day, my brothers and I woke to a surreal, and yet very real, story. There was a limit to what the adults would divulge to us kids at that time. But it went something like this:

Kristin had been rescued from the St. Joseph River in the middle of the night. How did she get there? On her way to the housing projects next to the field, a man emerged from his hiding place in the shrubbery, held her at gunpoint, then forced her into the trunk of his car. After some time, he drove to the bridge over the St. Joseph River. He bound her hands and feet, gagged her, and threw her over the side of the bridge to die.

There are photos from the day after. My family is gathered at a table. My grandparents are there, too. We are all sitting or standing around a cake, in an attempt to complete the celebration of Mark's birthday, which had been disrupted by the events of the day before. Were it not for the strained and sullen looks on the faces in the photo, it would have seemed as if nothing had happened.

Kristin: "Grampa took the photos. We are all around the cake. Then he took more photos of me two weeks later. And again one month later. He labeled the slides "two weeks later" and "one month later." He wanted to record what happened and how I was doing. He was worried about me, whether I'd be okay."

Over time, more details came out. Kristin landed in deeper water, then floated to a sandbar where the ropes binding her hands somehow fell away. With her hands free, she pulled the gag from her mouth. Standing in the shallows of the sandbar, with her mouth just above water, she screamed for help. It was dark, the middle of the night, around 4:00 a.m.

Kristin: "As I went down, I prayed. I did pray a lot. I had trust in God at that time. I talked to the man about coming to church. I tried to humanize him by asking him questions about his family. Before he gagged me, I pleaded with him not to push me over the bridge, but he did anyway. As I went down, I prayed, 'Help me,' and I think the water sort of helped me and the ropes on my hands fell off so I could stand and I could pull the gag off my mouth."

A young couple had just purchased a house on the river and had been working through the night to clean it up. They were taking something out of the house into the back yard when they heard Kristin's cries.

Using a rowboat moored at the side of the river, they rescued her and called the police. In Kristin's mind, the couple who pulled her from the river that day were angels, but they were only two of many angels she feels saved her from dying that day.

Kristin: "I still do believe that spiritual beings were with me that day. I thanked St. Joseph because it was his river and bridge and he is known as the protector of children. I felt like St. Joseph was there to help me, as well as Mother Mary. There was a song from vacation bible school that I sang over and over to myself. And there were other angels."

In the trunk of the car on the way to the river, Kristin somehow kept the presence of mind to stick her fingers out of a hole in the trunk of the car and wiggle them. At a stoplight, a woman saw her fingers, called the police, and described the car and the license plate. The man was apprehended soon afterward at his home, not long after Kristin was rescued from the river.

Kristin: "The lock to the trunk was broken out, which made a hole to the outside. It was the only way I could breathe. When the car was moving, there was air sucked in through that hole. If the car was stopped, I couldn't breathe very well. It was a hot day. So I stuck my fingers out when he stopped the car at a light and a woman saw my fingers wiggle. Can you imagine seeing that? She hollered at him and said: "There's someone in your trunk!" and he sped away. Well, then she reported it to the police, with the car's license and description and everything. So she was another angel."

Some inexplicable truths saved my sister that day:

St. Joseph, the namesake of the bridge and the river, is the saint who watches over children.

The ropes unaccountably fall away from Kristin's hands, even though the perpetrator was a tree trimmer who knew how to tie knots.

Kristin lands in deep water and so escapes injury in the fall.

She floats to a sandbar.

A young couple just happens to be awake and working outside their house at the side of the river at 4:00 a.m., and they hear her cries.

There is a rowboat on the shore that didn't belong to the couple.

The lock is broken out of the trunk of the car, creating a hole through which she can breathe and signal for help.

A woman at a stoplight notices two small fingers sticking out of the holes in the trunk.

It is hard, given all of these circumstances and real-life and spiritual angels who appeared to save my sister's life, not to believe that there was an element of the miraculous at work. But for me, the most incredible thing was that Kristin, nine years old, has the inner strength and presence of mind to try to save herself even as she is terrified. She sings. She prays. She talks to the man.

Kristin: "Years later, I made up my own angel. She's like this ten-foot-tall angel, a dark-skinned Indian woman dressed in blue that came to champion me as I was going through it. And to bring me out of it. She's an aspect of myself that helped me get out of that whole day feeling championed. It's someone I conjured up in my adult life to help me feel empowered rather than victimized. It's a part of myself that helped that child, helped me as a child to come out of it."

To my mind, that "ten-foot-tall dark-skinned Indian woman dressed in blue" that Kristin conjured up as her champion was a formidable and determined part of my sister. That part prompted her to signal for help from inside the trunk, to talk to her perpetrator throughout, asking him about his family in order to dissuade him. And she helped Kristin feel, in her words, "that I wasn't totally alone."

☘

My father, not long afterward, would portray the events to the media as a miracle, a moment of God's grace. This was how the Christian radio station that interviewed him wanted to hear it. Church members had prayed and the prayer had been heard.

Kristin: "There is a tape of his radio interview. It was all about how grateful they were to God that I was back. The community all prayed and they were all glad as Christians to be praising God. Nothing about fear, anger, shame, how we were all affected, how it's going to take time to heal, none of that. He said what the radio program wanted to hear. Everyone said, 'God saved you for a purpose!' So what is that purpose? The idea that I was saved for a purpose by God still haunts me. It felt like people wanted me to witness for God's grace. That he saved me. How else do you explain something like that, when fewer than 1% of children are found again when something like this happens to them?"

Beneath the seemingly miraculous aspects of the story, was the very real trauma. There was the unspoken truth that this event would take many years for us to come to terms with and to begin to heal. It would also take many years for the full story to come out. What the adults kept from us at the time was a gap in time between her perpetrator forcibly abducting her from the field and throwing her over the bridge. During that time, the man had taken her to a remote location and raped her. He bound her to a tree and left her, and returned more than once, until he took her to the bridge.

Kristin, over forty years later: "He hit me on the head three times when he first took me in the field. He treated me badly and did things to me sexually that I didn't understand at age nine. But I knew it was shameful and bad. I think the biggest psychological thing for me was that he threw me over the bridge like I was a sack of trash, disposable, not needed. It created a core mantra in my life that I don't matter. I'm not seen.

"Maybe I was saved by angels and circumstance, and spiritual helpers and all that, but why was it even allowed to happen? And why all of the destruction that's happening now on the Earth? It all seemed, and seems, so overwhelming to innocent people like us. I know we have our shadow side and we're not totally good, but it seems like there's so much bad, so many people traumatized. We just barely know how to take care of that. And the Earth can't even help us heal anymore because it's just trying to heal itself."

"It was a tornado," she said, "that swept into and through our lives and caused a whole world of chaos in its wake."

Chapter 5

Rupture

My parents were so distraught during the time that Kristin was missing that they were sedated with drugs, especially my father. He was unconscious when the call came that Kristin had been rescued from the river. My mother went with a man from the church to meet the police, and to take her home. Understandably, before they left to go pick her up, my mother collapsed, crying on the couch with relief, just to know Kristin was alive. And yet, my mother was told by the police and well-meaning friends who were present, "Don't cry now; now's not the time to cry; you should be joyful. Go and get her, be happy!"

My mother, years later: "It was a different time. If your father and I had had only a fraction of the psychological and emotional resources and the advice about how to deal with trauma that are available to you kids today, we might have known better how to cope, how to tell the story. And it might not have been such a family secret that we didn't talk about for all those years."

Kristin, and the story of her kidnapping and rape, made national news. But seething beneath the public persona my father projected in the news media, that of faith and gratitude for her "miraculous" return, was a different story, one of rage at the perpetrator and of betrayal by a God he had sworn to serve. His journals would only refer to the perpetrator as "the fiend." There was no mention of miracles.

Some did see Kristin's survival, of course, as a miracle, proof that there was a benevolent God watching over her. God's grace had saved her. Kristin herself, as I wrote earlier, felt more that there were other spiritual helpers, angels, who got her through it. Others, my father chief among them as it turned out, struggled to come to terms with a God who would allow this to happen to an innocent child. The God of love my father preferred to preach about, even in spite of his Calvinist training in seminary, became a suspect deity. It may have felt like a miracle that Kristin was returned to us alive, but her violation was something difficult to come back from, and her loss of innocence could never be regained.

It would take fewer than three years after my sister's kidnapping for that safe bubble of believers to fully burst. It showed signs of strain immediately. A little more than a year after Kristin was taken, my father moved us to a new church, partly, he said, to escape the memories of the place where it happened. We moved from South Bend, Indiana to Des Moines, Iowa. But a new church and a new start couldn't erase the trauma. His ministry would end scarcely two years after our move to Iowa.

There were already signs in him of disaffection with the ministry and the church in the months leading up to the kidnapping. He had grown increasingly unhappy with church duties. Every week, like clockwork after preaching two sermons on Sunday, he would be down with a migraine headache that would sometimes last until mid-week. What happened to Kristin acted to accelerate the rupture. In the interim, during the time between the kidnapping and his break with the church, my father simply recycled his old sermons. There was no new material, he said. He had burned out on the message and the theology.

As a seven going on eight-year-old boy, my main feeling at the time was shame. But I wouldn't identify that feeling until I was old enough to understand what shame was. Something bad and dirty had happened to my sister. I thought she was never coming home again. And so, along with the shame, were fear and trauma, and then the shock of my father's sudden break from the safe bubble of believers. After a period of confusion and adjustment, the collapse of my father's faith, as well as my own, would set me on an early spiritual search.

Having lost the safe and stable community of my youth, I found solace in the natural world, in solitude, even if I didn't know what my draw to nature meant at the time. That solace relieved me of the weight of sadness I felt but couldn't fully articulate. Sadness at the loss of certainty, at the loss of innocence, and anger at the violation of my sister.

I remember numerous church excursions to parks and other natural areas for youth activities. There were also family gatherings in celebration of certain holidays and birthdays. In those places, the allure of the surrounding woods and fields was much stronger in me than the uneasy comfort I drew from human company, which I never felt I could fully trust. I found myself wandering off frequently in search of the companionship I found with the trees, the birds, the insects, the creeks and rivers, the wind, and the animals. I puzzled at the indifference I sensed in others to the natural wonder all around us, to the beauty of light filtering down through a forest canopy, to the mystery and magic that seemed to saturate the natural world. It wasn't just the thrill of discovery that drew me. I felt held there, safe, accepted. For Kristin, given that she was taken to a remote natural area and tied to a tree, the story was more complicated.

For years, I knew little more about that day than the events as recounted the day after to me and my brothers. I didn't know she had been sexually assaulted. I knew little about her perpetrator. And yet, there was nothing that carried more charge for me emotionally when I spoke to friends about it over the years. I sensed a window for healing and growth if we could confront the trauma. Kristin's trauma was my family's trauma, was my own. The secret, bit by bit, over the course of many years, began to work its way into the open.

The perpetrator of the crime against Kristin, although caught, would never go to trial. He was sent to a facility for the criminally insane. Years later, when she was in high school, he was deemed competent to stand trial. FBI agents arrived at our house to ask if Kristin would testify, to which she assented. But he died in the institution from an intestinal ailment before standing trial.

LANDSCAPE INTERLUDE
Magic in the Glade

The disc slowly glides, then starts to bank away from me. I run a few steps and take a flying leap, catching the frisbee just before it hits the grass. I fall into a barrel roll, frisbee in hand, then leap to my feet, unscathed. I hurl the disc back to my brother Mark.

My family is out for a picnic, celebrating some holiday, probably Memorial Day. After frisbee playing grows old, my Dad and siblings play badminton for a while. Then, at Mom's behest, we sit down to a meal of hamburgers, potato salad, and baked beans. Afterward, the food and the late afternoon warmth bring on a sudden lull in activity.

As others drowse, I can't resist a beckoning footpath that leads into a boggy grove of large elm and hickory trees. From where I stand on the picnic grounds, I can see an eerie, amber light filtering down. The allure is too much. I follow the path to an area of semi-shade where the ground is carpeted by some broadleaf plants with leaves twice as big as my palm. A light breeze shakes the leaves in the dappled sunlight, creating a hypnotic shimmer.

As I approach, I am stunned to see dozens of dark creatures hovering above the plants. About as long as my index finger, their black gossamer wings whirr around slender cobalt blue bodies which glitter as they pass in and out of the late afternoon shafts of sunlight. I knew the beeline flight of the dragonfly. I also knew the flight of butterflies. This movement is slower, less erratic, an elegant dance, soft and graceful. As one of them comes to light on a dark green ivy leaf, it folds up its wings as if in prayer and seems to regard me with its ebony eyes, brought to life by tiny pinpoints of light.

What in the world am I seeing? There is nothing in my eleven-year-old catalog of animals to answer that question. To my child's imagination, I am seeing the storybook fairy in the flesh. Remarkably, as I stand gaping, one alights briefly on my arm, then flits away. The swirl of dozens of them hold me entranced and to this day, I still feel the warm inner joy of that encounter.

When I return to the picnic area and tried to describe what I had seen, my account was, of course, met by amused smiles from my parents and smirks from my siblings. Still enraptured by my discovery and wanting to share it, I lead my father down the path to show him; the light is gone, and so are the magical creatures. "It must have been quite something, son," is his gentle response, no doubt reading the disappointment in my face.

It wasn't until years later, on a trip back to Iowa in the month of May, that I learned the identity of my mythical beings. While on a bike path through similar terrain, I hit a swath of late afternoon sun illuminating a patch of broadleaf plants not far off the path. And there, hovering above them, were the ebony jewel-wing damselflies. What else could I do but dismount and let the dark and elegant flutter of their wings and the sheen off their iridescent blue bodies retrieve for me an old joy?

So I now had a name. I was grateful to the person with poetic sensibilities who had given this insect such an apt, and beautiful, designation. But a name is not an identity. It's just an identification so that we can use language to refer to the various events of being that we encounter. Identity is beyond naming, and that ebony jewel-wing, hovering and glittering in the half-light, will always have an identity for me beyond language. Something not fully of the sun, nor of the shadows, a twilight being somewhere in the interstices of storybook fairy and bug and the unnameable.

That not-quite-nameable aspect of things was what I felt as a pre-teen boy in the woods and groves, and the Iowa prairie, and the banks of the Raccoon River. It was an organically growing wonder and tenderness for all living things that sustained me. It's what I feel now, walking next to a great Valley Oak near my home in Northern California. I witness the tree, but before I reach for a name, there is a sudden flooding presence within me. It's the way my body knows the world. My awareness shifts down and down through my chest into my torso. As it spreads throughout my body, my eyes relax and my vision dilates. I'm home, grounded in something both old and familiar.

Midwest Reverie

From the upstairs bedroom window
of the farmhouse that breathes
in and out with the seasons
the boy looks out
onto the heat of summer evening.
A floor fan blows heroically beside him.

Below, in the farm pond, a bullfrog
bellows burlesque tunes from the cover of reeds.
The quiet air responds with a wave
and an echo, and the water—calm, clear—
reflects the redwing so faithfully,
that wind and word are one.

The boy feels himself a swallow
who lives in the eaves
and swoops over the pond.
The generous light of summer,
slow to depart, swings him aloft,
wind-bent into the wheel of his hopes.

He goes farther than he has ever gone,
beyond the murmuring hills. What he
finds in that far field
is whispered by grasses after dark,
in a language that usurps
the stories of his life.

Chapter 6

Leaving the Fold

Des Moines, Iowa, late 1969

"Your father's going away," my mother said one night as she put me to bed, "just for a while."

"Why? Going where?"

"There's a place. In Colorado. He needs a rest."

"Why is he tired? Why can't he rest here?"

"It's a hospital. He needs help."

"Why does he need help?"

"I don't know. He has headaches. He's not himself."

"Is he sick?"

"No. Well, not his body. He just needs some time. There are some people there who can help him."

I pictured the only time I had seen my father cry. Congregation members had donated food and money to our family because his salary as a minister wasn't enough to make ends meet. He rose to thank a group of them one day as we were picking up groceries in the church basement, but broke down mid-sentence. Then I remembered the only time I had seen him sick, after an operation on his back. I was nine. He was laid up at home for weeks and we kids took turns sitting with him during meals at his bedside. Flat on his back but propped up in a hospital bed, he ate with a tray across his lap. He seemed smaller.

One evening when it was my shift to eat with him, we both looked up from our food trays and out the window of the bedroom. It was just as the sun was low in the sky and the forsythia bush right outside the window glowed an outrageous yellow, almost as if it were aflame.

"You know, one day about this time that bush was lit up like that," he said, "and a bright red cardinal flew into it."

"A cardinal?"

"Yep, and then along came a blue jay."

"A blue jay?"

"It was *amazing*. Blue, crimson, yellow! How often do you think that happens?"

I could picture it, especially as I saw his face glow and his eyes light up.

"I don't know."

"It was a gift, son. A testament to the wonders of nature."

When he was back on his feet again, he seemed even taller than I remembered. Somehow, his height felt intimidating to me for the first time, because with it came with something menacing, unspoken, angry.

ψ

This sick father, off in a faraway place, was a new father, one I couldn't quite get used to. My idea of my father was one of strength; the leader of the church; nearly omnipotent like the God he preached about. Or the Big Star Lake father, earthier and more accessible. But not this. Too young to understand a spiritual crisis and not brought up to embrace emotions, I saw his absence as some kind of mental problem. That was the way it was described by the adults. At that time, because I lived in a culture that stigmatized the mentally ill, the feeling in me was shame. But I had no word for shame as a pre-teen boy in a family where feelings weren't much talked about.

His absence from the family went from days to weeks, and then months. This period of emotional and spiritual recovery at a rehab facility called Bethesda in Colorado, was paid for by the Christian Reformed Church. When he finally did return, it was as a stranger. His hair was long. He'd grown a goatee and sideburns. He wore loud shirts and love beads. He was smoking tobacco in a meerschaum pipe. Later, he acquired a used powder-blue Fiat convertible sports car. It was all so redolent of the 1960s rebellion, then in full swing. As a ten-year-old in a medium-sized midwestern city, the foment of the time was all but lost on me. My family weren't revolutionaries. They hardly took notice of the counterculture exploding all around us. It was all background to a sheltered world. This made my father's re-appearance and new dress and behavior all the more strange at the time. It wasn't until I reached high school that my siblings and I began to manifest the Zeitgeist of the 1960s in our own awkward ways.

My father's rebellion was against the strictures of his religious upbringing and the teachings of seminary. But he was also rebelling against his own choices — to be a minister, to be a father, to shun material wealth, to be Christian. So he left the ministry, and in the midst of that rebellion came the need to rebuild a livelihood and to support four children. He had to cobble together a living from an education limited to a particular religious worldview, and from a work history that qualified him for little more than being the shepherd of a flock. And so, he was soon off again, this time to get a Masters in Social Work at the University of Iowa.

We had moved to the small town of Prairie City after my father left the ministry, because it was more affordable to live in rural Iowa. We lived near enough to Des Moines for my mother to commute. For the first time in her married life, she worked. To make ends meet, she took a job offered by a church congregant and family friend who managed a supermarket. This worked out better when we were in school. But in summertime, my father away at school, what to do with two restless teenagers? My older brother, Mark, out of high school and soon to enlist to avoid the draft, was already working and out of the house. Kristin had fled Iowa small town life and moved to Michigan to live with our aunt and uncle and go to a Christian high school. That left my younger brother, Phil, and me in a free range existence for the summer, and we spent much of it in the fields and fishing rivers and farm ponds in the Iowa countryside.

My mother was only too happy to entrust Phil and me to the care of Mother Nature when she went off to work, at least in summer when we weren't in school. It was cheap childcare, and she received no complaint from us. She would drop us off on the banks of our favorite wild spot, Beaver Creek, and off we'd go. She worked a full day, while we spent the time wading the creek, enticing catfish out of deep waterholes underneath logs and snags with our spinning rods and reels, seining minnows out of the shallows, and generally playing at being Huck Finn, free on our own Mississippi. Late afternoon, she picked us up again in the parking lot of a gas station that sat on a pond adjacent to the creek. We had already popped the caps off Squirt and Nehi soda bottles and were downing Hershey's bars and potato chips. Mother always packed us off with water and sandwiches in the morning, but we had long ago consumed those. We earned the pocket change for these goodies by selling earthworms by the dozen and the odd lawn mowing job. We even set up an earthworm nursery in the root cellar of the old two-story clapboard home we rented in Prairie City. The nursery consisted of a long wooden box filled with the rich, dark Iowa soil and just enough adult worms to get things started.

We piled into the back seat of the Rambler station wagon, smelling of fish and mud, covered with chigger bites, and generally tired but happy from a long day on the creek. When I think about it now, it seems odd, given my sister's kidnapping years earlier, that my mother would be trusting enough to allow us this kind of unsupervised freedom. We were boys; and it seemed a more innocent time, and perhaps she thought we had each other. On the other hand, it may just have been that we had so little money, and she felt she had few affordable options.

For my part, the creeks and rivers of Iowa were a siren call to which I responded as often as I could manage. Winters were long dreary times spent dreaming of the other seasons and the adventures they would provide.

Vitis Californica
(Roger's Red Grape)

The roots of the wild grape vine,
after ten years
groping in circles, have burst

the bounds of the terra cotta pot,
which slumps away, an old shoe.
Free to roam its native soil now,

in search of older alliances —
rhizome to loam, fungi to rootlet.
new things come up to light:

the shawl of leaves, stitched
among the climbing threads,
its never been so full;

and tiny grapes for the first time
in the morning sun,
ripening into autumn.

Those November leaves!
Who knew the color of freedom
burnt such fiery red?

Chapter 7

Loss, Risk, and Creativity

Loss is not simply loss. It is simultaneously the elimination
of obstacles to the creativity that wants to flower forth.
—Brian Thomas Swimme
   Creativity and Cataclysm

The ultimate source and destination of creative work lies in
the wholeness of the psyche, which is the wholeness of the world.
—Stephen Nachmanovitch
   Free Play

In the summer of 1969, before my father left for Bethesda, my family motored off in our old beater Rambler station wagon on a vacation trip to Estes Park in the Rocky Mountains. I was thirteen, Kristin a year-and-a-half older. It was a trip where delight and hardship traveled with us as equal partners. On the one hand, the excitement of heading toward a place with mythic allure; our noses pressed to the car windows as a new and strange Colorado landscape streamed by; then the surge of fascination as the looming magnificence of the Rockies slid into view. On the other, unrelenting sheets of rain dogged us for days. Two of those days were spent stranded in a small town awaiting parts for a clutch blown under the stress of hauling a camper trailer and a family of six up and down too many Rockies foothills. And later, at the tail end of the adventure, a desperate attempt to escape the rain in a drive southward to Ojo Caliente, New Mexico, in searing hundred-plus degree heat. Having four crabby, spindly-legged teenagers in a car with no air conditioning were severe enough conditions to eventually reduce my younger brother, Phil, and my mother, to tears.

Despite these difficulties, or perhaps partly because of them, a lasting impression of the mountains and canyons stays with me even today. At one stop on our winding drive up the canyon at Estes Park, I found myself standing on the lip of the enormous canyon. Having finished a picnic lunch, my parents were dozing on a blanket. My siblings were otherwise occupied. I was momentarily alone. There was a breathtaking silence commandeering the canyon, coupled with the parting of pewter-gray clouds shuttled by the wind across an electric-blue pallet. A herd of elk grazed its way slowly along the river that wound through the floor of the canyon. Rays of sun poured between the clouds, glazing the vast sweep of luscious green canyon meadow below me. I felt an upwelling inside which exited suddenly as a gasp and then tears as I was overtaken by a sense of enormity that was both beyond me and within me. It seemed to originate from the depth of the canyon, carried upward on an invisible swell. That day, at age thirteen, marked my first attempt to capture the ineffable in a poem. The poem has since been lost, probably thankfully, in a jumble of discarded childhood scraps.

We continued our way up the canyon rim, snaking our way up the narrow road. Car repairs were behind us. The steady press of rain had lifted and with it our mood. Mom and Dad grew sunnier and more talkative, and my siblings and I, buoyed up, squirmed in a pile in the back seat, straining at the windows to see the view. Now and then Dad stopped the Rambler to take in a roadside vista. We reached our campground for the night, and after we settled in and had dinner, my attention was drawn by a small crag of rocks not far from camp. At the peak, stood a tiny but unmistakable yellow flag, planted there by some climber.

"Look!" I said to Kristin, pointing to the peak.

"Someone's been up there," she said, "and staked a claim."

"It doesn't seem too far," I answered.

"Not *too* far," she echoed softly.

We looked at each other for a brief moment. And then we were off.

The distance to that "small crag of rocks" was, of course, much farther than it appeared, probably a good half day's climb in retrospect. But Kristin and I set off down the path excitedly. The pines around us soughed in the summer breezes. The calls and hollow raps of woodpeckers lured us onward. Chipmunks skittered over logs and along the path. As we entered more deeply into the forest and late afternoon gave way to early evening, a darkness and a chill began to settle around us. The yellow flag atop the peak seemed hardly closer than when we set out. It was summertime, so we had longer light, but when the sun was gradually engulfed by the high peak, it grew darker by shades.

"Time to turn back," said Kristin.

"It's not that far," I answered, "we'll make it."

"You know there are bears out here. Mountain lions."

"They're afraid of people," I countered.

"We don't have flashlights."

She had me there. But my own excitement still overrode what should have been the same wise caution my sister was trying to impress upon me. I looked at that flag and just wanted to go there. There was something insurmountable in me that wouldn't let me turn back. Kristin pleaded with me several times, but finally turned back alone in the face of my recalcitrance.

"You'll be in trouble," she said, making one last attempt.

"Just follow the path back," I called out to her.

"I'm afraid," she yelled as we drew further apart.

"Don't worry. I'll be back to camp soon."

I continued up the forested slope alone, always heading in the direction of the flag. Before long, the path tapered out to an indistinct deer trail; then dusk came on stronger. I could no longer see the yellow flag, which just moments before had seemed lit up from within by the last rays of the sun. Remembering Kristin's words about bears and flashlights, I grew too afraid to continue. I headed back to camp, arriving just as full darkness fell.

My father was building a campfire. My excited account of the attempted ascent was cut short by his stern glare, and then completely silenced by my mother's vociferous and tearful rage. It was one of the few times I remember her, usually soft-spoken and reserved, being overtly furious or even very angry with me. Keeping the family together and safe was everything to her, but I was too young to understand the source or force of her feelings, her fierce imperative to protect us at all costs. It was part of her strength, her mother bear power, but it also carried a shadow side, one that I rebelled against over and over as I grew up, that of over-protectiveness and a risk-averse stance in life.

This family trip exists now in my memory as a kind of foreshadowing of a dynamic that would play itself out in various guises in my family over the years. To scale a peak in the lust for adventure in resonance with a deeper call. And yet risk and the fear of it hovering there as an obstacle in itself to be surmounted.

My father thought his belief would protect us from the world. This was largely true of my mother as well. Nothing bad would happen. But it did. The magical belief system, the thinking that we are great, we are the elect, straight out of Calvinism, crashed down. Both of my parents had come from families with varying degrees of piety, all of them with roots in the Dutch Reformed Church. My mother's side was more devout; my father's side less so. His religious fervor was more of a reaction to the death of his father than a call from the divine. My paternal grandfather, who died years before I was born, was a bit of a gangster, a gambler, a lady's man, and a drinker who was mostly absent from family life.

One day, when my father was about sixteen, my grandmother picked up the phone ringing in the front hall of the family home. From the other room, my father heard her muffled voice answer a few questions. Then she called out to my father,

"Tom! Come to the phone!"

"Who is it?" he asked.

"They say they're with the police," she said, "they asked to speak to you."

"The police?"

"That's what they said."

"Why me?"

"I don't know, Tommy. They asked to speak to a man, and your father's not home."

The police informed him that my grandfather had died in a hotel room far from home. My grandfather traveled a lot for his work, so this wasn't unusual, but the police indicated that he wasn't alone in the hotel, that he had died in somewhat scandalous circumstances. It was the latter part they were reluctant to share with my grandmother. When my father broke the news to her that day, he only told her part of the story. He went to his minister who told him not to say anything to his mother. That other part of the story was a secret my father carried in his body for most of his life, only sharing it with me and my sister in his final years. But my grandfather's questionable morality and the grief it caused the family sparked a backlash in my father and was probably a good part of the reason he became a minister.

We were supposed to be the chosen ones, was the belief. What happened to Kristin wasn't supposed to happen. I thought at one point that she was gone for good, never coming home. As a young boy, part of me thought it was all a game, the search party calling her name in the field in back of the parsonage, that she was just hiding and we would find her peering out from behind some tree, giggling. But another part of me was terrified, in disbelief that anything bad could happen to her.

I figured out later that my father believed that he had failed her. It couldn't have been God. God was omnipotent, and as my father preferred to preach, loving. And so it must have been something my father did wrong. He would say for years afterward that he never should have been a father. For a time I believed that he hated being shackled to family life, that he wasn't free as a father to follow his true dreams. But I came to realize that he was saying something entirely different, that he had failed to protect my sister, to protect us. The kidnapping assailed all the ways our family made meaning out of life. That magical thinking was attacked and our reaction to what happened created an internal sense of trauma.

I idealized my father as a kind of God figure, I "drank the Kool-aid," the idealization that I was special, that we were saved, that we were the Christian elect. And then we weren't, and all the promise of an eternity in heaven in a state of grace in the presence of an all-loving God fell to pieces. It is a story that was difficult for many years for me to fully understand. Because beyond the personal aspects, it is also a story of what it means to be American in a capitalist, consumerist society, growing up in the heartland thinking that we were special, chosen, above the rest of the world, untouchable from its dangers. Nothing bad is supposed to happen to Americans because we are exceptional. But this is also magical thinking that is destroying nature and our connection to others.

There are many similarities between my family's story and our cultural story. Kristin's rape and the violation of nature. The elitism of our religious faith that told us we were entitled to everything, special access to the glory of God, and a culture that spread exuberantly across the continent like a violent flash mob in the belief that Americans were entitled to all of its natural riches, now and forever. We went from a secure and safe existence held together by magical thinking to one in which the world isn't safe. There was an extraordinary effort on the part of my family to hold it all together by keeping things a secret, denying the reality that threatened safety.

And so, keeping the family safe became my parents' mantra. Don't take risks. My father feared travel. Stayed close to home. My parents always wanted to go to the Netherlands, to see the country of their origin. And yet, they never did. A planned trip fell apart when the vinyl roof to their aging Cadillac was crumbling and they had to replace it. So they didn't have the money for the trip. Owning a used Cadillac they could barely afford was a desperate attempt to stay in the consumerist, capitalist world, and it became more important to keep up appearances than to take the risk of a journey to their homeland. In a sense, my whole life has been an attempt to escape the tyranny of safety, to learn to take risks, to rebuild from cataclysm.

The incident at Estes Park bears out that tension, something we all face at one time or another. Kristin wisely turned back. I went on. Or I tried. When I reached a clearing with an unobstructed view of the peak, I just stood there, two different people, side-by-side, one facing upward and forward; the other back:

Darkness is pushing in around me. It isn't safe to go on alone.
I've come all this way.
There really are bears, and mountain lions.
The flag on the peak — "it's so close!"
I have no flashlight.
I can see by the light of the moon, almost full, showing me the way.
I'm alone.

In a sense that moment was emblematic of much of my life. Torn between the risk of climbing even a minor mountain and the aliveness that could come with it, and safety, good sense, the protection that camp and family could afford me. That night I chose family, return, safety, protection. There are times when I've chosen to ascend and times when I've chosen to sink back into the safety of the familiar and conventional. Each has its rewards. And risks. And sacrifices. Regrets. Choice is always there; so are limits, and wisdom more often than not comes after a fall. Risks well-chosen aren't the same as recklessness for the sake of proving something. And making the choice to risk isn't always rewarded in predictable ways. The gain sought but frustrated might make it seem like the risk was foolish. Or, it teaches me something about where growth is needed. It would be years before I could discern between the illusion of safety in life and a sense of security gained from being grounded in my own being.

Piano

An early memory. I am seven, seated at the piano, playing Handel's "Largo." As I complete the piece, I look up to see my mother and father standing in the archway between the living room and the kitchen. They are looking at me, their arms around each other, a look of pride beaming forth from their faces.

Years later, when I am fifteen, my mother and I are standing in the family room, shafts of golden sun lathering the old upright piano with a caramel glaze. The beautiful grain of the oak wood seems to sing like the music. My mother and I had worked for many months together in the basement refinishing the upright, removing a thick dark varnish that had obscured the bare wood beneath for decades. The repair of a few of the keys and replacement of the pads inside finished the job. We moved it into the family room upstairs where it took a central spot in the life of the family.

It was the piano I had played at age seven, and I had begun to play again as a teenager, after a few years' hiatus of not playing. Removing the dark varnish of a family heirloom, repairing the guts of the instrument to expose the beauty beneath. Little did I know how this simple labor of digging beneath the surface would reenact itself in time in a different way, within all of us.

One morning I approached the piano, excited to play. Brash sunlight fell in through the family room window onto the keys with a crash of dissonance. I wasn't seeing what I was seeing, surely. Several of the ivories, like knocked out teeth, had been torn off the keys. I sank into a nearby armchair, the weight of my father's dark fury pulling me down in a spiral until I couldn't stop falling. That which my mother and I sought to restore was met by a tempest within him, the tornado still sweeping through our lives.

The path of creativity

I started writing poetry because I liked the wildness of word, sound, and image much in the same way I loved bushwhacking the forests and prairies. There was the mystery in discovery that didn't happen on the more well-worn, familiar path of prose. Writing a poem led me sound by sound, image by image through the bramble of emotion and the sensual landscape into undiscovered terrain. I could follow the first line of a poem into a rainforest of emotion and come out energized. Very often, birds flew into my poems. I liked them there because they sang and soared, sometimes at the same time. My first poem came on the lip of the canyon at Estes Park. It was unbidden. It was the only way I could manage the energy roaring upward toward me from the play of light and cold wind on the canyon floor.

Creativity, community, and nature were a triumvirate of healing for me. Music and time in nature earlier on; poetry came later. I wouldn't venture to write much poetry of my own until I was in my thirties. There were a few angst-filled teenage poems as well as some romantic ones designed to get the attention of a new heart throb. But I didn't take poetry all that seriously as a way to make sense of the world, until later.

Eventually, being more of a bookworm and a poet than a rock

climber, I learned to look inward, or to the realm of ideas or creative expression for most of my adventures. I forged ahead with my own creativity, and came to see my inner life and the expression of the universe coursing through me as the flag planted atop the rocky crag. There was a tension between moving forward with one's creativity, asserting a separate identity and turning back toward the safety and haven of family, the "familiar." But what I eventually came to realize was that in order to go forward, I needed to go back, at least in a certain sense. I needed to learn my family history and to break the silence built around trauma in order to continue to forge my own path.

Always in my life was this tension between going backward and going forward. The need to differentiate and distinguish myself from my family, and the need to know my family's story as a formative influence on me. The need to know the cultural pathology I grew up under and to understand my own rebellion against it, my need to transcend it and to truly become an individuated cosmic citizen. The need to both challenge authority and to be seen by those in positions of authority, the need to both seek the limelight and to shun it. The need to risk, or to keep things safe. I have questioned the authority of mainstream culture because it couldn't begin to compare with what I knew of the radiant reality beneath it all, the awareness of which seemed to elude that culture in its devotion to consumerism and material success. I've been ambitious, but not in the conventional sense of the word. My ambitions lay in the successful expression of a deeper resonance through creativity and spiritual practice. It is a path that naturally goes counter to consumerist culture.

The dance between creativity and risk, between imitation and imagination, plays itself out in our lives over and over. One of the ways for me has been music. When I was seventeen, I took up the piano after a hiatus of a few years. Having had lessons for several years as a boy, I had quit playing, drawn away by playing baseball, girls, and other teenage sirens calling me away. When I returned to playing, it was with a passion I never felt as a child. Not long after I took up the piano again, a friend and I were listening to albums at his home. In between REO Speedwagon, the Eagles, and Jefferson Airplane, he slipped an LP of jazz pianist Keith Jarrett's "Bremen and Lassaune" piano improvisations onto the turntable. After several minutes, I slipped into an altered state that oscillated between stunned silence and uncontainable excitement. Listening to the raw power of Jarret's piano completely altered my experience of music. I was mesmerized, completely swept up. My best description would be that I completely merged with the music. I was no longer the listener, but a participant in the sound. I bought the album and couldn't stop listening to it. To create such profound beauty in a moment of free improvisation captivated me like nothing I could remember. I could feel the same primal urge within me and I just had to do what Jarrett was doing.

It wasn't long before I was shunning sheet music and attempting my own improvisations. There was only one problem. Almost on the first day I became a legal adult, I had moved out of my parents' home. And I didn't have a piano. The family piano at my parents' house was still there, but there were limited hours during which I could play. I no longer lived under their roof. Living on my own and barely able to make rent each month, I had no money to buy a piano. Eventually, my passion to play drove me to a temporary solution. My basement apartment was just two blocks away from Drake University. Drake had a robust music program and a massive music building with row on row of practice rooms stretching across three floors. Even better, they were kept open all night long. Some of these practice rooms had grand pianos and they were kept regularly tuned for the students. Any spare hour found me, often after working all day at the Pittsburgh-Des Moines steel plant, sneaking into the building and grabbing an open practice room, usually one with a grand piano. Once there, I could play undisturbed for as long as my energy held out.

Very often I sight-read classical pieces as I attempted to build my playing ability. But that never lasted long. The classical sheet music was a warm-up to what really energized me and drove me to trespass on Drake University property. I would begin to improvise, emulating at the time, as best I could, Jarrett's playing style. But I wasn't Keith Jarrett, and so my playing over time began to take on my own unique color and expression. One day, after I had been playing Beethoven sonatas for an hour or so, working on a particularly difficult passage, I spontaneously launched into an extended improvisation. It started with the passage from a sonata, but as I warmed up, I set aside the sheet music and just let myself play for the better part of half-an-hour. For the first time, I felt pure emotional energy surge out through my fingertips and into sound. A sound that came through me, unbidden and unaltered by inhibition. I finished, somewhat exhausted, but also oddly energized by a quiet joy.

Then came a light knock on the door. My heart raced a little. I thought, "I'm busted!" I was an imposter, an interloper in the strict world of formal classical musical training. I was trespassing, and I had always been a little apprehensive that I would be caught and bounced out of the building by some stern music administrator. I rose and opened the door. But instead of a bouncer I was met with the soft sparkling gaze of a young Asian woman, a music student, who asked me in a somewhat halting voice, "Could you tell me what that was you were just playing? I've never heard that piece. It was really beautiful."

I was a little taken aback, but managed to stammer, "I don't know. I was improvising, I just made it up."

"Oh, okay, wow," was her only response. "Sorry to interrupt."

I've thought about this encounter many times since. It has something in common with some other instances in my life that affirm the power of raw creativity vs imitation. My wife Diana and I once toured Frank Lloyd Wright's compound in Arizona, Taliaison West. Walking through the rooms of Taliaison was like hearing a siren call over and over again from the more sensuous part of my nature. I felt uplifted by the spaces there in a way that most buildings in our culture fail to achieve. Their design seemed to call on the surrounding desert landscape for their essential energy. There was a sense that they became the desert itself. Situated throughout the grounds were the bronze sculptures of Heloise Cristo. These works of art seemed to burst straight from the Earth and then dance with the other elements into vital and organic human forms. The human figures they depicted seemed enveloped and generated by the other forces of nature. The sculptures were a powerful complement to Wright's design.

Feeling the energies from these influences on our psyches, our small group eventually came to a small auditorium where Wright's grand piano was kept. He had almost decided to be a concert pianist instead of an architect earlier in his life, so he had a special connection to music. He had designed the auditorium so that no matter where you were seated, the acoustics would be equally resonant. Plucking up my courage, I asked the tour director if I could play. Having no sheet music, still under the influence of the architecture and artwork all around us, I improvised. When I pushed through the white-water rapids of risk, uncertain that I could even summon anything from the piano that sounded decent, I emerged into a calm pool on the other side. The convergence of the desert, the space designed by Wright, and Heloise Cristo's artwork came to a point of resonance within me as I tried my best to impart the feeling. There were a few moments of connection between all of us in the tour, as the music took on its own life and reverberated throughout the room. "Wow," was all I could think when I finished, "I played Frank Lloyd Wright's piano!"

People often resonate more emotionally with something that is created in an unscripted moment than with something that is well-rehearsed and prepared, no matter how masterful or polished the performance.

There is some immediate communication in an improvisation that happens, a purity of present moment awareness. There is no attempt to "get it right," only a feeling of intense aliveness. That raw expression has the potential for a deeper connection, and sometimes its beauty and power can be healing. Improvisation involves receptivity to the energy of the world coming into you. Playing an instrument like the piano with great technique doesn't make the music great. Surrendering to the spirit coming through is what lifts the music up and makes something really happen. That seems true of life in general.

Release

My desire for casting rubies like seed,
emeralds like green food for the world
is visible in the Sun's giving,
caught in the gleam in their flesh
as they tumble and turn
and sink into the eager Earth.

The eye beholds the light
and becomes the image
of a thousand burning stones
arriving fresh from their long
journey from the great enamorment.

Even these are not themselves
without the eye desiring the Beloved.
They do not shine
except with the inner flame.

These gifts of starlight
sit heavy in their leather pouch.
I only know relief
when I release their spark from my palm
and fling them far.

LANDSCAPE INTERLUDE
The Land Between Two Rivers

My love for the land between two rivers simmered slowly for years. It would only become a well-flavored broth when I had learned to become enamored with ghosts and transplants, to make the loss of the dispossessed my own, and to accept the strident claims of the present.

This land named Iowa — an expanse stretching between the Mississippi River to the east and the Missouri river to the west — was once riotous with diverse life. Hard maples and bur oaks dominated the river bluffs. Woodland ravines wore cloaks of beautiful ferns, interspersed with diverse softwoods and forest wildflowers like yellow ladies-slippers, jack-in-the-pulpit, and trout lily.

But Iowa was to become the most deeply altered terrain on the North American continent. By 1900: two thirds of the 6.7 million acres of forest cover in Iowa — gorgeous stands of white oak, red cedar, and hard maple — had disappeared; three thousand miles of rivers had been dammed and channelized; vast wetlands were drained out of existence. In slightly less than one human life span, a thirty-million-acre blanket of tall-grass prairie was reduced to one tenth of one per cent of its former size, a mere thirty thousand acres, by the moldboard plough.

The names are legion:

Bluestem, dropseed, compass plant, coneflower, gentian, and blazing star.

Successive waves of transformation — pioneer settlement, agriculture, gypsum and coal mining, the railroad, the creation of giant recreational reservoirs — swept through. Vast communities of prairie grasses and wildflowers became huge tracts of non-native grassland or mono-cultured farmland.

Frost aster, switchgrass, phlox, prairie anemone, hoary vervain, coreopsis.

With this habitat gone, abundant populations of elk, bison, wild turkey, deer, prairie chickens, bear, wolves, river otter, beaver, waterfowl, and shorebirds vanished.

White wild indigo, june grass, purple meadow rue, sawtooth sunflower, Scribner's panic grass... and more than two hundred additional prairie plants.

And yet, at sixteen, just coming of age in a small town in the heart of the state, something in this ravaged landscape won my heart. It began with a trip one summer day to an isolated rural spot on the Des Moines River.

To reach the Des Moines River valley, you drive due south from

Prairie City, past white two-storied clapboard farmhouses, A-frame pig sties, silos, tiny country churches, and patchwork fields of sorghum, soybeans, and corn. The road follows the contour of long rolling hills blanketed with some of the richest soil on Earth, formed from a departed sea of tall-grass prairie. Redwing blackbirds, brown-headed cowbirds, and English house sparrows dominate the farmyards and fence posts.

Just when you feel that this roadscape will roll on without end, you pass over the rise of a hill and abruptly hit gravel. The fields go wild and brambly and you osmose, as if through a membrane, into another realm. The old Rambler station wagon rumbles and clunks over the roadbed. Dust roils up and anoints everything in a kind of strange baptism. You grind it in your teeth and your hair turns bristly. The road is now little more than a dirt path.

The purr of the six-cylinder engine and the rattle of the springs accompany the drone of cicadas in roadside transplants: Ragweed, Queen Anne's lace, and now feral hemp planted in World War II as fiber for rope production. When you reach an abandoned gypsum mine now filled with water from periodic floodwaters and an underground spring, you stop and get out. You hunker down in the weeds on its banks and peer into the water. Bass, bluegill, and green sunfish hang in the crystal water as if on a string, turning slowly to meet your shadow. They glide and stop. Glide and stop. The stop is sudden and perfect, like blinking out a frame of the action. It is high summer and the carp have surfaced in raucous schools; their soft mouths extend to suck the surface. An Asian fish, you realize. More transplants, making their way, eating the eggs of natives. You toss a pebble and their scattering boils the water with a golden flash of scales.

You head across some rusted rail tracks, then down through a labyrinth of summer plant growth, emerging suddenly on the bank where the river does an almost hairpin turn. The flow is very deep here, so deep the river appears oddly still, even though you know the current is moving across the riverbed with sure steady strength. You imagine the murky world down there, picturing the giant bottom-dwellers you'd seen in the backs of pick-ups and in photographs in the Outdoor section of the *Des Moines Register*. These catfish hung, big as a small man, on stout poles between two people. It was said they came from a hidden place on the river, a well-kept secret from anyone but the locals. That place, your brother's father-in-law finally revealed to you, was this turn in the river where you stand. Years ago, a train had derailed here and the boxcars that tumbled into the river were left to the elements. "They spawn in those cars," was his only elaboration.

You pick your way across logs and rocks out to a perch on a rusty boxcar protruding above water. Feeling the dust and heat from the drive, you rashly plunge in. The current is more swift than you anticipate and before you're able to reach the far bank, you're swept downstream to a long strip of sand. You go to explore the trees lining the beach; but as you near them, you see that they are only the ghosts of trees, the shells of giant drowned bur oaks, gray, stark, and weathered against the sky. Their brittle branches are adorned with long ivies, the barkless trunks cloaked with brilliant green mosses. Blue herons retreat in lazy, lumbering flight on your approach. The dried mud crackling beneath your bare feet bears no footprints, only the tracks of receding floodwaters. This strange forest, with its unlikely beauty, was wrought from an Army Corps of Engineers project to create the Red Rock recreational reservoir in 1969.

❧

Years later, in the fall of the year, you return, perhaps to fish, perhaps just to turn over rocks at the edge of the water. This time the drive to the river passes the Neil Smith National Wildlife Refuge, a newly established five-thousand-acre preserve dedicated to restoring tall-grass prairie and savanna habitat.

A crisp October day turns by slow increments into a delicious suspension in time. You catch no fish, so you idly watch the sky as an endless, shifting, cavorting crowd twists and turns in strands and dots against ochre-lit clouds. The migrating waterfowl pass for hours overhead. Their calls and wingbeats move lucidly in and out of your consciousness, like thoughts and images in those fragile moments between sleep and waking. Something jars loose in you and runs untethered with the river. In its steady flow, you feel the tug, the relentless claim nature holds on all things, indifferent to possessor or dispossessed. An unaccountable beauty extends out of the mundane and the lost, shining out of the gray silence of bur oaks. You study the boxcars and discover that these intruders, too, have become an intricate part of the form of this place. You slowly realize that you are surrounded by your own kind. There is something in you of all of them — the transplants, migrants, and ghosts; the opportunists, the natives, and the dispossessed.

A pheasant, too near, crows loudly, startling you out of your reverie. Yet another transplant. You take this as a sign and head for home. Out of this wounded land, a river valley once nestled by prairie and shaded by forest, the steady sure pulse of life continues to combine, configure, adjust, and restore. A fragile beauty simmers, its strange and gathering flavors waiting to be tasted.

A Night on the Des Moines River

The river whispered baptism
from somewhere out in the night.
The sandbanks cupped our hips
as we slept. Our brows were
beaded with the muddy flow:
father water, catfish son, heron holy ghost.
They all respired of a piece.

Our teenage bodies
prone under the stars
not seasoned enough to know
any passage was made.
With day, we bore it all homeward,
anointed with dried mud
on our clothes and fingers,
dreaming only later of the sacrament:

the night, smell of fish and curl of smoke,
August, pale forms under stars and half-moon.

I remember our lines in the dark water,
waiting for the tug, the tug
that told us we were not alone.

[Here] is nature's cry to homeless, far-wandering,
insatiable human: "Do not forget your brethren
nor the green world from which you sprang.
To do so, is to invite disaster."

— **Loren Eiseley**, The Unexpected Universe

The eagle of his nest
No easier divest
And gain the sky
Than mayest thou

Except thyself may be
Thine enemy
Captivity is consciousness
So's liberty.

— **Emily Dickinson**

Learning
and Memory

Chapter 8
Wildness and Domesticity

What matters in learning is
not to be taught but to wake up.
—**Jean Henri Fabre**

It's a crisp October morning and I am face to face with an African lion. A large male whose every muscle looks to be on high alert. He looms above me on a rise. His gaze pierces me. Then he shakes his mane fiercely. Suddenly, a low growl rumbles out from deep within his tawny frame, his snout goes up, his great mouth opens, and the growl crescendos. The roar is so loud, it shreds the crystal clear morning, then rolls through me like breaking surf thundering onto the beach in a storm. Then, he repeats the roar several times in rapid succession. It is as if the voice of the lion hits me across the chest each time he issues a new roar.

He's clearly got the floor. Everyone around me is transfixed. The sheer size of the lion overwhelms me. I feel a shudder begin in my throat, then drop through my torso into my legs. A fleeting jolt of terror shoots through me when I momentarily forget that I'm safely on the other side of the deep chasm carved into the Earth that is meant to protect me at the Oakland Zoo. Everything in that instant tells me to run, and yet I am paralyzed with the magnificence of the sound. For that one raw instant, I remembered in my bones what my ancestors knew intimately out on the savannah when face-to-face with one of the great predators. With very little for protection but wits, reflexes, a sharp spear, or perhaps the tenuous safety of being one in a number of their own tribe or hunting party, it must have been a moment of sheer aliveness and presence.

We often view nature as if from outside, like the African lion in the cage, pacing, magnificent, wonderful in a way, but pent-up, controlled, contained. The beauty of the animal body is on display as spectacle. Landscapes are "scenery," backdrops, the stuff of tourism. The terror of the roar is titillation, entertainment in the face of our deadened sensitivities to the living world. A gulf exists between ourselves and the raw wonders of nature. And in the gulf lurks the illusion that we have contained the natural forces that have shaped us.

This kind of wildness has been caged and domesticated in a society that has mechanized, sanitized, and subdued the natural world. In this illusion of control, we think we have little to fear. The fears of the modern human are mostly due to threats from our own kind. We feel shielded by our cities. But the costs are high. The subjugation of wild nature has also subdued our wild and spontaneous inner world. The lion's roar, rather than genuine power, is little more than a futile gesture of outrage at the loss of freedom.

No other shaping influence in our culture has encouraged this "outside-looking-in" view of nature, this subjugation of our basic spontaneities, more than the education system.

Vagabond

There isn't a right way to become educated;
there are as many ways as there are fingerprints.
—**John Taylor Gatto**

In the middle of the sixth grade, my family moved from South Bend, Indiana, to Des Moines, Iowa. The kidnapping was behind us. My father was pastoring a new church in a new place. It was a fresh start, but also a harsh initiation for my siblings and me. The move took us away from our friends, all things familiar, and the landscape we knew. We were reeling from the transition from the relatively sheltered setting of Bethel Brethren Christian Day School to the rough and tumble of Des Moines public schools. I was twelve years old. The public school system set me outside the bubble of childhood in a different way. While the purpose of the Christian school was to inculcate me into a particular religious doctrine, the public school system was a different kind of indoctrination against which I had few defenses.

My public school education was scrubbed of spirit and if it contained wisdom, it was elusive and cryptic. It seemed little more than rote knowledge to be stored like a commodity. The Calvinist religion I grew up under, as well as my school education had tried to extract the human from the natural matrix and to offer incomplete and unsatisfactory answers to the mysteries of life. For many years after my family's break with the church, I was a kind of feral wanderer, a spiritual vagabond trying to find my way home. Although I wasn't wealthy, my basic material needs were met. But my sense of inner security was shaky due to the loss of a religious community I had known as a child.

My father would hold out for a little over a year in his role as minister before he left for Bethesda Hospital in Colorado for emotional and spiritual rehabilitation. When he did return, he was not rehabilitated as a minister. He left the ministry and was soon off again to get a Master Degree in Social Work. During that time, he had little to no income, so my mother worked for the first time in her married life. There was so little money that in the summertime, when we were out of school, rather than pay for a sitter, she left us in the care of Mother Nature. We fished the local creeks and rivers and swam in the gravel pits.

The domestication process called public education that I experienced in this country wasn't designed to foster independence. If it imparts values at all, they are those of a consumer economy. Neither my grade school education at a Christian school, nor my public education from sixth grade onward educated me as a child of the Earth. At Bethel Brethren Christian Day School I was taken on field trips to a Coca Cola bottling plant and a Whirlpool appliance factory. Early impressions are still with me of soda bottles shuttled down long conveyor belts and shunted into their cardboard carriers; washing machines and dryer tumblers row on row, gleaming and ready for their trip to American homes. These field trips were, in effect, a wedding of fundamentalist Christianity and capitalism, the perfect bedfellows.

Both my religious and public educational experiences encouraged a dualistic view. In the classroom, there was natural history, which was somehow distinct from human history. Humans weren't part of the natural world from which we had evolved. The planet was little more than a bank of resources and the universe was mechanical, pointless, and uncaring, not a source of wonder. The Christian schools transmitted a narrow religious set of values; the public school none at all, unless you count undying fealty to passive consumerism.

In grade school, I recall being taught the names of the countries of the world, not in terms of their geography, landforms, and unique plant and animals communities, but in terms of their "natural resources," those commodities which countries "possessed." The relative worth of a country had to do with the monetary value of their resource base and how effectively it could be extracted and exploited. There was a larger desire in the culture to turn all of nature into figures and formulae. Biology class wasn't about cultivating wonder at the bio-diversity and beauty of plants and animals. It was about a dissection, breaking animals, cells, and plants into their component parts, apart from their habitat, their families, and interrelationships with other species. My sensual experience of nature — the visual, audible, tactile, even the mysterious and ineffable — seemed suspect in the face of a larger belief that nature was simply there as a basis for a limitless, exuberant expansion of human prosperity.

None of this was conscious in me at the time, but something within me didn't take well to public education. I was an average student, unless the course was about writing or literature, where I excelled out of a natural fascination with words. If I wasn't acting out in the classroom and being sent to the principal's office for discipline, I was in a dream state at my desk, longing to be outside. I was the preacher's kid in rebellion, without even knowing at the time what I was rebelling against.

A feral state

One of the few alternatives to complete enculturation into consumerism is immersion in the primary text of nature. It's an experience that is increasingly rare for most of our children. Out on the banks of the Des Moines river, watching the herons fly, fishing the deep pools, I could feel its timeless flow within me. Out on the prairie, searching out wildflowers, walking the margins of the remnant forest, I could feel the earth under my feet. Seeing the shadowy glide of a great horned owl through a grove of oaks, I could feel the joy of flight surge up within me. My experiences of nature would always be an odd hybrid of the raw and the cooked, domestication and wildness, intellectual inheritance and creativity.

Thrust into early searching by a rupture with church and society, I existed in a feral state of self-education. Whenever I could, I was roaming the fields, forests, and riverbanks in the Midwest. Iowa was a vastly domesticated landscape, its thirty nine million acres of prairie mostly gone, along with extensive forests of bur oaks and cottonwoods. But any scrap of the wild would draw me into its charms. I was a bushwhacker, off-road and off-trail, following my nose and my curiosity through the scraps of nature still around. I could spend hours along a short stretch of creek or an intact grove of trees or an hidden and isolated marsh, searching out any wonders I could find. When I was younger and couldn't drive, this often took the form of fishing expeditions with my father or brothers, or family picnics. I ventured as far as I could before that, into stretches of creeks that hadn't been culverted and fragments of fields that were intact. By the time I reached high school, my hormones were directing my attention increasingly to the biology of the human female. But this was punctuated with time outdoors, swimming in local lakes and gravel pits, and fishing farm ponds and creeks with my friends and younger brother, Phil. This immersion kindled my love of nature on a bodily, experiential level.

Invaders and transplants

My early public education wasn't entirely devoid of wing and claw and fin and leaf. There was one exception, an enthusiastic young teacher for ninth grade Biology who fought valiantly to instill within us an under-standing of ecology. She kept a variety of live animals in the classroom and eschewed dissection as a teaching method. One day she took us on a field trip to a local creek which flowed into a slough that was brimming with aquatic life. One of my classmates had brought a rod and reel on the field trip and he lucked into a large carp. He convinced the teacher to let him put the fish in a cooler filled with creek water and bring it back to the classroom. She placed the fish in a giant sink basin in the back of the classroom. Midway through class, the fish was feisty enough to jump the confines of the sink and make for the exit in one last desperate attempt at freedom. It made for the most memorable day of the class.

The teacher took the experience as an opportunity to introduce us to the concept of exotic, invasive species. The Asian carp had established a firm fin-hold in the rivers and creeks of Iowa, she said. Its extreme hardiness made it difficult to eradicate. The carp had a profound impact on the native fish species in the rivers and lakes of the Midwest, eating their eggs and competing for food and habitat. "Trash fish," is the term used by the Department of Fish and Wildlife, she explained, and if you caught one, it was to be "destroyed," not returned to the water. In its native habitat, the carp might have been seen differently, but in the rivers of the Midwest it was seen as an unwelcome invader.

I would think back to the Asian carp from time to time. My brother Phil and I had caught carp frequently fishing the creeks and sloughs of Iowa. They were easier to catch than most of the native fish like catfish, bass, and walleyed pike. I developed a certain affinity, even a sympathy for carp. We weren't unlike them in our attempts to assimilate into a new environment. We were turning to nature in our own way in an unconscious adolescent attempt to initiate ourselves into a new kind of mystery, one to replace the certainties we had lost when our boyhood religious beliefs were called into question. This wasn't an easy task in a state that had been converted into a vast empire of agricultural mono-culture. We were, like most European invaders of the continent, hardy fish out of water, out of touch with a true mystique of the land as native peoples knew it. We nonetheless longed for that connection, and in our own awkward adolescent ways, tried to find our way home.

Self-education

The field of ecological awareness would get a sudden bump from the first Earth Day in 1970, about the time I entered high school. Then it got an even bigger bump from the transformative image of the Earth from space gifted to us by the Apollo 17 astronauts in 1972. There was our fragile-looking blue sphere, garlanded with white, set against the cold backdrop of deep space. But "ecology" wasn't a word that even entered my vocabulary until at least the ninth grade, and then not so much as a science but as a political movement. And why would it have been any different? Interrelationships, the foundation of ecology, would not have been an important part of an industrial education that formed the basis for an extractive economy where model citizens were considered to be good consumers. In fact, it ran counter to it. What is the point of extracting resources without consumption to drive it?

"Education is the most vital of all resources," wrote E. F. Schumacher. "If Western civilization is in a permanent state of crisis, it is not far-fetched to suggest that there is something wrong with its education." Scientific and engineering "know-how," he continued, "is nothing by itself; it is a means without an end, a mere potentiality, an unfinished sentence. 'Know-how' is no more a culture than a piano is music." The task of education if it is to be beneficial to the human and the Earth community, he concluded, should be the "transmission of ideas of value, of what to do with our lives."[2]

But from where do these ideas of value, of what to do with our lives, originate? And how do we make learning uniquely our own? How do we forge an identity from both the transmission of ideas and our direct observation? How do we engage in learning that fosters life? If knowledge is the piano, then we sound out the music by making the instrument our own.

My true education would not come fully from what I had inherited from others, but from how I internalized and made use of their words and ideas and made them my own based on my own observation. I had to belong to myself before I could find belonging with others again. My deepest sense of self would come not from studying nature in a biology textbook, but from feeling the wind on my skin and lying back on the grasses on the hillside. My writing would have to come from the energies of the Earth that wanted to feel their way through me, into the larger world.

Identity and nature

So a question grew in my mind over time from my discomfort with the mechanistic, reductionist, dualistic worldview: What does it mean to be initiated into the wonders of the natural world and to a sense of belonging in the cosmos? Or to instill in the child a larger story from which they might make sense of their life as they grew up and formed an identity? To educate a child in this way would be to sensitize them to meaning. And a sense of meaning is the basis from which to move beyond fear and alienation.

Domestication creates the basis for fear because it means to sever one's inner spontaneities from those of nature. This is tantamount to releasing an astronaut from their tether to the mothership. Imagine floating alone in the vastness of space, drifting away from all connection to everything that gives you life, gazing into a void. This is the human untethered from Earth and home, face-to-face with existential loneliness.

I felt this loneliness, this alienation from the community of life, throughout my primary education in the system of compulsory schooling. As I became a young man, I needed to forge an identity of sorts, an identification with the powers of nature around me. There were few mentors and guides along the way because the pathology of separation, duality, is culture-wide. I was living in a country that had its basis in genocide of indigenous peoples who knew how to live in reciprocity with the land and felt kinship with nature. The European exuberant expansion into the New World and the doctrine of Manifest Destiny had decimated the natural beauty of a continent in just a few generations. I had to come to terms with the fact that these were my forebears, and my cultural legacy.

In my effort to find spiritual repair, I went through a period of cynicism about my kind that bordered on misanthropy. This alienated me from others. It was a dark night of the soul, an emptiness during which I indulged a contempt for my own European Anglo-Saxon roots and the culture that arose from it. It was a necessary and difficult passage, eventually bringing me face-to-face with the divine in an entirely new guise and integration.

While I felt the need, as any young person, for elders, I also realized that I needed to forge a spiritual identity that also reunited me with the natural world. Years later, Dagara shaman Malidoma Somé would tell me when I interviewed him, "If an adolescent isn't initiated by elders into manhood through the mysteries and powers of the natural world, he will attempt to initiate himself throughout his life. Often he succeeds, in a way, but he can also cause a lot of damage in the attempt, both to himself and others."

If my education wasn't producing wisdom, how to live in the world in a reciprocal manner, with an eye to future generations, then it wasn't an education at all. Instead, it was a kind of sleep, a desensitization to the most fundamental dynamics of what it means to be human. It was as if the whole of Western civilization ran screaming from its knowledge that it was one species, one being, one animal, among many.

Education in this country could be a rite of initiation into wildness, creativity, and spirit. Instead, it is largely a process of acclimation to a particular idea of what a human being should be. The wilderness of learning that is human experience doesn't count for much in this educational system. Nor does it speak much to the wild nature from which we have evolved and that gives us our being every day of our lives. It is the taming of the instinctual, of spirituality, of the body, and of the imagination. There is a two-dimensional view of the human being, a pale, flattened version of what we could be, and of the future.

The African lion I encountered at the Oakland zoo was very real. But the situation in which I encountered him, was not. It was fabricated. And it represents our experience of the world today. I heard a kind of raw outrage in that roar. Outrage at the lack of freedom we experience through the domestication of our core spontaneities. My industrial education didn't help me make sense of the world. It didn't help me explain the violence within human nature. And it didn't offer the relationships in ecology as a way to make sense of evil. My bookish view of nature was like that of the lion in a cage—magnificent, wonderful, but simply there to be controlled, contained, domesticated. My bodily sense of nature corresponded with my internal landscape, uncaged, chaotic, but creative. A gulf existed between my thinking self and the larger magnificence.

Wilderness of work

Fresh out of high school, more schooling was the last thing on my mind. I wasn't interested in conforming to the societal norm of a fast track to college straight out of high school. My parents, although educated, were oddly noncommittal on the subject, probably because they had no money to pay for my higher education. I worked a variety of jobs until I was about to turn twenty-six, when I finally went to get a college degree. My driving imperative was a desire for independence. I was out of my parents' house just days after I became a legal adult, living on my own, and ready to throw myself into the work world and prove myself. I did take journalism courses at Des Moines Area Community College while I was working full-time, but I had no interest in being a journalist, and even less interest in a college degree. I only wanted to write creatively, and I thought of the classes as a means to that end.

I wanted to be doing something in the world, make a living, get my hands dirty. So I worked as a steelworker at Pittsburg Des Moines Steel, then on the crew of a massive printing press at Meredith Printing, a company that printed some of the major magazine titles in the U.S. I spent two years on a sales crew selling encyclopedias door-to-door. The irony of that was that our pitch to get in the door with people was: "We want to get your reaction to some new educational ideas." In reality, they weren't new ideas at all. In the pages of Colliers Encyclopedia were the same spiritless, consumerist ideas served up by public education. I was hawking the same educational wares that I had come to distrust from my primary schooling.

In spite of my distaste for free market capitalism, I had undeniable entrepreneurial urges in my twenties. I've heard it said that one character trait of aspiring entrepreneurs is that they often collect things. And I did love collecting things throughout my boyhood. Those collections ranged from stamps and coins to rocks and gems; to butterflies and beetles, and even a collection of what I called "rusty bits," which were bits and pieces of scrap metal that had corroded and oxidized into interesting shapes and hues. Those earlier urges translated later into a desire in me to sell things. I made pocket change in seventh and eighth grade selling greeting cards door-to-door that I had sent away for through the mail. When I was a junior in high school, there was a drive to sell magazine subscriptions door-to-door as a fundraiser. While my class-mates grumbled, ridiculed, or shied away from the task, I took it as a challenge, selling more subscriptions door-to-door than my classmates combined, and winning prizes of a black light and posters.

In the work world a few years later, I took a job as a route sales-man, first for Coca-Cola and then for a industrial uniform/linen rental company. I didn't even drink pop, but I asked for a rural route because it had few accounts and I saw it is an interesting challenge to "build up the route." I doubled the size of the route in the space of two years by selling new accounts. The same challenge was presented to me with the linen rental company. It was a small local company competing against the behemoths of national companies, and I relished taking accounts away from the big guys.

Many years later, even after I had completed college and was editor of a national magazine, the same entrepreneurial urges operated within me. I took the job because it brought my main interests, ecology, spir-ituality and writing, together in one job. However, once I was at the helm of the magazine, I found that I loved another aspect of the job as much as the writing and the ideas. I loved growing the subscriptions and soliciting donations every bit as much. A magazine is essentially a collection of stories, and I enjoyed soliciting articles from writers as much as writing myself. The job brought together my love of ecology and spirit with my entrepreneurial side in a perfect storm. For nearly ten years, I threw myself into the work body and soul.

ψ

At the steel plant in Des Moines, I worked alongside Perry, a man in his early sixties who had lost his family farm in the 1970s. His life on the farm had toughened him like the steel we worked with, and although I was much younger and physically strong, I struggled to keep up with his hardy work ethic. We worked on the plate shear, a massive machine that cut enormous steel plates up to ten feet across and one-fourth-inch thick with an enormous blade that crashed down, severing the plate in an instant. The snap of the thicker steel plates being sheared was loud enough to potentially inflict hearing loss. We were required to wear earplugs, hardhats, and steel toed boots for protection.

We were cutting plates for the Ruan Center in Des Moines, a skyscraper that was just being built, and for many years would be the tallest building in the city. The building would house insurance and banking offices, making it one of the country's headquarters for industrial capitalism. And so, in retrospect, I was helping to build a citadel of capitalism, just as not long before I had been selling encyclopedias that housed many of consumer capitalism's sacred precepts.

These jobs were part of my education. I loved the challenge of selling as well as the hard physical labor of the steel plant. It would be years before I would understand my unconscious participation in the industrial culture that was dismantling our green planet. That understanding would come only when I came up against the limitations of making a living in that world and would seek an education beyond its walls. The work world had been a wilderness of learning for me, a feral contrast to the domesticated and mechanistic primary school education to which I had been subjected.

In my search for a spiritual path, I fell in with a self-styled spiritual teacher who had taken the name Tatsumo Makami. I never learned his American birth name. "T," as he liked to be called, was into a combination of Eastern philosophy, Taoism, kung fu martial arts, the spiritualism of Edgar Cayce, reincarnation, the mysticism of the Essenes, and meditation. I see this now as the more feral side of my spiritual life. I was in a spiritual wilderness without an adequate guide. I would come to find out that T's esoteric approach was mostly ungrounded and self-serving. We parted ways, but I retained the practice of meditation for many years afterward.

There came a time, when I turned twenty-six, that I found myself at an impasse with the work world. I had become disaffected with the mild deceits required in any sales job where I didn't fully believe in what I was selling. As a result, my entrepreneurial energies fizzled. One night, in the whirlpool bath at a health spa with my lover at the time, Carol, I floated an idea: "Maybe I could go back to school, you know, finish the journalism degree I started out of high school." Carol pounced. She wasn't one to waste a good idea. Despite my reservations about formal education, she made sure that what was an idle comment from me, in a relaxed and vulnerable state, didn't simply evaporate with the mist from the jacuzzi. Several months later, I had moved to Iowa City and was enrolled at the University of Iowa.

Chapter 9
From Feral to Free Range

When I returned to the university after several years in the work world, it was because I wanted to be there. Even so, I didn't follow a path to a lucrative career. I took courses that fed my love of learning, not a degree that would take me down a more conventional path into business, law, medicine, finance, or public administration. And so, what had been a feral and unconscious state of self-education morphed into free range exploration. The structure of the university system provided some boundaries along with a degree of freedom to choose coursework within the liberal arts.

Studying history gave me a new context, and I began to more fully understand the roots of American capitalism. I read the natural history essayists. I shunned courses that felt devoid of my preferred contexts of ecology, history, or evolution. I struggled with Chemistry and its numbers, formulae, and reductionism, but adored Botany with its fundamentals of ecology and plant biology. That's where the elements came alive. Photosynthesis could take carbon out of thin air, nitrogen out of the soil, and photons from the sun and conjure a million forms. I thought of plants as the marvels of the living world. A course on Ecology and Evolution kept me up late at night all one semester with excitement as my readings brought me to a new understanding of evolutionary philosophy and ecological relationships.

Then I came upon a wild ecosystem of authors who would slowly but surely help me rebuild an identity that was more in line with my bodily experience of the world of nature. I discovered a flood of literature that was a bell sounding in full resonance with my own experience of nature: Henry David Thoreau's explorations of wildness and voluntary simplicity; Ralph Waldo Emerson's contemplations on nature and the human spirit; Aldo Leopold's exposition of a land ethic; Rachel Carson's dire warnings of our chemical warfare on the Earth; Annie Dillard's rapturous, if somewhat baroque, essays on her local watershed; Loren Eiseley's evolutionary prose, unsurpassed at the time in its eloquence; Wendell Berry's agrarian stewardship for the land; John Muir's love affair with the glory of California's mountains; Gary Snyder's Zen-like and deeply ecological poetic language; and many others. In a way, it was easier to get lost in the thicket of the prose of an author like Ralph Waldo Emerson or to stare down the maw of an Emily Dickinson poem than to find true wilderness on a subdued and exploited planet Earth. Many of these authors weren't even on the course syllabi at the university. I spent more time reading them than the assigned readings.

These writers were not found in the repertoire of readings my father was assigned when he was in Calvin College seminary in the late 1940s. Thoreau, Emerson, the American Transcendentalists, and their contemporary lineage didn't mix well with Christian fall-redemption theology. And so, they were newly explored terrain for me in college. Their articulation of a more viable way of relating to planet Earth was reaffirming the pleasure and sense of belonging I had already discovered in the woods and rivers. Their writings spoke to the healing and energizing powers and graces of nature, but they also echoed my uneasy sense that somehow my culture had lost the connection with the web of life on Earth. And it had done so to the point of pathology and at its own peril.

My time at the university was like passing through a portal, an initiation of sorts into a better understanding of the planet through literature, but also through courses on ecology and evolution, botany, and zoology. I was discovering new articulations of landscape and the human imagination. As I absorbed and internalized environmental philosophy, I became unapologetic when it came to my love of writing and desire to articulate the same love for the living world.

My allurement toward writing eventually landed me in the Iowa Writers Workshop, where I learned to navigate the sometimes treacherous, sometimes uplifting, terrain of peer criticism. But it wouldn't be the rigors of the workshop that would ignite my path as a writer. It would be a course offered by Robert Sayre. Professor Sayre was the great nephew of Zelda Sayre, F. Scott Fitzgerald's wife. His course in expository writing challenged us to explore family and animals as grist for the writing mill. I knew from reading Sayre's writings that he and I were kindred spirits in our respect and love for the natural world. It would turn out to be the most dynamic course I took in almost five years at the university.

"Write about family and animals" was Sayre's only assignment. It seemed an unlikely combination to me then. On the family side, my sister's kidnapping, my father's crisis of faith, and my family's subsequent fall from grace and loss of community. On the nature side, stag beetles, forest mushrooms, creeks and rivers, a world of birds and salamanders and the tall-grass prairie. But I wrote about all of them out of the same well of longing for answers. My fascination for the natural world grew like fungi from the leaf litter of trauma in my past. The fearsome pincers and imposing size of the stag beetle and the soothing wind across a prairie landscape were ways of reimagining loss and creativity, nature as fearsome risk and safe haven. My love of writing and of nature came together in a new way that began to give me a sense of healing a rupture I was only partly aware of at the time.

It was around this time that I first met Barry Lopez when he came to the University of Iowa on the occasion of his *Arctic Dreams* book release. Reading the book and listening to his account of writing it, I heard the clarion call of a new orientation in my life—nature essayist, poet, a defender and champion of all things wild through the written word. What Lopez brought home to me in the spare, crafted, and poetic prose of his books *River Notes* and *Desert Notes* and *Winter Count* was that language, imagination, and landscape were an energetic matrix that could give rise to meaning. As Westerners carrying the legacy of an invader culture, perhaps we could relearn the language of the heron and the salmon and the mountain and find a way home. But only if we come out of the confines of our rational, analytic mind and bring it into a balanced, direct experience of the living world. And only if we learn to listen to nature and to the indigenous peoples who inhabited this land for thousands of years.

One of the things that I learned from Lopez and other writers in the nature essay genre was that the human imagination can be a powerful agent of change in one's worldview. Language, writing, ideas, and books engage a certain dimension of one's being. But these only supplement our experience as embodied beings on a living planet; they don't supplant it. Our capacity to reinvent our relations to the community of life comes both from the imagination and from feelings of awe, the beauty and terror that reside at the vibrant ground of our being. The craft of Lopez's writing and the power of story affected my imagination deeply. When we met again, years later, I told him: "Your book *Arctic Dreams* showed me how language can not only transform an idea of landscape; it can create an internal shift that permanently cuts through how we have been conditioned to see the other-than-human world. I'll never think of a polar bear, or the Arctic, or a narwhal, or the people of that landscape in the same way." His response was a simple bow and a smile.

Earth's body is my body

My avid birding life began during these undergraduate years in Iowa City. It prompted a series of expeditions around the Iowa City area with my friend Kazunari Ueno. Kaz was Japanese and at the university to do research, and we were roommates for a time. Kaz was also a photographer; I was newly into birdwatching, so we explored remaining scraps of Iowa's wild nature together.

One of these outings began in the pre-dawn hours at a lake a few miles west of town. Kaz wanted to catch the very earliest light for his photos. We pulled into a parking lot at the lake through thick fog. A short hike up the steep flank of a hill on the western shore of the lake took us to the highest point in the park. Along the climb, the fog parted here and there, revealing the bright yellow flash of a goldfinch or the dark-crested silhouette of a kingbird. Robin song burbled out of the mist, punctuated by the rough caws of crows. Warblers cast out their first tentative trills and mordents, and yellowthroats volleyed their jubilant triplets back and forth.

The light was just beginning to cast its first pale streamers across the scene below. From the rise, we looked down on a dimly lit yellow and pink blanket stretching all the way to the horizon. The Sun gradually painted the humped and slowly-rolling back of the fog bank in a strange array of pastel hues. It was a sight that insisted that we slow down; that we breathe, and witness. The first sliver of the Sun's rays appeared furtively, like tiny shining ships over the far lip of the sea. Time slowed, but the turning Earth did not. Once that first shimmer appeared, the Sun was no longer tentative; it seemed to shoot up over the horizon so rapidly that for the first time in my life, I felt the great heaving roll of the planet deep within me.

The Sun didn't rise that morning. Instead, I rode the back of a giant turning body, and my body was one and the same with the planet's. Together, we were racing toward the Sun as if to the arms of a lover. And as we rolled as one, the Sun unrobed. And then there was morning and the birdsong began anew, as if jolted into astonished praise of that long love affair of Earth and Sun that had brought all of this life into existence.

To say it was a "turning point" seems to make "light" of the moment, and yet there it was, an experience where I pivoted even more deeply toward a felt sense of myself as one with a planet that had spun itself into a panoply of life the likes of which the encircling arms of the Milky Way galaxy had never seen. Searching root, aspiring branch, floating crust, fiery center, flowing magma, oceanic cloak of water, rising mountain, green aprons of forest; they were all churning within and around me. It was a moment of deep and abiding love, strange and wonderful. I felt the enormity of the event that is our planet and its riot of life. And the birds were the Earth singing out of joy, of her own glory.

How Stories Appear
—*Loess Hills, western Iowa*

The hills are ochre powder ground from glacial
melt-waters, carried by the wind over the banks
of the Missouri, laid down like silk scarves, poured
like anointing oil. There are no rocks in its fine grain,
not even a pebble, smooth as foam,
colored like the demeanor of the people there.

Some walk across the rare hills, naming them,
remarking the toad, the snake, the bison,
the oak, the elk, the shooting star,
recalling their histories. And throughout, the sound:
"loess, loess"
departs from the lips of hissing grasses.

Having been nursed by the river, the hills follow
its banks, toddlers not weaned, lie down
and suckle its flow, strain to hear their father's
scrape and grind—a glacier gone off, descended
beneath Earth's crust like an old god,
leaving the land bubbling with its dying.

They say if you find a rock here it is from
somewhere off-planet. You can touch it
and say, "visitor, you are found out."

How a place is made, how stories appear, walking,
how the land endures. This is what the body knows.
Set in the flank of a loess hill, they speak,
the spirit of grass and hoof and wing,
held in place by a tale of stars, river, wind, glacier,
soil, by people walking with open ears.

Chapter 10
Prairie Heart

Gratitude surges through me, and the
cast of grief holding me rigid is broken.

I instinctively froze, then I ran for all it was worth. I've never really been that quick on my feet, but that day I could have won the hundred yard dash. A beast as big as a small bear with a massive head was my motivation and it was headed directly at me. Soon, it was hot on my heels. Each of its periodic growls loomed closer and louder as I scanned the terrain ahead of me for the safety of an oak or a maple. There weren't any good options. I was nearing the boundary of the cemetery. Ahead of me, about ten paces away, was a rusty barbed wire fence about four feet high. Should I vault it? Or turn and face my pursuer? Something told me to turn. I stopped, whirled around, and braced my hands on my knees and glared in the direction of terror on four legs.

The Rottweiler approached full tilt, skidded to a sudden halt in the thick grass, then dropped its forequarters in a stance of play. The universal signal transformed my fear to relief, and seeing the drop and the tail wag drew out a laugh that shook me and caused me to slump, a gasping heap to the prairie floor.

I was twenty seven years old and studying English Literature and Cultural Anthropology in college. This was supposed to be a quiet, reflective day away from my studies in search of native wildflowers. I was in one of the few remaining patches of native prairie in the state of Iowa, a cemetery in the tiny unincorporated town of Rochester in Cedar

County. I had my 35 mm camera and close-up lenses and I'd gathered images of shooting stars, columbine, buttercup, iris, and phlox. The beauty of spring wildflowers normally would have been uplifting, but the truth is, until the sudden appearance of the beast, I was brooding. I had been reading the story of the prairie's demise in the state of Iowa and a sense of tragedy was fresh within me. Foraging for scraps of the tall-grass prairie's former glory in the state only drove me further into my grief over the loss of such a rich biological treasure under the uncompromising and insistent blade of the moldboard plough.

A few of the thoughts and images preoccupying me: Perennial grasses, wildflowers, stretched like an ocean as far as the eye could see; thirty million acres of prairie covering 85% of what is now called Iowa; there were over four hundred species of flowering plants, roots as deep as six feet, some of them perennials with life spans of over one hundred years; the soil was of legendary fertility, created over aeons by generations of self-organizing, self-perpetuating plants and soil microbes under a blanket of ancient loess soil. The plant community supported over one hundred mammal species, including bison and elk, and countless birds, many of which nested and bred only in the prairie.

This natural wonder of the Iowa prairie was reduced from thirty million to less than thirty-thousand acres in just eight decades, from 1850 to 1930. In the name of an idea of that had taken root in the European mind. The plough was the accelerant. The dense soils and tangle of tough roots weren't at all easy to convert, but the steel moldboard plough, brought into existence in the 1850s, tolled the death knell for most of the prairie. The moldboard allowed the steel blade to cut through heavy soil without having the soil constantly adhering to the plough. This type of plough was a repurposed implement, hewn from one of the very saw blades that had been part of the take-down of most of Iowa's five to six million acres of oak-hickory forests. It happened in even less time than it took to decimate the prairie. Vibrant stands of bur oak, white oak, red oak, and shagbark hickory forests were reduced to less than 1.5 million acres by the turn of the century.

The prairie is not technically a super-organism, which is an aggregate of members of one species like a termite mound. But it's not difficult to see the vibrant mesh of plant and animal communities of the prairie as one living being, one so extensive that it would have been visible from space. If the planet can be seen as living, the prairie was a key organ of the body of Earth. The intricacies of the plant and animal relationships and the vast area of thirty million acres would have made a profound impact on the topography, weather, and lives of countless mammals, insects, birds, amphibians, and other life.

What I longed to see was hill after hill of prairie rising and dipping, wave after wave, billowing with the hand of the wind and glistening under the face of the sun. But I could only see it in my imagination. It was in just such a forlorn state, camera slung over my shoulder, alternating between self-pity and outrage, that I trudged to the crest of the hill where I would encounter the hulk of a dog with a massive head. I didn't even know the breed at the time, had never seen a Rottweiler. What I did see was a black and brown carnivore barreling straight for me and barking thunderously. A quick scan of the area told me that we were alone. There was no mediating master to rein in the dog's animal whims with a sharp command.

I pulled myself to my feet and watched as the Rottweiler spun itself around twice in a frenzied dervish, then jetted off for the far side of the cemetery. Dizzy with adrenaline, I lunged after him, pushing myself to the limit to keep up. Just as I felt I was losing the race and would have to stop and rest, the dog spun to face me and stopped. I was learning the game now. I took off running with all my might. I could hear the rustle of grasses behind me as the dog gained traction and quickly gained on me. This time, as his growls and barks grew closer, I felt exhilaration well up and it made me push harder and, even though I didn't know I had it in me, to run faster. I thought my lungs would burst, but I was giddy with the thrill of the chase. Then I spun around again, and faced my playmate. Instead of stopping, he changed his trajectory, leaping in a long graceful arc that took him in an oblique direction. I was hot after him, shouting out my own kind of bark, feeling I was giving him the same pleasure I had felt a moment before. There is something about being pursued like you are the next meal that can light up your blood and make you forget yourself.

I don't know how many turns we took around the cemetery, or how much time passed. I was lost in the game. But I felt my endurance was unbeatable and my stamina eternal. It was my playmate who suddenly barked three times, as if to say, "It's been real!", then turned and loped over the hill in the direction from which he'd come. He disappeared as mysteriously as he had materialized, as if osmosing between worlds. I was perhaps just too slow to hold his interest for long. But the rangy visitor had pulled me out of my moody torpor and made me feel alive.

The wild heart of a domesticated dog; my own wild heart dancing with his, and the heartbeat of the ancient prairie still beating in this remnant patch of native forms and wildflowers, somehow preserved amidst the manicured plots of the dead, domesticity among wildness, the raw and the cooked; life and death commingling in a place where people came to honor their dead, their ancestors or progenitors, to remember something of them that still lived within them, and so lived on. I was remembering somewhere in my own blood and bones the vast organism of the tall-grass prairie where I could run free, pursuing my animal heart, and turning to be pursued in return, fleeing, hunted, chased. The exhilaration of it was beyond reckoning. And in the background, a mystique of local story and ancient wildness and a lost landscape.

☙

Local lore flourished around this cemetery like the wildflowers in the small patch of prairie it protects. There was the story, for instance, that the famous actress, Sarah Bernhardt, born in the Rochester area to the King family and then orphaned while still quite young, visited the grave of a her adoptive mother, slipping into Rochester by night train, then horse and buggy, masqueraded in a veil and a hat. Disowned by her extended family who raised her for her fixation with the traveling theater that came through when she was a young woman, she ran off, but returned on this particular night because she was playing a nearby theatre.

Rochester was a site that sheltered runaway slaves too. There was the Green house, owned by a local railroad conductor where a patched-up brick wall was discovered years later with tunnels beyond it that led to the Cedar River where there would have been waiting boats in the middle of the night. And there was a belief that the departed spirits of the slaves guarded the town and its abolitionist descendants from harm.

These capacities for remembering through story, of resilience, the pursuit of justice, protecting the innocent, are part of the human too, as much as our capacity to destroy. As such, they are part of the prairie landscape. The ability to develop new sensitivities and learn from the wisdom of the past is a lesson of the prairie. With wild patience and persistence, quadrillions of plants, microbes, and animals built the fertility of the prairie soil over millennia. Bison, passing over the landscape, pruned the grasses and wildflowers with their hunger and aerated the soil with thousands of sharp hooves. Lightning strikes brought regular fire and Native Americans built soil health through controlled burns. The entire expanse of what is now Iowa was a sea of intricate relationship and symbiosis, a bio-diverse and resilient organism.

Even in the face of the drive to dominate with the plough, there were those very early in the process who began the work of patiently preserving the land. Conscientious souls who loved and valued the tall-grass prairie began preservation efforts of its remnants as early as 1900. The Walnut Creek National Refuge (renamed the Neil Smith Prairie Reserve) is just such a restoration effort (not original prairie, but reintroduced native plants), begun in the 1980s. Bison now also roam this Reserve and are part of the restoration efforts. The prairie may never return to its pre-settler glory. But with the right sensitivities there might yet be a fruitful marriage of what was and what is that will ride the creative tension of human and non-human into fuller being.

My playmate departed, I lay back, flat against the patch of prairie, and gaze up into the green and gold-tinged leaves and branches of a huge sheltering sycamore. Beneath me are the searching roots of prairie wildflowers and grasses. All around me are the bones of my own kind, people who knew this place and perhaps even loved it, commingled with the rich soil of millennia of life and death, of plant and animal bodies that had flourished and returned, over and over again; centuries of mutually generative relationships, thousands of generations, toiling, living, dying. And us, the newcomers, a scant few generations into the adventure of the Great Plains.

Breathing lightly, with my eyes closed, I sink down into the body of the prairie, and hear a deeper voice in the interval between thought and feeling. When I roll over, I find myself face to face with a small patch of shooting stars co-mingling with yellow buttercups and red columbine. In my depleted but happy state, their magenta and yellow faces glow fiercely in the waning sunlight of early evening. The black points of the star blossoms hang, as if poised to etch their story into the palm of my hand. Their fluted blossoms shake with the urgency of remembering. Precious and endangered, yes, but their precarious state no longer draws me into forlornness. Instead, gratitude surges through me, and the cast of grief holding me rigid is broken.

A fellow traveler on Earth had bounded up and reminded me that I had a body, that I was healthy and alive, that what is lost only truly stays lost when we are frozen out of possibility by our forgetting. And there are survivors, wild and waiting to regenerate when we learn to make the right choices. Although domesticated, who's to say that the heart of a Rottweiler, or that of a grieving human being, doesn't beat with the same wildness at its core as that of the bobolink or the bobcat, the great prairie toad or the burrowing night crawler. Or, the whole of the wide and wild prairie?

Life-unto-death-unto-life cycles over generations become the self-perpetuating body of soil, the fecund intelligence of Earth herself nurturing a swarm of life, a vast living being that once mantled the face of a continent. Rain and fire and wind and birth and death all shape and feed; a feast of ages called Prairie. The fecundity isn't lost as long as there is a playful and wise awareness that kindles its evolution. Who knows what can be born out of that relationship between the awakened human and the prairie soil, seething with life?

On the Seam

Walking the rock road between
pasture and wild oak,
I stop at the stile, its two
weathered feet planted
on each side of the wire fence.

One foot in the well-grazed
and pasteurized, the wire-strung,
hoof-trammeled, wheel-rutted.

The other foot in the raw-boned,
leaf, twig and memory-crusted,
the moss and lichen-sculpted.

A pregnant bobcat hunts
the pasture side,
stalking her own form of fire.

My hunger, fired by spring,
is beyond food—
the animal body arriving
to find its poem
right here, on the rocky seam.

Chapter 11
Abroad

The dance between landscape and the human imagination stayed with me long after my undergraduate studies at the University of Iowa. I moved to France in 1985 and would live there for almost two years, traveling from region to region, getting work where I could. I was looking to immerse myself in another language and culture. For a time I visited family *chateaux* in the French countryside out of a curiosity about bread ovens in local communities that were once common points of community gathering and cohesion. My sense of the French was that their connection to the land was older than my own. There weren't many remnants of the natural world left in France or in its neighboring countries of Italy, Belgium, and the Netherlands, which I also visited. The wild was there, but latent, braided within stories, or buried under centuries of human habitation. They had the ocean, the small villages of the Loire Valley, and the Alsace region, where I spent some time.

I visited the great cathedrals of France, incited by writer Henry Adams's observation a century earlier on the psychic energy in the human imagination that was driven by the Virgin Mary. What could possibly be a substitute for that energy in my own time? What archetypal figure could erect something as grand as the medieval cathedrals? The cathedral at Chartres, as with Adams, held a special interest for me. "Of all Mary's miracles," wrote Adams, "the best attested, next to the preservation of her church, is the building of it; not so much that it surprises us as because it surprised even more the people of the time and the men who were its instruments."[3] Adams goes on to describe the Herculean labor of the people involved in the building of the cathedral at Chartres, beginning with the quarrying of the stone which was "excessively hard," cut into enormous blocks. These giant blocks then had to be transported and set into place at Chartres, which was about five miles distant. This was done with "feverish rapidity" but in a spirit of pride, devotion, and inspiration, even religious zeal. This was not the slave labor used for so many other great human edifices, like the pyramids of Egypt, unless you deem slavish devotion to Mary, the Queen of Heaven, as such. Then there was the devotion of the architects, the glassmakers, stone masons, and carvers, something that Adams chronicles in great detail in the chapters following "The Virgin of Chartres."

This had special meaning to me as I thought of what modern equivalent of the cathedral calls to be built today, if any. Could devotion to the Earth as Gaia drive the building of, say, the green city, rising from the plains of my native Midwest? Could the dreams of visionaries like Paolo Soleri, Lewis Mumford, and Richard Register be fed by the power of the Earth Goddess? I doubted it. The American imagination was too secularized, too steeped in Manifest Destiny and the exuberance of an extractive economy drawn toward the Puritan image of a golden city on the hill. This vision saw the United States as exceptional and exemplary, an idea that had little room for reciprocal relations with the living world of a vast continent.

My reading of Adams's *Monte Saint Michel et Chartres* began for me a years-long query about what currently drives that psychic energy to be able to build a modern-day equivalent of the great cathedrals. Although the Virgin Mary was not a key part of my Protestant upbringing, I was fascinated by the idea that she was the source of so much psychic energy. As I visited the great cathedrals of France, as well as numerous churches in towns throughout the French countryside, I couldn't miss the pervasive presence of Mary everywhere, even the church I was married in at Limoges. These questions were never far from my mind after I left France and ventured into the Canadian wilderness. Nor would they leave me and my subsequent travels to the West Coast of the United States. I would later turn from the story of the golden city on the hill toward a different story emerging from scientific cosmology based in our evolutionary origins. But for now, I couldn't envision even a modern-day simulacrum of the Virgin Mary. She was a thirteenth century shibboleth, run underground by an increasingly secular America imagination and by the modernization of the church by Vatican II, with its antipathy toward Mariolatry.

I was married in Limoges to Melinda, an American who was teaching in France under a Fulbright scholarship. We had known each other at the University of Iowa, but arrived in France separately. I was there under a four-month work permit. I had fallen in with a group of French college students, picking apples by day for work, partying at night. In the evenings, we hung out in a large barn on the orchardist's property, smoking pot and Gauloise cigarettes, and banging out bad rock music on a couple of guitars and an electric piano. Three of the students who hoped to form a band had somehow managed to scrounge up the instruments, hauling them with them in their beat-up van.

When my permit ran out, I was looking for ways to stay in France. For one thing, I had not bought a return plane ticket to the U.S., and had not made enough money to buy one. When I contacted Melinda in her studio apartment in Limoges, after some months living alone, she eagerly invited me to join her. I found work "under the table" where I could, teaching English to students at the local lycée, then in a soup kitchen at one of the town's churches. When a knife fight broke out between two patrons under my watch one night, and I had to break it up using my broken French, I quit and worked odd jobs for a circus while it was in town.

Our wedding was an event that the French in Limoges found mildly amusing. "You had to move to France to fall in love. But then it is only to marry one of your own countrymen," Madame Rancée, the wife of the school headmaster, teased. But they also found it romantic. We were married in a gothically beautiful eleventh century church, St. Michel des Lions, so named because of two Gallo-Roman stone lions, removed from a nearby cemetery, that guarded the entrance. We were almost broke, and couldn't afford much of a ceremony, but the townspeople pitched in wherever they could. Madame Rancée forced cherry blossoms to bloom on branches from her yard, just in time for our wedding. The chef at the lycée, also a baker at the local patisserie, baked us a three layer cake at no charge. Another teacher from the lycée arranged for us to take a honeymoon in her family's country home on a small lake for a couple of nights. "*Les petits Américains,*" they called us even though at my 6-foot-4 and Melinda's 5-foot-eleven we towered over most of them. They found it charming that we chose Limoges for our wedding ceremony. People we didn't even know attended our ceremony, just for amusement, or out of curiosity. We were the talk of the town, at least for a weekend.

When Melinda's teaching fellowship in Limoges ran out, we set out for the Netherlands to see what we could find out about my Dutch ancestry, then to Italy to explore her ancestry. If I couldn't find answers about the activation of energy in Europe's devotion to the Virgin Mary, perhaps I could start more humbly, with a look at my family's origins.

ॐ

"This guy had no progeny," said the genealogist whom Melinda and I had met just hours before. He was pointing at the crypt in the floor of a church in the tiny village of Blije in the Friesland province of the Netherlands. The genealogist, Pieter Nieuwland, had generously offered to drive us to Blije after we visited his office in search of information on my Dutch ancestry, and we discovered that he and I had some common ancestry.

The remains in the crypt were those of Janke van Unema, who died in 1520. He was depicted on the sculpted cover of the crypt as a knight, wielding a sword and wearing mail armor.

"It wasn't unusual back then for the farmers working the land to take the name of a nobleman who owned the land when he died and left no heirs," said Pieter.

"And so my ancestors weren't nobility," I answered, "but farmers."

"Yes, and it appears from the records that they were Mennonites."

Well, this was a turn. And one that met with a lukewarm reception from my living relatives. This was because for years a story, both written and oral, had circulated in my family about Janke van Unema's exploits and adventures. How he was a Dutch nobleman, the owner of a castle which would later become the Unema farm. And how by dint of his sword and strong right arm he had stormed a citadel and rescued a young woman who had been abducted from his castle by marauders. The result was marriage to the damsel, and so this adventurous character was our ancestor, went the tale. Everyone liked that story on my mother's side of the family, the Unemas. It was fun to retell it at holiday family gatherings.

Standing over the grave in Blije, I immediately took to the revised narrative that we were descended from farmers, people who worked with their hands and the elements, the salt of the Earth. I found this appealing in the same way as you might come to love the more spare beauty of a native wildflower over the splendor and ornamentation of a rose cultivar.

My father, after I returned from Europe, also took an interest and he sleuthed out our ancestry on both sides of the family, then drew up a family tree. A name floated up from my father's side. Egbert Boer, my great-grandfather. "Boer means 'farmer' in Dutch," said my father. "When Egbert died, the older of his two sons kept the name Boer. The younger son, your grandfather, took the name of his stepfather, Smit, then later, Smith."

This was the prompt for me to eventually change my name. I reclaimed the name Boer and went from the rather generic last name of "Smith" to "de Boer." I added the article to make it "Lauren the farmer," a further connection, I felt, to the land. Instead of my first name at the time, Kurt, I began using my middle name, Lauren, because it was what my father called me when he was feeling affectionate toward me.

"What do we really know about our ancestors? Who were they, really?" I asked my father one day as we were poring over his patchwork of scraps of paper that formed a sprawling diagram of ancestral names and dates.

He regarded me. "I guess we don't know much about what they thought and felt as people," he responded, "just a few anecdotes and odd facts." Beyond that and a handful of names on the family tree, I know nigh unto to nothing about them. No trunkful of letters or enduring artwork or artifacts were passed down. What came down to me from them lives inside, silent, inscrutable.

I thought of my grandfather on my mother's side, Peter Unema, who died right about the time we visited the church in Blije. I had begun to notice that I had some of his mannerisms and traits — his quiet laugh, the tilt of his head when listening, his tendency toward baldness. Not long ago, wearing a wool hat passed down to me from my father, I caught myself mimicking my grandfather's nervous habit of turning his wool hat around in his hands by the brim when talking. But what of his inner life, his fears and joys?

The best I could recall were quiet moments with him in the basement of his home where he had a shop, warm sunlight reaching down through a window well onto a pockmarked table where he sifted through penny postcards, stamps, and coins with his thick fingers. He would give me one keepsake from his collection each time we visited.

My grandfather came from that line of Mennonite farmers in Blije. He was a shoe repairman, humble, earthy, as were the smells of leather and dye in his basement shop. He wasn't a king or a captain of industry or a celebrated artist, but he was real.

Eventually, after over a year-and-a-half living in France, we ran out of money and options for staying in Europe, so we returned to the U.S., then moved to Canada, where Melinda had chosen to do graduate studies at the University of Toronto. North of Toronto were the vast wilderness areas of the Ontario province. The contrast of the wild areas of Canada to France could hardly have been more stark, secondary in my mind only perhaps to the contrast of the heart of New York City to the far northern reaches of the Arctic. The Arctic wasn't far from my mind as we moved north. Barry Lopez's description of the landscape in his book *Arctic Dreams* had lit a fire in me for visiting the region. But traveling to the Arctic took money. I would have to settle for the Algonquin wilderness north of Toronto.

We landed in a boarding house run by a tiny but tough Serbian grandmother. From there we would look for housing, get set up in Toronto. But after only a day or two under her stern gaze and prying questions, we lit out for an outing in Algonquin. We rented a canoe and with our tent and sleeping bags, set out to find an island in one of the patchwork of small lakes in which to camp. It was a bit audacious with no guide, but we found a site, pitched camp, and had enough daylight to eat a simple meal.

In the tent, in the middle of the night, an eerie cry reached us from across the lake. As the wind picked up, a snuffling sound started up not far from the tent. Worn out from strenuous canoeing, Melinda went straight to sleep, while I lay awake, letting my imagination run wild. I had bears on my mind because for some now rueful reason on the drive up to Toronto, I had read aloud to Melinda from a fictional, but historically accurate, account of harrowing bear-human encounters. The snuffling sound not far from the tent sounded for all the world like a bear rifling through the campsite. I finally plucked up the courage to stick my head and a flashlight outside the tent. Eventually, the beam of light lit on our canoe which was tied up to a tree root. A wind had come up in the night and the sound of a bear was nothing more than the canoe rocking lightly against the shore of the lake. And the eerie cry from across the lake? A mystery never solved.

In the morning, we found that the food bag we had hastily and ineptly jerry-rigged onto a tree limb using a rope threaded through one of our jackets was on the ground. What little food we had with us was gone. We'd had a night visitor after all and from the size of the paw prints, it had to be a bear. Out of food, we struck the tent and headed back toward the lodge where we'd rented the canoe.

Soon we faced a decision. We had accessed the lake through a narrow winding channel of water. But as we reached that edge of the lake, we discovered not one channel, but several, and we couldn't agree which one we had come through. We took one of the channels, neither of us certain it was the right one. After an hour or so of canoeing, an uneasy feeling crept in that we had chosen wrong, followed soon after with a dawning dread. It appeared that we were lost. In our haste, we hadn't packed a compass. The crude map that the outfitters had provided was nowhere to be found. We were lost. In a wilderness area with no food. There were no landmarks to guide us. Our only hope was to run across other canoeists, but the day before we had only seen a single canoe other than our own. We spent a good part of the day searching for the right way back to the lodge. At one point, following a channel, we broke through to a second lake. Was it that same lake where we had camped? We weren't sure we hadn't gone in circles.

In the center of the lake was a small island. A small curl of smoke appeared at the far side, a sight that drew us out of what had grown to be a state of panic. We headed toward the smoke, rounding the point of the island to see a small encampment. A man stood over a fire wearing thick leather garden gloves, a thick crop of silver hair, and a full beard. Beside him was an Airdale terrier, tail wagging, barely containing his energy at the approach of two strangers. We glided in as the man towered over us, pulled the canoe up onto the sand bank with us still in it, and then extended a hand to Melinda to help her out of the canoe. We must have been visibly relieved because he just said, "You two lost?" His eyes had laughter in them. After we told him our plight, he said, "I'm just making dinner. You can join Josh and me, if you'd like. He likes the company, isn't that right, boy?" He petted the Airedale roughly on the head, then pulled the leather gloves back on to manhandle a beat-up cooking pot onto a triangle of logs over an open fire. He reached into a small cooler, retrieved two large packets of stew, and emptied them into the pot.

"This was going to last Josh and I another two days. Guess we'll all have to hunt and gather the next two days," he joked. As it turned out, he was due back the next evening to Toronto.

We were lucky to cross paths with Sid for a number of reasons. He was a retired high school teacher in his late fifties, still young and fit enough to be guiding wilderness treks. He was a fantastic storyteller with a magnanimous personality. His stories were all things Canada and beyond. He was a kind of wilderness Mountie without the uniform, had grown up on the edge of Algonquin, and knew the area intimately. He had taken his students out many times and after we got to know him, he was only too eager to take two young Americans under his wing and into his favorite areas.

That day on the island, Sid's propensity for storytelling took an improvisational turn as he told us a story about an Algonquin being who had the power to shape-shift landforms in order to confuse travelers throughout the region. As the story went, according to Sid, there was a man who had been banished by his tribe for the crime of theft to live alone in the wilderness for some time alone. A spell of bad weather came in and he perished in a storm before his banishment ended. His spirit came back and, seeking revenge, roamed the region, changing the waterways and shorelines just enough to cause confusion among travelers and his former tribe so that they would lose their way. Some perished, some learned the land and survived. The area became known as the Lost Islands and the cries of the lost could often be heard in the night, bemoaning their fate. Sid told the story with a lot of embellishments, but as fantastic as it sounded, he had our attention. He admitted later that he had made up the story on the spot out of our adventures because it amused him.

Our final piece of good fortune with Sid was that he owned a house near Hyde Park in Toronto and had a two-room studio just coming up for rent in the upstairs. And so, we found ourselves with two new friends, Sid and Josh, and soon we were back in the Algonquin wilderness, this time with a competent guide. We canoed into and out of the lakes and inlets, and camped on an island far in the interior, using it as a home base for several days. Often, at dusk, a solitary bull moose appeared near our camp in the bog, silhouetted against the fire of the setting sun in the glasslike surface of the lake. At the end of our final day, hot and tired from paddling all day, we swam in a deep pool just off the edge of the island. The water was inviting, but so icy that our bodies never quite adjusted. Sid stood near the fire, laughing, hands covered by those thick leather work gloves as we ran in blankets, gasping and shivering to the fire. He cooked a simple meal of beans, quietly amused by *"les petits Américains."*

Chapter 12
A Turn Toward Life

Between doubt and hope, your life
is oriented toward landscapes that
coincide with something that is within you.
—**Silo**
   The Internal Landscape

The tragedy of the modern Western mind
has been our inability to generate
cosmologies that are life-enhancing.
—**Suzi Gablik**
   The Re-enchantment of Art

The Canadian wilderness contrasted sharply with Iowa, one of the most domesticated states in the U.S., and with Europe, which had also tamed nearly all of its wildness. Going to France, to the Netherlands, attempting to connect with my human ancestry, finding out that they were mostly Mennonite farmers working the land, all that was going back. Our expeditions into wild Canada felt like a move in the opposite direction; forward, not back. There was all this space, miles of forests, lakes, and streams. I had a growing sense that to be cut off from wildness is to be cut off from our natural spontaneities, our instinctual energies, and our generative powers. The beauty and rawness of the Algonquin wilderness further ignited a flame within me to understand more about the link between landscape and the human imagination. As did my deeper exploration of thinkers in ecology and anthropology. This felt like another move forward.

So when Melinda finished her studies in Toronto, and said to me one day, "It's your turn. Where to next?", I had a ready answer:

"Gainesville, Florida."

"Gainesville," she repeated softly, then looked at me quizzically and added with a hint of alarm in her voice: "Not what I expected."

I had been reading the work of a cultural anthropologist, Marvin Harris, who taught at the University of Florida in Gainesville. I wanted to more fully understand the relationship of the rise of human culture to the natural world. Harris had a school of thought he had termed "cultural materialism," which in its essence theorized that the origins of all cultural phenomena arose in response to the material conditions in which people lived. For Harris, all culture had a materialist base. Mystery, magic, wonder, story, spirituality, religion, the arts, could all be reduced down to creative adaptation and explained as a survival response.

In its own way, Harris's system of thought was attempting to explain how culture arises from the power and effect of the environment on the human imagination. That was, in essence, what drew me to his work. Harris's work seemed a natural extension of my interests in how our connection to the natural world was key to the formation of our identity as human beings. I thought this would make fertile ground for my exploration of landscape, imagination, and identity. I had no basis at the time for questioning the materialist foundations of Harris's thinking, and so I applied and was accepted to do graduate studies in Cultural Anthropology with him in Gainesville.

Then one day a packet of information landed in my mailbox from my sister Kristin. Included was an offering for a week-long workshop with Dominican theologian Matthew Fox in Greensboro, North Carolina on the topic of Creation-centered Spirituality. I had first heard of his work some months earlier, not long before I had sent off my application to graduate studies in Gainesville. The workshop with Matthew Fox and some of his faculty was to take place just about the time my wife Melinda and I would be passing through North Carolina, headed for Florida. So we signed up. We packed a tent, sleeping bags, cooler, camp-stove, and everything else we owned into a powder blue Plymouth Valiant we called "Old Blue," and set off on a two-month-long adventure that would take us first to Montreal and the Gaspé Peninsula in Quebec, then to Nova Scotia and around the island of Newfoundland. We finally headed through Maine and down the coast toward Florida. We both thought Gainesville would be our home for the next two or three years.

On the morning following the workshop in North Carolina, Melinda and I struck camp at first light. We drove from the campsite into Greensboro and caught a sunrise breakfast on the front sidewalk of a cafe. We were ready to strike out for Gainesville, but decided to stretch our legs with a walk alongside the Haw River before the long drive.

"You haven't brought up Gainesville for three days," she said.

"What's to bring up?"

"It's all you've talked about for our whole trip before that."

"Well, not all. Canada. I've talked about Canada. Newfoundland, which is where we should move some day, by the way."

"Almost every new place we visit is a place you want to live some day ."

"I know. I fall in love too easily."

"I'll try not to take that personally."

"Well, you know what I mean."

"I'm just saying, University of Florida has dropped off your radar this week. Every time I bring it up, you change topics."

I studied her for a moment. "Go on."

"Well, what about this week? Something in you came alive."

"I could say the same for you."

I was picturing Melinda after an evening event for women, Native

African Rites for Women. She was glowing, animated, yet secretive. There was some mystery she couldn't, or wouldn't, talk about. I could only read it in her changed demeanor and the light in her face. Something like that was in me too from a week of "Art As Meditation," "Dances of Universal Peace," and workshops with names like "Cosmos as Primary Revelation." And these were punctuated with talks by Matt Fox on a new paradigm that braided the wisdom of Medieval mystics with ecology, scientific cosmology, indigenous wisdom, and a vibrant spirituality.

"Think Golden Gate Bridge," Melinda said, "Bay Area. You've always said you wanted to go to California."

"Look, I know you're not crazy about the prospect of Gainesville. But I'm accepted. We've got housing. Financial aid. I'm into Marvin Harris. I think he's onto something with his ideas on culture and the environment."

"I know. It's just a thought." She grabbed the crook of my elbow and pulled herself close, looking up at me.

I knew by this point in the conversation that the prospect of canceling graduate studies with Marvin Harris and taking a westward turn toward Oakland, California where Matt Fox offered a Masters degree at his Institute in Culture and Creation-Centered Spirituality was more than just an idle thought. I was already in deep with the idea. The still-early sunlight and the slight cool breeze blowing off the river were inciting the florescent leaves of the riverside elms and maples to an impetuous dance. A glittering sweep of wind raked across the surface of the water and seemed to rush toward us with one big gathering wave of dazzling *yes!*. Even so, in my growing excitement, I wanted to savor the birth of that raw feeling you get when you make a decision you know is daring, maybe a little reckless, but that aligns perfectly with your gut and your capacity for adventure in that moment. It's like hearing a melody that moves you, calling you home to a latent or forgotten part of yourself. And so I strung Melinda along for another ten minutes, selfishly relishing the rush of excitement, raising just a few more objections, logistics, and questions before blurting out "Okay, let's do it! California here we come!" Melinda ran ahead several steps, leapt in the air, and pirouetted down with a fist pump: "Yes!" After a conversation with the admissions director of Fox's Institute, Jim Conlon, and a call to the University of Florida, we were on our way west.

The dangers of blundering into the Algonquin wilderness without an adequate guide had its equivalent in the spiritual wilderness in which I found myself after a break with my religious past. I could go without a guide, but there was a strong possibility I'd lose my bearings, or lose myself. At first, I didn't think of my growing interest in landscape and the human imagination as a quest of spirit. But the power of the land drew me. A need for healing was at the core of that allurement, a longing for intimacy with place, even though it would take some time for me to acknowledge it. "When the student is ready, the teacher appears," says the old adage, and a guide soon appeared.

Matthew Fox's maverick spiritual vision appealed to me on two levels. The first was that it reframed my religious upbringing, something I had attempted to leave behind in the wake of my father's leaving the ministry. The second was on a socio-political level. My family had never been overtly engaged politically. But I came out of undergraduate school at the University of Iowa newly educated about history and outraged at my own country's genocidal past and neocolonialist interference around the world. Seeing the revisionist history I had grown up with in a new light, I became politicized. I grew increasingly cynical of capitalism and its contradictions. Donella Meadow's book *The Limits to Growth* left me questioning the whole paradigm that fueled the exuberant explosion of European settlers over the continent and that was still at the root of the American economy. The idea of Manifest Destiny had destroyed exquisite native populations and natural wonders the continent over. The golden city on the hill felt utopian, non-ecological, and religiously over-zealous.

This was at the tail end of the Reagan administration in the 1980s. I had been part of the apartheid protests at the University of Iowa, where a group of us had been arrested occupying the university president's office demanding divestment from South Africa. I had protested the bombing of Libya, the Iran-Contra scandal, and U.S. interference in the governance of Latin and South American countries. In France, I found myself answering questions from the French who were curious about my views of the Reagan Era foreign policy with a kind of apologetic loathing for my own government's actions.

Further back in my past was the rupture of my family with the Christian church. What I learned of political and cultural history at the University of Iowa had not only politicized me, but had made me even more suspect of religion. I found Karl Marx's assessment that religion was an opiate of the people at least credible at the time, if not a bit over-simplified. But for me, religion was also in bed with American capitalism and a party to environmental destruction and social injustice. Protestant Christianity, as practiced in the U.S., provided a perfect justification for rape of the natural world. It also bolstered the idea of American exceptionalism. It justified violence against other countries in the form of political coups and covert support for paramilitary groups with the aim of undermining legitimately elected governments that the U.S. power elites deemed unacceptable challenges to American hegemony.

This was the framework, the worldview, with which I came into the weeklong workshop with Matthew Fox: outraged at my country, or at least at the corruption of those in power; disturbed by its genocide of native peoples; tending toward misanthropy because of my sorrow at the destruction of the natural world. Part of the reason I sought to understand the connections between human imagination, spirit, and landscape was, mostly subliminal at the time, an attempt to heal a second rupture in my life and the lives of my entire culture, that of the rupture of humans and a sense of belonging in the natural world. I couldn't understand our innate capacity to despoil and plunder the planet at every turn. Couldn't people see that this beautiful garden planet was dying at our own hands? And why did so few people seem to care? Or even take an interest in the beauty and healing found in nature? The nature essayists I was reading offered transcendent views of nature, but little in the way of understanding the pathology underlying humankind's troubled relationship with our home planet.

Seated in the audience in the campus auditorium at the University of North Carolina, I tracked Matthew Fox as he entered the room and mounted the stage. Animated, bespectacled, silver-haired, somewhat more diminutive than I expected, he strode quickly but unassumingly to the podium and welcomed us. My head was full of ideas from his book *Original Blessing*, which I had been reading to Melinda in the car as we drove around the island of Newfoundland and down the eastern seaboard, but I had never heard Matt express them in his unique cadence and tone. His voice rose and fell in a rhythm that alternated between urgency and passionate intensity when he was critiquing the failings of society's institutions and modern Christianity, and warmth, reflection, and compassion when he spoke of the rich and earthy spiritual traditions that he was attempting to reintroduce to a culture alienated from its roots.

That night he seemed to speak directly to my rage, disappointment, and grief toward my culture, my country, and my kind. This part resonated within me. But then I felt a different energy stir within me when he spoke of the Medieval mystics and their passion for justice, their sense of spirituality that was inclusive of nature, their perspicacity and prescience. It stirred again when he spoke of how the native peoples of the North American continent and the world over had maintained a sacred relationship to the natural world, saw animals as kin, and passed down their wisdom generation to generation through story and ritual. And again when he spoke of how our estrangement from the natural world from which we were born was pathological, not inevitable. As any disease, it might potentially be healed. Perhaps it wasn't yet terminal. Most powerfully to me at the time, he spoke of creativity in a new way, one that appealed to the nascent writer, poet, and composer within me. Creativity wasn't some marginal or peripheral activity sequestered to weekends and holidays, sidelined by the career-oriented, materialist, consumerist thrust of our society. It wasn't meant to be commodified. It was central to who we are as human beings, an integral part of a creative universe unfolding, and a capacity within us that was to be honored every bit as much as our widely-touted intellect. In fact, it enriched that intellect.

As the ideas simmered within me, I began to feel less alone, less marginalized. Some of my anger abated and for the first time since my childhood, I felt the real hope that comes with seeing avenues for action. There were hidden sources of wisdom to turn to — the feminine face of the divine, native peoples, the world's classical religious and philosophical traditions. And, there was science as I had never considered it through the lens of my education and enculturation. Matt spoke of cosmology, the power of story, and how a narrative given to us through scientific discovery might unite all peoples because it was our common story. Science could be a wisdom tradition, not merely a method for amassing data about the universe. The epidemic of addiction in society, from substance abuse to consumerism, was largely due to the lack of a functional cosmology. As was my culture's fealty to violence on every level.

I had trouble sleeping in the tent that week, not from the hard ground beneath my sleeping bag or from feeling troubled, but from excitement. Melinda had told me with some degree of envy when we were first married that I "slept the sleep of the just." Now I was an insomniac, my mind racing with thoughts about justice for the Earth and her people. I was awake in a way I could not have fully described at the time because it was still in formation within me

The evening ended with a dance of cosmic celebration in the same auditorium, to world music and images of the universe, animals, the stars fading in and out on a big screen. It was a good way to channel the energy of new ideas at the time. What I didn't know that evening was that it was the beginning of a dance back into the heart of community, a turn toward life that would take me down unforeseen paths.

The workshop in North Carolina was an inflection point where I veered away from materialism toward an earthy spirituality. I arrived to do graduate studies at Matt Fox's Institute the same year he would be silenced by the Vatican for what the church hierarchy saw as heretical views. He was a fervent feminist, they said; he called God woman, and he refused to return to the Dominican order and to stop teaching a theology of original blessing as opposed to original sin. The official doctrine of the Catholic church had significant kinship to my own Protestant upbringing. Fleeing as I was from Calvinist doctrine of the Christian Reformed Church with its roots in fall-redemption theology only primed me to feel that if Matthew Fox had incurred the wrath of the Vatican to the point of their silencing him, he must be getting something right. But for me, it was really more of an internal resonance. Matt may have been a maverick in the modern-day Catholic Church, but he was faithful to the wisdom tradition of Christian Medieval mystics. His attempt to resuscitate this much older "Creation-Centered" tradition of the church was an affirmation of life, nature, creativity, the body, and the sacred feminine, and pointed to a generative, not destructive, role for the human. Matthew Fox turned the fall-redemption theology of my youth thoroughly on its head. Instead of being born into original sin, human beings came into the world as blessings. His four-fold spiritual path was a welcome integration of competing emotional and psychological states in my life.

The first three paths

The paths aren't simply a formula for spiritual growth. They describe internal states, and all four together represent healing, the wholeness of the human person. In their most mature form, they constitute the fully realized self, the human as cosmic citizen.

The first path, the *via positiva*, is a celebration of the human being as a participant in Earth's life community and our evolutionary story. On a more real, bodily, level, it is a sensuous grounding in the present. This is more profound than the experience of our physical senses, as energizing as that can be. It's an internalized sensuous experience of the world that gives rise to an empathic connection to all of life. Even more, it is an awakening to the inner life of the Earth. This is a way of knowing that I call "cosmoriginal" (chapter 27), a depth of understanding that unites one's heart with the heart of the universe. There is an intelligence of the body that has a natural resonance with a vaster store of knowledge than the head's intellect can contain or articulate. My early meanderings in Iowa's landscapes, my desire to be out in nature wasn't just an infantile regression or an escape from the difficult challenges of human society. It was my birthright and my grounding, a connection to the internal radiance of matter, one which many of us in industrial culture have lost.

In the Landscape Interlude "The Cosmic Citizen," I relate an experience on a creek in Iowa when I was an undergraduate. My senses that day were incredibly alive with the power of the place. The sight of the moving water and the dance of foliage. The sounds of the wind and birdsong. The feel of the sun and the hand of the wind on my skin. But beyond my senses, I came to feel something more profound, a sensuous radiance underlying everything. Many of the Landscape Interludes in this book relate similar sensuous experiences I've had in particular landscapes. This is our blessing and our birthright, the *positiva*.

The second path, the *via negativa*, welcomes and taps into the energies of the feeling dimension within us. It involves a willingness to gaze into darkness and unknowing. There is a letting go into uncertainty, an acceptance of change and loss. My grief was real. I felt the loss of my innocence, my boyhood community, and my faith. But I also deeply felt both loss and anger about the ecological destruction accelerating around me. My heart was breaking for my culture, but also for the planet. The *via negativa* helped me to value the feeling function within me, not to run from it or denigrate it. To feel deeply, to grieve as well as to know joy, is necessary and normal, not weak. Joy happens when there is an emptying out of images, when there is a suspension of outmoded beliefs that obscure our feelings of belonging, when there is a stillness within, a silencing of noise.

In our culture, there is a concerted effort to expurge the darkness. There is a flight from nothingness, stillness, and receptivity. For example, one of the more endangered experiences of our time is a pristine view of the night sky. There are few locales where a patina of artificial light doesn't obscure all but the brightest of stars. Our cities gleam and shimmer under domes of undifferentiated and milky sameness. To experience the wonder of the stars, we need to travel to remote areas of the desert or far off-shore in the ocean. There are few sanctuaries free of artificial light that remain. This pollution of the night sky serves an apt simile for the state of our consciousness as we are pulled ever more deeply into the hyper-illumination of the cyber-age. As an unstructured flood of information washes over us from every direction, we are experiencing an eclipse of depth because of a flood of artificial light. Our attention, much like the light pollution of the night sky, has become colonized with cyber-noise and uncensored data. It's as if we are attempting to power-wash the dark out of existence with constant distractions like consumerism and social media. Deeper illuminations from the depths of the unconscious are still there. Joy is there as well, but more difficult to feel. But like the stars, it's just harder to perceive them. Ultimately, killing the mystery of the night sky impoverishes our imagination.

The third path, the *via creativa*, is an awareness that human intuition, our very creative nature, is in unity with a generative universe. The very arc of the universe is creative, and human beings are integral to that unfolding. This rethinking of the nature of the universe energized my own intuitive paths of music, poetry, and writing. They were no longer isolated and quirky activities, but gifts that were integral with the reciprocity found in all vibrant communities. Our cultural myths of creativity—that it is the elite domain of a gifted few, that to do art is to suffer, and that the drive to create is merely a weak compensation for some neurosis —fell away or lost their power. Higher creativity is aligned with a more positive trajectory of the universe. For me, as a daily practice, a kind of meditation, the creative act reaffirmed my connection to mystery, to beauty, to the source of our existence. It peels away layers that insulate us from the essential radiance around us. As a generative activity, it gives me a sense of a future.

The fourth path: bowl of the cauldron

As I was working on this part of the book and puzzling over how to present the four paths, an image came to me in a dream. In the dream, I was on a journey with a small band of people through a dark forest. We were quite hungry and on a search for food. As nightfall neared, we came to a clearing and at its center was an ancient, three-legged Chinese cauldron placed over a campfire. Etched into its side were images of fish, birds, plants, and animals that were all in motion. They swam, flew, and ran in a teeming profusion of life. I could feel the warmth of the stew as I approached and peered into the bowl of the cauldron. The bowl was open to the sky but also grounded by its three legs to the Earth. As I gazed into the bowl, I saw my face and the faces of my traveling companions intermingled with points of light like distant stars.

One way to interpret the meaning of this dream is that the image of the cauldron was a non-verbal expression of the four paths of creation-spirituality. Each leg represents one of the first three paths which culminate in the bowl of the cauldron, which is the fourth path, the *via transformativa*. As a dynamic convergence of the first three paths, the *via transformativa* is an image of the whole human person. This fourth path is where the other paths find their fulfillment, their mature form. Within the human person, it is the fully-realized self. This path represents our capacity for thought and action that transforms injustice and imbalance in the world into right relationship.

The first leg is a bodily connection to the world, the intelligence of the body through the senses, but more correctly, through a sensuous connection to the spirit permitting everything. The groundedness of the yin, the earthy feminine needed to balance the yang of the heady intellect of the masculine. The second leg is feeling as a valid energy with which to navigate the chaos of the world. A feeling orientation is the ground of empathy and compassion. The third leg is trust in the intuitive, creative energies, that they are the actual powers of the cosmos finding expression through each one of us. Learning to trust these will provide a rich offering in the bowl of the cauldron. Within the human person, the cauldron represents the realized self, feeding the world with a nutritious stew.

A new compass

Matt Fox was uncovering a hidden history, an underground vein rich with the ore of the spirit. Whatever patina remained in my consciousness from my childhood faith was growing thinner. My experience of the environmental movement of the '70s and '80s was a highly secularized one, so much so that I was forced to segregate my sense of the sacred from my love for the natural world. It was Cartesian dualism coming through in a dispiriting way. I could, and did, volunteer for Greenpeace, the Sierra Club, and similar efforts, but there always seemed to be an unspoken agreement within these groups to check your spirituality at the door. It was at best something left to conversation around a campfire or over a beer. Saving the environment had little to do with one's spiritual life.

The grounded spirituality that Matt and his faculty brought to the table wasn't a mere exercise in comfort and conformity. It wasn't an attempt to start a new religion. Nor was it a cult, because it was grounded in ancient wisdom traditions and there were no coercive tactics or expectations of adherence to prescribed beliefs. In fact, Matt Fox encouraged people to renew their own traditions through the insights of Creation-Centered spirituality. It was a direct challenge to the anthropocentric orientation of the Western mind, one that integrated light and celebration with darkness and the shadow side of human nature, and that brought creativity to bear on transformation and erotic justice. This affirmed my deepest allurements as a poet, composer, and essayist. But it went beyond mere affirmation of my creative nature. It set it within a larger cosmology, a story, and life's work. I had a choice: my creative contribution could further the vibrancy of the Earth community, or it could continue, as with the larger culture, in the service of death.

So Melinda and I pointed Old Blue, like a compass point magnetized toward an invisible but irresistible force, toward the West Coast instead of south to Florida. We landed in California, where I completed the Masters program at Matt Fox's Institute in Culture and Creation-Centered Spirituality. The program was meant to educate the whole person; to help people mine their traditions for lost wisdom; to honor both the intuitive right brain and the analytical left brain; to awaken thought, creativity, wisdom, and a desire for transformative action in the world.

Some years after I completed the Masters program, I interviewed Matt, using his new book at the time, *Sins of the Spirit, Blessings of the Flesh*, as the focal point. I shared with him at the time that I had experienced something of a transcendent experience reading a portion of the book called "Litany of the Universe." The litany listed an amazing inventory of scientific discoveries about the universe, any one of which could, with some degree of contemplation, elicit awe. His response spoke to the choice we make about whether to turn toward, or away from, life: "I have to confess that I had a transcendent experience *writing* the litany. What I hear you saying, Lauren, is that if you prayed this litany every morning, you'd be building your muscles of biophilia. This book came out the week of the Columbine school shootings. In it, there's a line from Eric Fromm: 'necrophilia increases when biophilia is stunted.' That line really names our culture, which is very involved with necrophilia in many levels and subtle ways. How do we bring biophilia back; how do we pump it up? How do we help people cut through cynicism and despair?"[4]

By the time of the interview, I was beginning to answer that for myself. I had come to believe that our role as human beings was to deepen our sensitivities and love for all of the life community. The destiny of the human would be to further evolution through the development within the human of a more compassionate nature. I was called to do work that would help heal our culture's rupture with the Earth community. We needed a more mature awareness of nature and our place in the universe, one more akin to that of native peoples, where there is a marriage of science, heart, and spirit.

Chapter 13
The Question

Beginning in adolescence, not long after the tornado that swept through my life and that of my family's, I had carried within me a question; I wouldn't articulate it as a question until my studies with Matt Fox, but it was there. On the far side of its longing was the issue of trust. Suspending my belief in a deity had left me with uncertainty about what kind of universe we live in. If we live in a random, uncaring universe, then the trauma of my sister's kidnapping was a bad roll of the dice, a meaningless and arbitrary event. If we live in a universe that is headed somewhere predetermined, then the trauma was nefarious in its justification of violence against the innocent. If the universe is neither random nor predetermined, but creative, then human beings had agency as part of its creative unfolding. We could choose to turn toward life and participate in bringing forth a vibrant future.

Is the universe a friendly place? I had learned that the universe could be a brutal and violent place where seemingly random events occurred that violated the very heart of innocence. So for me, this question translates, given the trauma-inducing events of my past, as: Do I feel safe? Any young child has to have a connection to a caring adult to feel safe. Feeling held gives a child the freedom to then explore, to play and to discover who they are. My parents were stressed by the events of the kidnapping so they couldn't provide me and my sister, Kristin, and my brothers, Mark and Phil, with the safe haven we needed when our community and sense of safety were ruptured.

I took on that stress and a tried to cope with it through self-soothing and self-denying behaviors. For years, I battled various kinds of addiction, from alcohol to experimenting with drugs to bingeing on movies. The alcohol and drugs dulled the emotional pain, but also heightened my happier moments, but only temporarily. Ultimately I was left with the same pain. I immersed myself in the stories in movies in part because I was unconsciously trying to find a story that worked better than my core life story. I was particularly drawn to stories that depicted the struggle between good and evil.

The other way I tried to cope was by pushing down my emotions, particularly anger and grief, but also joy, resulting in recurring bouts with depression. The universe had become a threatening place. To express my authentic self was too great a risk in an unsafe universe. I risked rejection, even within my family unit and with friends. In love relationships it expressed itself as distance. I could rarely show my deepest self, even to a lover or partner. When it did happen, I had glimpses of my more authentic self, and a deeper connection took place.

My lifelong dedication to creativity has been the healthier part of the survival strategies I've adopted over the years. It was an attempt to be my authentic self through music, poetry, and writing, to find and assert my true self. To express myself authentically was too great a risk in a family that had become risk-averse. My parents were so stressed they couldn't see it in me because they couldn't see it in themselves. This was partly due to the times. Thus, the message: "don't cry! You should be joyful that Kristin has been found and is safe!" And "Don't do anything about Kristin, just watch her. If she acts out, go to a professional." It was also due to my religious background which didn't encourage celebration, joy, and expression of emotion. My northern European ancestry also cultivated a certain emotional reserve within me.

Could I trust a God, a universe where there had been such a betrayal of innocence? Could I even trust myself, my gut instincts? For years I had a quote from Ralph Waldo Emerson taped above my desk: "Envy is ignorance; imitation is suicide." I'm only now beginning to understand the appeal that quote had for me. It was about being faithful to my authentic self. All my life I have ridden out the tension between the need for approval from people in authority and my need to rebel against them and reject their power over me. It was the battle between my need for attachment and a deeper need for authenticity. Both were survival strategies in the face of a traumatic past.

And yet, I feel like I have found my way. My gut instincts found their expression through creativity. My heart intelligence was affirmed through a connection to the living Earth. And my head intelligence found its fulfillment through story, a new cosmology, a retelling and a reboot that usurped the core story of my life that had to do with the wound of trauma.

I came to understand that perhaps friendliness wasn't precisely the correct way to frame the question about the universe. Maybe the question had more to do with trust. At the very least, the universe could be trusted to be creative. And trust forms the basis for faith. What I came to learn through a meaningful cosmology was that as active agents in that creativity, human beings were supported by the very powers that had brought us into existence. Faith in these powers gave me energy. I felt a renewed intimacy with the community of life. I could choose to become a beneficial presence on Earth, and in that choice is empowerment.

The next section, "Trajectory of Healing," describes a pathway toward a new faith in the human, and with it, a journey toward wholeness.

LANDSCAPE INTERLUDE
At Home in the Breath

Each step is a breath. Each time my foot touches Earth, my attention distills downward through my soles. My heartbeat clings to the sheer granite wall to my left and the rock comes out to meet it; our uniting becomes my balance, my focus against fright. On my right, only a one-thousand foot precipice and the wind. I am climbing to the peak of Angel's Landing at Mount Zion National Park. And I am thinking of turning back. The chain handgrips embedded in the rock and the diminutive footholds just don't inspire my confidence.

A gust of wind wells up from the canyon and cascades over me. I close my eyes, grip the chain, and deeply breathe the Zion air several times into my shaky frame. Then at the peak of my fear, I feel the wind expand within me. My vision warms and seeps downward into my chest. I feel my bones and blood flow outward into the quartz of the red canyon wall—my blood, its iron oxide; my bones, its calcium carbonate. An unaccountable steadiness infuses me and my steps begin to feel like a prayer of praise, not beseeching. My movements grow impeccable; I feel that I can't fall, and if I do, no matter. I will surrender to the wind, as I have to the rock. In that moment, the wind streams through me, out my fingertips into the canyon, and is swept up on the wings of passing vultures.

Far below, the Virgin River continues its thirteen-million-year labor of cutting the gorge of Zion canyon. The Navajo sandstone of the towering cliffs across the chasm glows burnt sienna in the late afternoon wash of sunlight. "Mukuntuweap," the Pahutes called the canyon, meaning "straight arrow." They regarded the canyon as off-limits to farming and hunting. It was too spiritually potent. Early Mormon settlers, their breath swept away by the sheltering beauty of the canyon, renamed it Zion, a Hebrew word meaning "place of safety and refuge." At six thousand feet, the peak of Angel's Landing, I breathe over the canyon, melding my breath with Zion's. I am at the lip of a precipice, but I feel at home.

Holy Spirit Wind, to the Navajo, steadies us in the world and allows us to move through it gracefully. Their word for it is *nilchi'i*, writes Barry Lopez. Among the complexities of its translation into English is "the Wind that is Creation's first food, the source of all motion and change, giving life to everything, including the mountains and water." It is the underlying force that unifies everything and the means of communication between all elements of the natural world.[5] Barry Lopez, through the voice of a fictional character writes: "Other native North American peoples have refined similar ideas; but the Navajo conception is particularly successful in relating the idea of the individual to the concept of a stable society...through *nilchi'i*, individuals participate in graces or powers that surpass those of the individual... those graces or powers keep one secure in the world and confirm one's indispensability, one's necessity in the world."[6]

We are more secure in the world when we carry a sense of belonging to something greater—a place, a clan, the community of beings on Earth. It begins with a realization: that we are indispensable, that not only do we belong, we are needed. We are here to fulfill a role, and to do so is our greatest generosity; the only thing required of us, to be of service, is to seek harmony of thought and action. There are forces that come to our aid, like *nilchi'i*, which, when it passes into us, becomes our spirit. The word spirit comes from the Latin *spiro*, meaning "to breathe." Wind is considered to be the highest expression of divine Spirit in many spiritual traditions. Combined with our own being through breath, it becomes our deepest expression of beauty. When I hear people speak about "connecting to nature," I've come to believe that they want to breathe again, to know the marriage of Sacred Wind and their breath within, to become "in-spired," enlivened again by Spirit.

My mind easily falls into the perception that this participation is an abstraction rather than a bodily truth. Perhaps that is the very reason for our profound sense of alienation from Earth's community of life, a wind lonely beyond compare. To cut ourselves off from the truth of our existence is to have the breath—our sense of balance and harmony, of beauty—knocked out of us. We lose our wind and our secure footing. To bring myself back is to breathe in the Sacred Wind of remembering. Aligning my breathing with the pulse of the Earth's breath, the Sacred Wind, steadies me in the realization that I am essential, needed, that my role is integral to the story of planet Earth.

When I felt Zion in my blood and bones, it wasn't a trick of mind using metaphor to create meaning. It was an actuality in my body. I carried Zion within me, and yet more accurately I entered Zion by means of the breath and remembered what is always constant and true—I am of Earth's body. My very thought and breath come from that participation in powers and graces that belong to the larger body.

I am also of the body of the universe. And in terms of breath, from the present backward throughout deep time, I have a connection to unlikely ancestors long forgotten. These tiny progenitors pulled off a feat of creativity, the invention of respiration, which amounted to a moment of evolutionary grace in response to crisis. It started when a cyanobacteria, about two billion years into the story of life on Earth, began to produce oxygen in copious amounts, feeding off the limitless energy of the sun. Oxygen was toxic to life at the time; nevertheless, one of our bacterial ancestors evolved into the mitochondria which processes oxygen in the cells. This was an enormous new source of energy and it would evolve into aerobic breathing that would drive the advance of multicellular life. With each draw of air, I can remember those ancestors and feel gratitude for my life, for my breath, for the flame of oxygen that powers my thought and my body.

There are a hundred winds I've known in my life, but I have no name for them. English isn't one of the more nuanced of languages. We have all known more avatars of wind than we can describe and we could use more terms to name them, using names that evoke their experience in our bodies. There is the fresh wind, for instance, that relieves us of staleness: "Cool Maiden Makes New Again." There's a wind that ruins good fishing: "Puts Fishes to Sleep in Afternoon." Or the fearsome wind that caught me and my brother off-guard once, imperiling us in the middle of a lake in a boat during a lightning storm: "Turns Quickly in Dark Light." There's "Cicada Counterpoint at Twilight," the wind that stirs magic on summer nights in the Midwest, alternating its voice with the song of the pulsing insects.

I can mark key events in my life that have brought a sudden wind shift. At times, it's a hard gust. Often, it's the subtle, almost imperceptible puff that clears the mist from my awareness to reveal some dormant truth about my life.

Today, there are gale forces that blow beyond our control not only as individuals, but as a nation, and as peoples of the Earth community. Among them: economic globalization, the breakdown and co-optation of democratic ideals, the betrayal of our trust in politicians and policymakers, climate change, and a degradation of life support systems the likes of which the planet has never experienced.

To return to steadiness, as a culture, we must find our Sacred Wind, the soul of the country, the spirit that unites us to other peoples and species of Earth in a sense of kinship we can't deny any longer. One direction we can look is to Earth's winds because they unite us: the bora of the Hungarian Basin; the foehn of the

northern Alps; the bayamo of the south coast of Cuba; the brubu
of the East Indies; the mistral and sirocco of the Mediterranean
basin; the chinook, or snow eater, of the Rocky Mountains.
They are the spirit of Earth circulating, renewing, giving life
to everything. We can call on them, unite them with our own
breath, and surrender, in that unity, to this larger wisdom: to be
secure in the world is to flow with *nilchi'i*, the Holy Spirit Wind.

Not long ago, I found myself humming an old hymn under
my breath, "Breathe on Me Breath of God." I pulled the old
hymnal from the shelf by my piano and read the lyrics of the
first of three verses:

> *Breathe on me breath of God,*
> *Fill me with life anew,*
> *That I may love what thou dost love,*
> *And do what thou wouldst do.*

Here is a fourth verse in this time when our planet is in peril and
our unified efforts are never more needed to change the direction
of our collective wind:

> *Breathe on us, Sacred Wind*
> *Fill us with life anew*
> *That we may walk upon this Earth*
> *United in all we do.*

The sorrow, grief, and rage you feel is a measure of your humanity and your evolutionary maturity. As your heart breaks open there will be room for the world to heal.

—Joanna Macy

Authenticity's only dictate is that we, not externally imposed expectations, be the true author and authority on our own life.

—Gabor Maté

What hurts you, blesses you.
Darkness is your candle.
Your boundaries are your quest.

—Rumi

Trajectory of Healing

Chapter 14

The Transformative Power of Story

Ecology without mythology will be defeated.
—**Michael Meade**

About two years after Melinda and I moved to California, I completed graduate studies at Matthew Fox's Institute in Oakland. We were young, excited to be on the West Coast, and I was still brimming with the energy from the program. But we were on the edge financially. A Masters degree in Culture and Creation-Centered Spirituality with an emphasis in Geo-Justice didn't offer immediate or obvious work opportunities. And so, I was working an office job at a public hospital to make ends meet.

One morning, on my way to the job, I decided to grab a coffee and pastry to go at my favorite cafe. I made the purchase, but as I turned to leave, I found my path blocked by a panhandler who had planted himself between me and the exit. I sidestepped him, and brushed by, with only a brusque grunt of acknowledgment. I was running late, and irritated. The forward momentum of my day was disrupted.

I sped down the sidewalk, but halfway to the car, I slowed down, and then came to a stop. What had just happened? I slowly started to turn, while searching inside for some anchor for my behavior. How could this encounter have gone down differently? Then, unbidden, the familiar figure of Jesus emerged into my awareness from my childhood, followed by a question: "What would he have done?" He would have seen the man, I thought. He certainly would have given him the gift of his kindness and presence. He might have asked: "What happened to you? What is your story? What is your pain?"

What came home to me that day in a new way was how the power of story can become an inner guide to behavior. Christ, as a key part of the mythos of my childhood, emerged spontaneously on a sidewalk in Oakland when I was challenged to be kind, to acknowledge another person's humanity and dignity, to be less self-absorbed.

For so many years and so many reasons I had rejected the religion of my youth, running from it. But what I couldn't run from were the values that were instilled deeply within me from the stories of Jesus's life. Nor could I deny their spontaneous irruption into my psyche. Christ as a salvific figure never resonated with me; I've never felt the need to be saved by Jesus. His death by crucifixion, the sacrifice of his life for the sake of vicarious atonement for sin, was a faint glimmer against the more luminous gifts Jesus had imparted through the example of his life. He saved me long ago in childhood through the mythos of his all-encompassing compassion, the power to heal, the creativity of his parables. They were the most compelling part of my boyhood mythology. This mythos was how I oriented myself, how I made sense of people, the world, and the universe. I embodied it imperfectly, but its power over me grew and developed.

As a boy I carried around a red, zippered Bible given to me by my parents. All of Jesus's words were in red. The parables, the Sermon on the Mount, the Beatitudes, his admonitions to his disciples, his words as he was dying on the cross. And as well, my father's sermons, vacation Bible school, readings at the dinner table every night, all centered around the same mythos of Jesus.

Then came the rupture and the consequent spiritual search in my life. What I could not have anticipated was the return that happened, a higher order of integration that took place over the years. The journey included encounters with various spiritual traditions over the years, from Taoism to Buddhism, from Christian medieval mystics to Native American sweat lodges. Then hours and hours spent in the natural world, in the presence of magnificence, giving myself over to wonder. I came to see that the tenderness that I felt for all living beings was not simply regression to some ancient animistic state, but a new order of complexity, a higher expression of the compassion I had learned from the example of Jesus's life. It extended beyond the human to plants and animals, the planet, even the stars that had birthed me. At the base of my loathing of injustice and cruelty was a passion for healing and erotic justice, not just my own but for the community of life. Jesus modeled that as a healer. My impulse toward creativity was the primal pulse of the universe wanting to express the "I am" within me and to find my unique forms of creativity. Jesus modeled that as a storyteller.

Master storyteller Michael Meade, to expand on his epigraph at the beginning of this chapter, talks about our "storied nature:" In an interview I did with him in 2004, he said: "Our nature is to tell stories in order to find the meaning of our own lives. It's what I call our 'second nature,' what's second nature to us, humans as part of nature. I don't accept the idea that there is nature, and then us. In our second nature, you find that we are woven with greater Nature. That weaving, with its surprises and cycles, are what we call stories. Meanwhile, Nature is feeding back to us its bio-version of the cosmic story. Nature is talking to us, we are responding with stories."[7]

I had to learn to listen as Earth spoke to me on many levels before I could weave it with the stories I grew up with, and that had an undeniably formative influence on me. Then I could begin to respond with a new story that supplanted the old, one that drew on the lexicon of Nature speaking to me from within.

Over the years, I've had a number of what I think of as transcendent experiences. These were moments in my life when I've been free of fear and alienation, and permeated with undeniable and all-encompassing feelings of connection and love. One of these took place when I was twenty one years old. I was working a blue-collar job at a printing company. The company printed magazines on enormous printing presses, some as large as a ranch home. At the time, I worked as a book stacker, which meant that as pages of the magazine came off the press, I would pull a pile of them off a moving belt, carry them over to a table with a vibrating surface, stand them on end, and shimmy them into neat stacks. Then they were put on pallets and shipped off to the bindery. I also filled the ink wells and changed the giant paper rolls on the presses.

We worked two stackers to a press. Our work schedules on these presses were such that, when the books were printing smoothly, I would work a half hour, then have a half hour break. I took the opportunity during many of these half hour breaks to meditate. This meant that on some days I would meditate for two or three hours. A perfect place for meditating was in a large room not far from the printing press that housed giant rolls of the paper that fed the printing presses. These rolls were four or five feet high and ten to twelve feet across and laid over on their sides, making them a perfect platform upon which to sit cross-legged and meditate. The hum of the printing press in the background created a soothing white noise that at times would put me into a kind of trance state.

Often, instead of meditating, I would read for my half hour break. At the time I was reading books on the wisdom of the mystics down through the ages, as well as sacred Buddhist texts and Lao Tzu's *Tao te Ching*. I was also reading a book on Jesus and the Essenes, a Jewish mystical sect that was thought to have had a strong influence on him. In a way, I was attempting to rehabilitate and recalibrate my relationship to Christ since my family's break with the church. He had meant so much to me as a boy and was still a powerful force in my psyche, even though at the time I wasn't fully aware of it. To see Jesus in a mystical light, rather than through the accounts of the historical Jesus in the Bible, was refreshing and intriguing for me.

I came back from one of these breaks one day in a very calm and focused state from having meditated. I started to work stacking the books, and I soon entered into the pleasurable flow of physical work. The combination of meditation and physical activity seemed to be the perfect storm for what came next. As I stood at the vibrating table, I felt a sudden palpable, radiant presence very close behind me. I felt a warmth enter my lower torso and then up into my chest cavity. Light and warmth infused my entire body and I heard the words "I am here, within you, always." I felt the presence very clearly to be that of Jesus, and I felt myself slip into what would be an ecstatic state that would last for hours. I felt utter connection to everyone and everything around me — to the workers on the press, the press itself, all of the sounds, lights, and activities on the work floor. A deep feeling of love radiated within me. Everything around me was infused with light. I even felt this love for two co-workers who had, for reasons unknown to me, bullied and intimidated me for weeks. My coworkers noticed an immediate change in me. One of them commented on my radiant face and disarming smile. Another wanted to know if I was "on something." It is a state that is impossible to describe fully, as many mystics have pointed out. But I knew the utter reality of our inter-connectedness in that moment. I had no antagonism toward anyone and felt a complete trust in the universe. I have no doubt that my feeling of Jesus as the spiritual presence within me that day came out of my religious upbringing and a deep familiarity with the stories of his life. My internal spiritual guide at that time consisted almost entirely of an image of Christ.

It was an experience of profound self-acceptance that moved me beyond fear to a sense of belonging. I felt I had a place and a role in the universe. I have since had two similarly transcendent experiences. One was in the midst of millions of migrating ducks and geese at a wildlife refuge. The other was in the heart of the city of San Francisco on a street packed with people. These were hours during which I felt no mediation between myself and the world. The commonalities between these experiences were a pervading feeling of compassion and an absence of fear.

Ripples from this experience at the printing plant have passed in and out of my life in the years since it happened. I haven't always been conscious of the connection. And yet, in thinking back, I see that it is a kind of keystone experience, an awakening to the truth of our connectedness that took on a life of its own and to which I return to orient me in challenging times. My feelings of reverence for all living things; my sense of awe at the wonders and terrors of the natural world; my amazement at Earth herself, spinning her story out into the vastness of the cosmos; these were all infused with an intimacy through the figure of Christ that went far beyond my knowledge of the historical Jesus. A faith had grown within me in the very powers that had brought me and my kind into existence. The essence of the Christos permeated the world of nature, from the galaxies down to the micro-world. As distorted and perverted as Christianity had become, all of the suffering and depravity that had been perpetrated down through time in the name of Christ by those who professed to be Christian but who waged endless war on the planet and her people, couldn't pollute this basic essence, the core of Jesus's message — compassion and love. Heal, don't destroy. Feed the hungry, become a feast for those hungering for connection, meaning, and belonging in a world addicted to consumerism. Be present to suffering with an open heart. Seek to mend the brokenness caused by a dualistic worldview. Rebel against the injustices of a culture of greed and ecological destruction.

For me, the archetype of Christ incarnated, having become the body of Earth, had extended divine love to all of creation through the light of human consciousness. As a species, we are aware that we have developed a unique, perhaps unprecedented, complexity of consciousness. And so, we possess the will to choose. Our most fundamental choice, the one affecting the future of life on Earth, is the choice between compassion and violence. This will isn't powered by our intellect, but through increased sensitivities to signs of the sacred within and around us. "Only the Earth can adequately will the Earth," wrote geologian Thomas Berry, "If we will the future effectively it will be because the guidance and powers of the Earth have been communicated to us, not because we have determined the future of the Earth simply with some rational faculty."[8] This requires that we surrender to a deeper wisdom that we can't fully understand with the intellect.

Sometime in the early 2000s my soon-to-be wife, Diana Brooks, introduced me to the work of an Argentinian philosopher, Mario Luis Rodriguez Cobos, who wrote under the pen name of Silo. He wrote of the importance of configuring within oneself an internal guide, a figure that represented strength, wisdom, and kindness as a way of creating what he called "valid action" in the world. Valid actions were those which are in unity with one's thoughts and feelings.

Having grown up a minister's kid, my own configuration of an internal spiritual guide had been primarily shaped by a Christ mythos, personalized by Jesus. But it evolved over time to include the divine feminine. In a tale (later called a guided experience) written by Silo, a new archetypal spiritual figure merged with that of Christ in my internal configuration—the Protector of Life. This figure is a radiant woman in a grotto beside a clear flowing stream. She became for me an expression of the divine feminine, the feminine face of Jesus, a healer and protector of the innocent, of the *anawim*, the poor ones, the voiceless. She also represents a healthy love for the body as a gift of nature. "Everything in your body is rhythm and beauty," she counsels, "Take care of your body so that it can serve you well, and be guided in this only by the opinions of those who are wise. I, who have passed through all the ages, know well that the idea of beauty is ever-changing. Do not harm your body with illnesses that exist only in your imagination. If you do not regard your body as your closest friend, it will become sad and ill—therefore you must accept it completely. It is your instrument for expressing yourself in the world."[9]

As the feminine counterpart to Jesus, she was a manifestation not only of a tenderness for Earth's community of life, but of self-compassion, a love of Eros and the body, and the nurturing and self-healing part of my nature. She was also a figure for my own healing, both emotional and spiritual. This was not only a healing of personal trauma, but also the healing of a spiritual rupture in my culture, the loss of connection to the larger community of life. This had begun over ten thousand years ago when ascendent northern patriarchal cultures worshipping a male deity began to overrun the Neolithic goddess cultures. Feminine consciousness had gone underground in Western culture and the resulting imbalance was causing planet-wide ecological disruption and alienating us from our roots. An intuitive, life-giving, matriarchal, receptive wisdom had been repressed for centuries due to the enthronement of masculine rationality driven by an ethos of domination.

Nor could I find a compelling image of the divine feminine within Christianity. The Virgin Mary of the Protestant Christianity of my boyhood had nowhere near the power of the Mary of Catholicism. Protestant Mary was the mother of Jesus, but little else. I had visited the great cathedrals of France, and witnessed, as had Henry Adams a century before, the psycho-spiritual energy the Catholic Virgin Mary had inspired. How could one not feel a sense of wonder at the manifestation of that power in the soaring architecture, the beauty of the glass, the massive presence of stone, the transcendent light? But to simply witness it wasn't to believe, or to feel the Virgin within me as a healing archetype. I was even more at a loss than Adams as to what modern equivalent could inspire that level of psychic energy. Nor did I have a clear sense of what the modern equivalent of the cathedral might be.

For me, the Protector of Life is a manifestation of the divine feminine similar to Quan Yin, the *bodhisattva* of compassion from Chinese mythology, who also played a part in my spiritual archetypal configuration. Quan Yin is seen as a fierce protector of women and children, the "one who hears the cries of the world." Hearing the cries, a *bodhisattva* chooses to stay in the world and not enter nirvana in order to save suffering beings. I searched for quite some time for a stone likeness of Quan Yin to place in my home, one that I felt carried an expression on her face that spoke to me of the love for all life. Once found, I first placed her in my home in front of the hearth. But she now seems more at home in my garden among the plants, lizards, frogs, and insects, where she is a constant reminder to me of the call to protect and cherish the living.

My boyhood conception of Jesus grew out of crisis, a subsequent quest, and then a return to a larger, fuller integration of a Cosmic Christ. To heal is to re-integrate; the Latin root, *integrare*, means "to make whole." My way back to wholeness is a love for planet Earth and the community of life; and for the evolutionary unfolding that gave us life. Earth as Christos is the embodiment of compassion for the web of life. And it is through the human that the planet can grow to a greater expression of love ... or not. Through the phenomenon of our conscious self-awareness, we have a choice. And violence is still the choice we make far too often.

There are four main attributes of Christic energy that for me can help the human return to wholeness.

Compassion, or love, is the main attribute and taken to the cosmic level, constitutes a circle of compassion for all beings. It is the Christos as ultimate communion, an intimacy with the Earth and the universe that opens a pathway to fuller being and greater beauty in evolutionary unfolding.

Creativity, another attribute of Christ, is an expression of cosmogenesis (our origins and creative unfolding), from which we each derive our unique identity and expression. "Creativity is the fundamental law of the human psyche which constitutes a microcosm of the universe," wrote Matthew Fox, in his book *The Coming of the Cosmic Christ,* "In beginning to imitate the law of the universe, human communities and social institutions will need to reinstate creativity at their core."[10] Jesus used parables, the power of creativity through story, to shift consciousness.

Rebellion was a third attribute of Christ. Jesus rebelled against the authorities of his time, because their power was based in injustice. The truth shall set you free. Speaking truth to power is the only way to spiritual freedom in a culture that is based on systematic injustice. In Chapter 17, I write about *EarthLight,* the magazine I edited for many years. *EarthLight* was all about rebellion, and in some respects the editorship was perfect for me, because I was not only going against my religious past, but calling into question the assault of industrial culture on the natural world. I was also rebelling against the injustices of American society. I was never ambitious in a conventional sense. Making a lot of money never occurred to me. My ambitions lay in the spiritual and artistic realms. I rebelled against the limitations of my family by moving far away. I rebelled against my father by refusing to accept collapse as the main theme of my life. In a sense, I rebuilt his ministry in the form of the magazine and an entirely new worldview it was based upon. And when the magazine collapsed financially, I re-channeled my creativity into new forms, using poetry, music, and writing to continue the work.

Healing is the fourth main attribute of the Christ. Jesus healed the sick and infirm through the power of their own faith. "Thy faith has healed thee," he tells the woman who reached out to touch the hem of his garment as he passed through a crowd and found herself restored to health. In today's disenchanted world, a sense of wonder is the basis for faith in an evolving universe, and the main source for healing in a cosmic sense. We can reach out and touch the tapestry of life again with a sense of wonder. And our faith can heal us. Faith in mystery, that life finds a way. Faith is the basis for trust.

What I came to learn from the work of Gabor Maté, and from my own process of healing, was that the experience of trauma is not simply defined by a particular incident, but in the consequent alienation from the self that occurs. The events of my childhood induced that, as well as the need for recovery. Recovery meant a quest, finding the self again. Simultaneously, my culture has been suffering from a general feeling of alienation from the world of nature. This loss has engendered widespread longing in the human soul to be embedded again in community, in place, in the creative spontaneities of nature. The transformative power of story is that it creates community. It brings people together in a common purpose.

The configuration of an internal spiritual guide in figures of compassion like Jesus, the Protector of Life, and Quan Yin, were a big part of my road back to myself. More importantly, they became a road, one which I still travel, to a renewed sense of belonging to a larger ecological Self. And with cosmology, our common story, comes my constant sense of astonishment and wonder that we are here at all.

Lady of the Grotto

Somewhere in these pinyoned hills
a grotto breathes
and the breath is a lady.

Her weeping has been mistaken
for coyotes by strangers
and the cups of her hands
praying for water confused
with the boughs of trees.
Her hair has been thought to be
canopies swaying at dusk.

But her laughter is in the willows,
the moon pearl oil her bath.
She hears the cries of the world,
her footfalls whisper your name,
calling you back,
echoing what you already know.

Chapter 15
Secrets and Stories

There are myriad sounds and images from my early midwestern landscape that are imprinted on my psyche. I carry these pieces of my childhood within me, clear auditory or visual glimpses that trigger an immediate feeling response within me. A flicker landing on a low branch, piercing me with her sharp call. A box turtle moving slowly, but resolutely, through the tall grass. A dark gray horizon torn by a searing flash of lightning, then healed by the answering roll of thunder. The pulsing buzz of cicadas and locusts on balmy summer nights. The crisp autumn air turning leaves to bursts of orange and crimson. The slow, warm, murky slither of rivers and the silver scramble of creeks gushing across gravelly beds. The stark, silent pallet of snow, ice, and leafless oaks in winter.

Each glimpse has as its companion a feeling. Closing my eyes, letting these glimpses roll through my consciousness, I get a sense of myself as the sensuous land itself. I am complete within my joy and my grief. For a moment, I am whole.

Even to this day, these memories surface from deep within my body into my conscious awareness, often between sleep and waking. One of these images inhabits my dreams more frequently than most. It comes out of the minimalism of the winter landscape in the Midwest. And yet, for all its starkness, it has no less power over me than other, more glorious, landscapes. Bodies of water in an Iowa winter—farm ponds, gravel pits, sloughs, small lakes—become milky plains of ice and snow beginning in mid-to-late November. Then, in the faux-spring of the

January thaw, or later, in true spring, there are places where those white sheets begin to clarify. The snow melts and runs off. The ice thins to transparency. Here and there, horizontal windows appear on the land, affording a view of a subsurface world beginning to stir. Out walking, I would seek out these windows along the fringes of small lakes and ponds, or in the beds of frozen creeks. Beneath these panes of clear ice were movements, shifts, hints, awakening currents lightly nudging the shapes of fallen foliage, some still decomposing, turning to food. Insect larvae, clams, turtles, the mud dwellers. Peering down onto one of these icy windows in full daylight could be like gazing into a mirror. I wanted to shatter the ice, look down into an older identity, forget the self. An uncontrollable urge to excavate and expose would eventually lead me to shatter the window with a foot or a rock or a stout stick.

That this image still haunts my dreams indicates a certain longing for primary knowledge, something the body knows and the soul recognizes as truth. I sought to break through the cold, the icy boundary, the illusion of the self that prevented me from understanding the depth. I wanted to know the bottom of a pond coming out of winter's sleep, the strange life frozen in the muck of a pond bed, then released by the warmth of spring. What stirs out of those depths when the ice melts, what awakens? And when the sun's fingers reach down, what secrets are exposed?

Whenever I visit my home state of Iowa, I feel a familiar tug within me. It happens the minute the landscape comes into view, as the plane approaches the runway or the Amtrak slides past the green fields, or I drive into town. It's a feeling unlike any other. Standing before a spectacular vista can elicit awe, but the sight of the muddy Raccoon River on the edge of town is bone deep. There is an immediate recognition, like seeing a friend again after an absence.

There came a time when another kind of inner tug drew me to my home landscape.

"I want to come home for Thanksgiving this year," I wrote Kristin in a letter in 2004. "Strange that I still call Iowa home after all these years away. I hope you will tell me what happened to you. Because it happened to all of us. Maybe we can come together as a family and talk about its impact on our lives." Over the many years, whenever I tried to talk about Kristin's abduction to a friend or counselor or spouse, I fell into a well of emotion that felt like it had no depth. Grief, anger, shame, mostly. But over that well was a veil of silence in my family. For decades, there was a cold winter as bleak and barren as a snowfield. I was peering down through the ice, but I couldn't make out what was there.

I remember a black and white photo of Kristin taken about the time of her kidnapping. She is wearing a plaid dress, her blond curls fallen down onto her shoulder, a slight smile her lips. Every time I saw the photo, I felt shame. Something had happened to her that was beyond bad. Then there is another photo, one of myself as a young boy. What I see in that photo is joy. There is a spark in my eye, a light shining out from my face. After the trauma, a moroseness crept into my photos, the light dimmed and diffuse. Dark circles under my eyes accentuated a strained sadness.

It would take a breaking of the ice to begin to see with any kind of clarity what stirred below. A lifting of the silence was just the beginning of healing from shame. Healing begins with not turning away from the reality of a trauma-inducing event. Growing fully into the possibilities of one's life isn't possible without a gaze into the truth of a situation, even if it is difficult. Knowing the true story is the place to begin.

My letter was long overdue. Kristin's response to what happened to her, her trauma, was my family's trauma, was my own. And yet, she carried it alone for many years. "No one asked me what happened." she told me years later, "And so I kept it inside. I thought I was protecting you. I didn't feel like anyone wanted me to talk about it. I didn't hear anything from anybody, so the burden was all on me. Not only to deal with what happened to me, but to keep the secret, to protect other people from the tragedy. Mom did reach out to a psychiatrist and asked what to do. He recommended that they not talk about it unless I brought it up." It was the early sixties, a more ignorant time in psychiatry and the culture. Little was understood about the effects of trauma. We remain a culture that is largely inept at addressing the pathology that comes from unacknowledged trauma. Gabor Maté, whom I wrote about in the Introduction, puts this approach in perspective by contrasting it to that of some indigenous traditions, like the Lakota people.

"In the Lakota tradition," he says, "when somebody gets ill, the community says 'thank you.' Your illness represents some dysfunction, some imbalance in our whole community, because we're not separate. Your body is not separate from your mind, and your mind is not separate from the rest of our minds. We co-create each other. Your healing is our healing; so thank you."[11]

There are so many people who have experiences that have induced trauma in their lives. To the extent that we can listen, as in the Lakota tradition, to their stories and honor their, and our, need for healing, we can begin to move toward cultural wholeness. In spite of the silence over the years, our family owes Kristin our gratitude. Her trauma was our trauma, and her healing is our healing.

My family did come together on November 23, 2007, over forty years after the ordeal. Meeting with a family counselor, we sat surrounding Kristin as she gave us a detailed account of what happened to her on that day. It was more horrifying than I knew or had imagined. Broad impressions and mistaken assumptions fell away, replaced by that sudden release of energy that comes from recognizing a suppressed truth. I could actually feel muscles in my face and chest relinquish long-held tension. Her ordeal stopped feeling like some distant fantasy.

She also shared what it was like for her just after her rescue. "I had nightmares for months afterward," she said. "I would wake up many times and shake my head back and forth to try and get him out of my head." Even today, I close my eyes and my own head wants to shake back and forth as I think about my ten-year-old sister trying to cope with the trauma within her.

My parents knew some of the story from counseling sessions with Kristin over the years. After I wrote to her in 2004, we went together to see a couple who had been counseling her. She told me more of her story at that time. But for all of us, much of the information was new. What I remember most from that session was Kristin's request that she feel her three brothers surrounding her. She asked us to lock arms and stand around her in a circle, embracing her. For years she had been protecting all of us from the truth. "It felt like a fortress of protection," she said. "It was very powerful for me to have you stand around me."

As for my father, he had been mostly absent. He didn't talk about it, either the day of or for years afterward. He was sedated into unconsciousness while it was happening. The day after, he stoically preached a sermon. On the radio and in the media, he presented a miracle to the public, but harbored different feelings. He found ways to continue to sedate himself over the years, not so much through substances, but through denial, avoidance, dark moods, unpredictable behaviors, and migraine headaches that debilitated him.

But on this day, my father, upon hearing Kristin's story, held her on his lap and whispered over and over to her, "I'm sorry this happened to you. I'm glad you're back home. I'm glad you survived. I will protect you."

Secrets and stories

It is very difficult to heal what we cannot name. There are small day-to-day secrets, things we keep under wraps out of a fear of truthfulness, of hurting someone. But then there are bigger secrets, ones that shut down growth and connection, and keep a life from flourishing. In my life there were two bigger secrets. Both involved paths to healing, but not until hidden truths were revealed. The great secret of our family was finally out and exposed after nearly forty years.

The other secret is a collective one, and has its own hidden story. People around the world down through the ages have had origin stories, cosmologies that oriented them, gave them a sense of belonging, and reminded them that they were part of something larger than the individual person. The collectively best-kept secret of the Western world for centuries now has been that we are, in reality, deeply connected to Earth's community of life. Not just physically, but psychically, through a unifying field of consciousness. We belong here, every bit as much as the wren, the redwood, and the tiger. We are participants in a story that goes all the way back to the primordial fireball. The universe literally lives within us because we are formed from the stars. In our mistaken belief that we are not of one body with Earth's community of life and with a magnificent story, we continue to enact the trauma of severance from our origins.

Those who refuse to or cannot heal continue to inflict psychic trauma on themselves and others, even if it is in silence. It's the secret that makes us ill, that causes the greatest harm. My father, for example, carried secrets with him throughout his life. He flew from the trauma of losing his father just as he was coming into manhood at age sixteen, right into the arms of the church. He never told my grandmother that his father died with another woman in a hotel room. Then, when the refuge of the church exploded with the kidnapping of my sister, he flew into the chaos of the sixties rebellion and came out the other side resentful of his decisions to be a minister and a father. In his later years, he did spiritual work, but would always remain in some form of denial and refusal to acknowledge his earlier wounds. Part of my own healing has been to find forgiveness for the emotional abuses my family and I incurred because of his own brokenness and inability to heal.

The psychic trauma inflicted by both secrets had to do with not knowing the story. In my larger social, ecological, and cultural community, the healing of the human cannot really begin until we know our larger story. What Thomas Berry has termed a "radical discontinuity" between the human and the web of life is the greatest collective trauma a human society has undergone in history. As long as the "secret" of our unity with all life remains suppressed, we are all impoverished and half-blind to human possibility. If we refuse to heal as a culture from that severance from our roots, we will continue to inflict trauma on the natural world and on each other.

My family gathers two hours later at the home of Kristin and her husband, Lynn. Her story is still swimming around us and through us. Some of us are sitting quietly in the living room. Others are on the deck that overlooks their back yard of stately walnut and oak trees. Kristin is sitting on the couch next to my mother, holding her hand as she cries quietly. The doorbell rings. Kristin gets up to answer. A woman is at the door. She has been visiting each house in the neighborhood with some news. Kristin speaks to her for a minute or two, then turns and walks over to us, a look of disbelief on her face. "A young woman is missing," she says, "the family and police think she's been abducted." She has the same initials and last name as Kristin when she was abducted. We look at each other, not knowing what to say. Of all the moments in all of the years my sister has lived in her home, this visitation happens after our family secret has been released and we are together, trying to process it. A mystery that may never be solved. Later, we hear that the outcome for the young woman and her family and the community was not good. She did not survive her abduction. I struggle to hold the strange mixture of sorrow for the woman's family and gratitude that Kristin was returned to us within me. We are connected in ways we may never fully understand.

Several hours after my family met to hear her story, as we sat around a table in Kristin's kitchen, a folder was brought out of clippings and photographs from the day. For the first time, I saw the face of the man who had taken her. It was a yellowing image from a newspaper clipping. He was being led away by FBI agents. He seemed unremarkable some-how, ordinary, and yes, a little rough-shaven and scruffy-looking, but not the monster that had inhabited my imagination.

And yet, as I gazed at his face, I felt a sudden firestorm surge up within me. All of the rage and grief of the event and the cascade of destruction it had caused ever since converged on that one point, his face. I saw the trauma with utter clarity and it was in the face of her per-petrator. An electrified force moved up from deep within that I couldn't contain. It propelled me from the room as I yelled something in my rage that I can't remember. I flew down the hallway and into the bathroom. There, it felt literally and physically as if a demon was departing my body. My entire frame shook with a profound grief. The feeling that surfaced when I spoke of the kidnapping to others came on me full force. I was completely in my body, all mental resistance melted away. And then, after a time the sobbing subsided and a profound quiet came over me. For months afterward, although I felt emptied out, I could finally speak my truth. My heart was breaking for the violation of innocence. It felt, for a time, that even my creative Muse had left me, and I wondered if she would ever return. Oddly, Kristin's perpetrator lost his power over my imagination once I saw his face. In its place, an emptiness, a place of uncertainty where I could only observe and wait. It was an emptiness, but there was an internal movement as well, not unlike that of a giant slowly turning whirlpool. In that turning, my imagination would need time to recover. Slowly, over time, I began to compose and write again. A new coherence grew inside me, as I noticed that there was less urgency in my creative expression and more reflection and focus.

Chapter 16

The Lens of Deep Time— the Question Revisited

It never occurs to us to wonder how the Earth sees us.
Is it not possible that a place could have huge affection for those
who dwell there? Perhaps your place loves having you there.[12]
—John O'Donohue

The question I first brought up in Chapter 13 persisted: Is the Universe a friendly place? I wasn't sure. All of my family's perceptions about what made the world a safe place had broken down. We came to doubt our own authority, because authority had mainly come from outside us— from the creeds, elders, and dogmas of the church, from the unquestioned authority of the Bible, and from the certainty that there was an all-powerful, all-loving God watching over things. My trust in my own perceptions would have to be rebuilt over time. I wanted to make the choice to affirm and protect life, to risk again, not to let despair drag me into cynicism, not to self-medicate with alcohol or other addictions. But trust and acceptance would take time to work its way into my heart.

My primary way of coping over the years had been to search out the one community that would not visit gratuitous violence on me or those I loved. That community was the natural world. Given the potential severities of the natural world, this can seem counterintuitive. But I could simply be on the riverbank, without judgment, without shame. I could walk the deciduous forests that remained in my home state without expectation or critique. It was an uneasy sense of ease.

There was a certain paradox or irony to my comfort and ease in nature. Kristin told me that because her perpetrator had taken her to the woods and tied her to a tree, she feared being alone in isolated natural areas or to be out after dark. And yet, I took refuge there. My experience as a white male is quite different from that of most women, as well as many Black Americans, whose relationship to wilderness in North America is vastly complicated by a history of lynching and other acts of extreme violence that haunt their collective and personal memory. "While most African Americans have never seen a lynching," writes professor and environmental science scholar Carolyn Finney in her book *Black Faces, White Spaces*, "the act of terror perpetrated on a Black person in the woods is remembered both for the place where it happened and the act itself."[13]

America's genocide of native peoples and enslavement of people of African descent added to the collective trauma of our estrangement from nature. In fact, it is that particular rupture in the human experience that allowed the pathologies of genocide and enslavement to arise. Our ongoing pathology and continuing trauma is our denial of this basic truth. We forgot that we are connected. That very separation we feel from our roots has allowed Western culture to objectify whole races of people and whole ecosystems of living beings. To be capable of enslavement, killing, of clearcutting a forest, or destroying millions of acres of native prairie, you must first objectify what you are destroying. As long as there is silence around these pathologies, the trauma around them will be made to seem normal. It will seem like it is just the way of the world, when in reality it is an aberration that keeps us from healing.

And yet, we cannot project human violence onto the natural world in general. The living world is the common legacy and locus of healing and connection for all peoples. Injustice in all its forms—from racism to subjugation of women—is a violation of that birthright, not emanating from within it. Part of the work of our time is to find ways to restore that legacy across peoples and species. This reimagining happens through direct experience in nature, but also through works of the imagination, and a spirituality that reminds us of our fundamental connection to each other.

Not long ago, my sister and I both read Richard Powers's novel *The Overstory*. The novel tracks the stories of four people over time and their rich and nuanced relationships to trees. She feels that reading the novel helped her change the way she thinks about trees. "Trees had a bad association for me because the perpetrator tied me to one," said Kristin. "I was left alone in an isolated natural area. Trees have had to witness terrible acts. I've felt sorry for them. They've been accomplices even though it wasn't their fault. And it wasn't nature's fault. I've had to overcome the feeling of being unsafe in the woods or areas people can't see into. But I've begun to see trees differently. The trees in my life are more allies, not enemies. There are magical things happening in nature that we aren't aware of." Powers's novel is part of a growing canon of literature that is "reimagining human-Earth relations in a mutually enhancing way," to use Thomas Berry's phrase.

Kristin shared with me recently that nature has become part of her healing journey. "My experience with nature has changed so much in the past few years. When I was younger and lived in Iowa City, I would go to Hickory Hill Park. I would get good ideas walking in the woods and along the streams. I had a lot of fears because of what happened to me, but I did it anyway because I wanted to face my fears."

"I have a yearning for feeling good about the land. It used to be, when I was driving in Iowa, I would see the land, but it was mostly agricultural, owned by someone else. There was no wildlife in view, just mostly farm animals and mono-crops. One of the things I've seen recently is more hawks. The red-tailed hawks have come back. I see them on the fence posts along the highway. I see them as my guardian angels keeping me safe on the highway. They are a vehicle for feeling close to the land again."

"I feel that with my local creek too. They took all the curves out of the creek years ago and the creek would constantly flood. Now our city has changed the creek's contours and made it curvy again. They put a big bend in the creek near our house so the water wouldn't rise so high, and it created a wetland. We started seeing all this wildlife that wasn't there before. Ducks, beaver, deer, muskrat, herons, cattails, frogs, dragonflies. But especially the beaver. When the city came in and cut down trees to create the bend in the river, I thought they were destroying life. But it actually brought life back. Like the way beaver create pools and bends and the land heals."

Kristin has a special affinity for deer, especially the doe. "I feel close to the mother doe," she said, "I feel that she's my animal friend. After some deep emotional work, I took the name Joyful Dancing Deer. I've been told that I have doe-like eyes." She laughs. And she does have eyes like a doe.

Nature had its trials, its severity and extremes that could challenge my own need for security and safety. Death was a part of life, my own included, a necessity for new life to emerge. Gaia could just as easily kill me as look at me. And yet, I also felt held and loved by the Earth. In a general sense, I didn't have to fear being taken out by a predator. My kind had essentially neutered that possibility by slaughtering the apex species wholesale. Nature as "red in tooth and claw" had a certain truth, but it isn't the whole truth. Cooperation and symbiosis are just as prevalent, if not more. My intuition was that violence in nature wasn't violence in the way human beings perpetrated it. It was out of necessity and the imperative to survive, not out of a sense of lack, uncertainty, or alienation.

Perpetrators and victims didn't really exist in nature. Animals killed to eat, survive, protect their young; only humans killed out of weakness, depravity, lust for power, psychological pain, and desperation. Violence wasn't even a concept that could rightly be applied to nature, because predation wasn't a violation, but a consummation; it wasn't personal, but a condition of our existence. Only human beings killed for no reason other than the thrill, or some notion that killing an animal would give you their power.

Human imagination brought incredible ingenuity, much of it good, but it also brought unspeakable evil. Human creativity had brought about wondrous inventions, and it could heal; but it could also bring cruelty and destruction. We built cathedrals and found medical cures, but we also built missile silos and perpetrated torture and massacres. And in general, the destructive aspects of patriarchy have robbed most of us even of the healing potential of the natural world.

It was this very perversion that would come to consume me. I had to find a way to see the human being as something more than a pervert cut loose on a garden planet. It wasn't easy. I grew up in a time (the 1960s and 1970s) of the ascendency of the environmental movement. With it came images of the human as a cancer on the planet in the minds of many who cared about the future of life on Earth. I understood this notion on some level, the outrage behind it. But I also knew it wasn't a blueprint for a viable future. The human had been formed from the creative travails of the planet down through millennia, and there was just too much poignancy in the view that we were just a blight, a cancer, an evolutionary experiment gone bad.

I've always felt a tenderness for living beings, and in-born desire to protect, to nurture, to allow them to flourish. To defend them, not against the conditions to which all life on Earth is subject, but against industrial culture as perpetrator. My father had taught me to fish as a boy, but even this fell away, as I found I much less heart for harming the fish. For the extent of a living being's life, no matter how brief, I felt they had a right to thrive and to inhabit and bless the Earth with their unique manifestation within the living world. Each is an expression of the divine. The ultimate act of sanctity for the human is to allow life to flourish, and if need be, to preserve the conditions for that to happen. Even if the duration of that life is but a few months, days, hours, the freedom to thrive and procreate, to swim, fly, crawl, slither, climb, tunnel, run, and bear young, to feed, and die and decay and emerge again as part of Earth's life community is a sacred right.

That feeling of tenderness, of generativity, the need to protect the innocent is marginalized by the machine, by a mechanistically based culture. To have these feelings as a man in such a cultural ambit is difficult, and yet its absence is a wound that takes away the most precious part of a man and threatens to rob him of meaning and value. To violate that sanctity is to go against evolution, diversification, against the emergence of beauty as a manifestation of the divine. One of the supreme ironies of human life is that in order to survive, to eat, to flourish, we must kill.

Part of the tenderness and desire to protect that I felt within me was about my need to protect the innocent, including my sister. She received protection from St. Joseph and other angels when she was a girl undergoing something no one should ever have to endure. The "fortress of protection," her brothers standing around her, was, she said, one of the most healing symbolic acts she has experienced. "In a society where trauma and abuse are rampant, we are still learning how to best protect our daughters, sisters, and mothers," she adds.

And so, for a time in my life, fall-redemption theology took a new twist. Humankind truly had fallen from the primal graces of nature. If the human needed redemption, it was from the sin of despoiling our garden planet. We all bear responsibility. If there is a sin, it is *acedia*, or "non-action" against injustice and senseless violence. To atone for the crimes of exploitation and extraction beyond all reason and past the point where the Earth's life systems can recover, has yet to happen with human beings generally. And yet, I sensed that this tweak of the fall-redemption worldview had all the weaknesses and shortcomings of using old paradigm thinking to solve the problems that an outmoded system of thought has created. Solutions couldn't be found in contempt for my own kind, and by extension, of myself. If you fall, you need a savior, and require redemption. In a creative, emergent universe, we are not fallen, we've just forgotten who we are. And so, along with a sense of place, of being held by the Earth, a sense of deep time is needed. *When* we are is as important as *where* we are.

Deep time

In a culture that has forsaken its roots, learning is remembering. Physical erasure is nearly universal. Only rarely are things preserved, as in a fossil. For anything to be preserved in this way is rare. And yet, there is a way in which the past that formed us is retrievable because it is not fossilized, but imprinted, etched into our bones and veins and flesh. What is contained in the bodies of the living requires a different kind of excavation. The bodies of our ancestors, formed from stars, have disappeared into prairie plants, beetle larvae, grouse feather, and the flesh of worms. This isn't complete erasure, but transformation.

We are the living Earth expressing herself in human form. The world is evolving within us as well as around us, through our inner landscape of dreams and emotions. Those two evolving worlds are not distinct from each other. They grow in tandem. Just as we are an expression of the biosphere in a particular place, we are also integral with the biosphere in deep time. The legacy of the planet's evolution is expressed through us, and each one of us is a unique emergence. Whatever we are facing, whatever trauma or challenge, is exactly what we need to evolve as a person. This is true in a collective sense as well. Our trauma and our capacity to face it is what our collective evolution needs. This is why facing the wounds of the past, to break the ice of denial and secrecy, is to embrace the future.

When I say in this book that I "spend time in nature," it's a clunky and not very apt description of what I feel is really going on in terms of my healing. To begin with, the more I am "out in nature," the more I realize that I'm not just in nature. I *am* nature. I am the biosphere evolving through me and within me. To spend any length of time "out there," is to awaken to the reality that we are nature evolving. My inner life is every bit the "natural world" as the wilderness I trek. That is a deeply healing realization. But it's not only about place, or about ecology, or about relationship in the present. There is also the healing aspect of deep time, or a remembering of our ancestors that brings to us a renewed sense of belonging. It is our deeper identity as the Earth evolving. The wounds of the past are also part of us. To follow a healing trajectory collectively we need to reconcile with our collective trauma. Running away from those wounds will only deplete our life energy. Knowing and telling their story places us in deep time and benefits the whole of the Earth community.

When I asked Kristin to tell me her story, what I really needed was to release my life energy from its frozen state. The intensity of feeling that I experienced when I talked about the trauma with friends and acquaintances happened because I was just beginning to connect with that life energy. I sensed its great power as I spoke of the trauma. I also knew that capping it with secrecy for those many years was a diminishment of the energies not just within me, but within my whole family. The only way I had to connect with that energy over the years was through the creative act. Although this was an unconscious act, it was a natural effort to heal.

The massive rush of energy that issued from within me after I heard her story and then saw the face of her perpetrator, was a release of that great well of energy. It was a sudden breaking of the ice. In a sense, it really was a demon released, because an energy suppressed only grows in malevolence and power. Frozen, it becomes a distortion of the life force. The sense of emptiness I felt afterward, that my Muse had gone, that I was in completely alien territory, uncertain and shaky, was a natural state following release. It was the emptiness of the *via negativa*, a natural vacuum created from the departure of an occupying force. The vacuum would refill over time. And it did refill and reconstitute into more mature and less desperate forms.

The work of Joanna Macy helped me to understand the well of energy that exists in knowing the story of our evolutionary past. It represents both an excavation of deep time and an excavation of the internal, primal energy source of human emotion. It is a process of remembering that helped me to process my grief, not just the personal grief of my family's past, but especially the grief I felt at the destruction of the planet. Her approach felt honest, authentic, and multi-layered. It begins with gratitude, which opens the space for generosity and reciprocity. And it provided practices for communally and personally activating energy in the face of loss. It addressed transforming despair and collective trauma into empowerment, and sustaining our gaze on what is happening to our world, even though it breaks our hearts. This helped me sustain both my grief at the ecological loss, but also that of my personal family trauma. "The sorrow, grief, and rage you feel," she wrote, "is a measure of your humanity and your evolutionary maturity. As your heart breaks open there will be room for the world to heal." I also found that when the heart breaks open, you can find purpose in your rage and sorrow. Joanna was an editorial advisor for the magazine I edited (see next chapter), and generously wrote a column for part of that time, and her vision deeply informed much of the content. Her work facilitating the Council of All Beings connected me to the web of life, the deep time of our evolutionary story, and to my own grief and recovery. It was an enactment and a ritual that taught me to step outside of the limitations of my human identity and live in empathy.[14]

Connection and courage

"People who are traumatized," says Gabor Mate, "tend to take on others' views of themselves."[15] And so, gaining a strong sense of oneself is part of healing. One of the best ways for me to know my own authority is to slow my life down to the speed of contemplation through a meditative practice of stillness and attention. Then to observe thought and feeling, bringing them into unity. Otherwise, how was I to know what were my perceptions and the resulting unconscious formations in my consciousness? When I felt sorrow and rage, I could let myself feel it through attention to my body, and then I could learn to relinquish my own thoughts into a larger sensitivity. This was a transformation of energy, and a recovery of my sense of self.

The loss of a sense of self is the essence of trauma. Time spent in nature was one way of figuring out what my true perceptions are. It was a contemplative practice, about knowing who I am. I was never one who had grand goals as an outdoorsman, someone who has to cover a lot of ground, collect grand vistas like possessions, or to scale mountains in order to feel thrilled to be out in nature. In fact, the most aimless and goalless time in nature yielded the greatest treasures; and it opened me to love. I could achieve a stillness in the silence, and being in the presence of animals and landscapes I didn't need to question motive or fear malignant intent. What's more, I could open myself to voices other than my own, ones that didn't carry an agenda, but which resonated with my deeper being.

These were the graces of the natural world. The only way I could know whether I could trust my own perceptions was to be still and listen, to quiet the din of images competing for my attention in the consumerist culture. Far from being a retreat from life and society, this was a desire to find union, a deeper intimacy with the living world, and an experience of fuller being. If I can truly know who I am, then I can feel that I belong. I can not only love my home place, but feel that the place loves me. Knowing *where* I am is knowing who I am. I *am* nature, and the universe unfolding. There is another aspect to knowing oneself within the matrix of the living Earth. It generates courage and confidence. The contemplative life always suited me, not because it set me apart from human society and closed me down, but because it opened my heart, energizing me and giving me courage. And cultivating attention when I was in the natural world developed the same capacity in me when I was in human company. I found I could listen more attentively and begin to trust.

To the extent that I could open myself to what the Earth was saying to me, I could know a deeper aspect of myself, and then maybe I could make a difference. It wasn't only through some rational faculty that I and others like me could bring it about. It was also through a deepening sensitivity to the powers and graces of Earth herself, to the primal spontaneities of the natural world of which we are a part, and through the wonder and terror in the mystery of Earth's processes. Reason had a role, but it was in partnership with, if not subservient, to heart and spirit. Human intellect, one of our shining gifts, was only a gift insofar as it was free of hubris and in humble service to an animated spirituality and a heart open to the living beings of the planet and her cosmic heritage. The healing of the rift between human and Earth is a reciprocal process. To be whole, to thrive, we must cease the assault on the one source of our healing — the planet that birthed us.

What I found was that attention to my own rage and sorrow did open my heart, and in doing so, it energized my intellect and my will to action. It activated an Earth Warrior archetype within me, and a power of discernment was activated in my intellect. Choosing life, I was able to face my own fear. And this is where we find freedom in its truest sense. When we are taught in our culture that we are essentially alone, we tend to think about the self, the ego, that we are essentially an individual with private thoughts and aspirations. We see freedom as independence from others. But this is where fear wins. And yet, none of this is our reality. It is a small and limited conception of who we really are. Connection, not independence, is the foundational nature of our reality; and attention and presence are the keys to connection. To let the Earth speak to us, we must pull the stoppers from our hearts, so that we can hear the song that will sing us home again.

Awakening

The sun bathes the bare stalks
bakes out the sprouts
and smells of earth ripening
from the boggy meadow.

From beneath the wind's net
a quail call sails. The rush
of the stream comes
coaxing up from the valley.

Ice clears to a looking glass,
the sun's fingers reach down
to the muck of pond bed;
dark currents stir sleepers awake.

The trees slough off
the hardy hold of winter,
laughing from inside
their bark. So the hour's

come round again
when the emissaries of life awaken,
cross the shadow threshold
into the dream of spring

and I stand captive,
speechless, still, and again.

LANDSCAPE INTERLUDE
Radical Presence

Is not beauty something that takes place when you are not?
—J. Krishnamurti
Ojai, California, 1985[16]

A Broad-billed Hummingbird hangs for a few seconds, not three feet away. The brilliant sapphire gorget flashes for an instant, and then the tiny bird is gone in a shot, his raspy cry fading like a lost thought into the oaks. I close my eyes and try to feel the impact that the hundreds of hummingbirds I've seen over the past few days have had on my psyche. The swirl of their presence, their diminutive size, their radiant color, their adroit quickness, their bickering flurries, all seep into me, and finally well up into awed appreciation, just for their being in the world. Past, future, and self fall away. In that moment, I've become the planet-as-human, in wonder at hummingbirds, feeling them as part of the splendor of life.

I am having this moment in one of the most diverse landlocked plant and animal communities in the world and I'm thinking about flight, how it might have come to be that life learned to transcend the bounds of gravity. I'm also thinking about energy, its sources, our need for it, and how access to it is integral to the flourishing of all of Earth's community. These two preoccupations—flight and energy—didn't rise up in me arbitrarily. The canyon I'm in, part of the Chiricahua Mountains in southeastern Arizona, boasts the highest concentration of bird species in North America. My love for birds is why I came here. And the relationship between flight and energy takes on particular meaning because of my third preoccupation: the bond between hummingbirds and flowers; there are fourteen species of hummers that frequent the canyon, the highest count anywhere in North America.

Few, if any, activities in the animal world are as energy intensive as flight. And no species of bird has used it so extravagantly as the hummingbird. No other bird has mastered backward flight. And hovering, something hummingbirds do with unparalleled grace, requires extremely rapid and energy-intensive wing movement. Other birds are more economical in their use of energy in flight, like swifts, for example, who have long slender wings that keep them aloft with minimal wing movement for weeks, even months at a time. And yet, hummingbirds hover, even when it exacts a high energy cost. Their reward is access to nectar, and lots of it.[17]

The hummingbird's draw to nectar ignited a unique kind of co-evolution that has heightened the diversity of bird-loving (ornithophilous) flowers on Earth. The next time you stop to admire penstemon, or fuchsia, or similarly shaped flowers, thank the hummingbird for its love affair with nectar. That fascination drew out the forms and hues of a vast array of flower petals. The hummingbird's singular obsession with nectar also gave rise to a dazzling array of color in the hummingbird's plumage. The resemblance of a hummingbird's feathers to the color in flowers' leaves and blossoms is thought to help protect it from predators. The colors aren't due to pigment in the feathers themselves, but to refraction. The hummingbird's gorget appears to be a uniform gray in the shadows. But sunlight is bent as it strikes the plumage and then bent again as it is released as specific fragments of the color spectrum. The curvature of light becomes beauty as dazzling color in the eyes of the human.

We can stop to take this in, to reflect on it through our symbolic consciousness, and then release it through language. My first glimpse of the purple flash of a Lucifer hummingbird's throat took my breath away. I wanted to put it into words, to share it. The hummingbird's "coat of many colors" has incited a linguistic cascade from the human imagination in our attempt to capture its allure; a sample in English, out of more than three hundred: Long-billed Star-throat, Mountain Gem, Black-throated Mango, Fork-tailed Wood-nymph, Blossom-crown, Little Wood-star, Empress Brilliant, White-chinned Sapphire, Horned Sun-gem, Purple-crowned Fairy, the Magnificent, Black-hooded Sunbeam, and the Sparkling Violet-ear.

A hummingbird aptly named The Magnificent veers out of the shadows. The chartreuse of his gorget shimmers. His crown and breast flare up in deep purple as the feathers refract under a flood of sunlight. He hangs, almost motionless for a few seconds, over a trumpet flower bush. In an age-old dance of enamorment, he visits flower after flower. I'm back from my preoccupations of mind and self, surrendering myself to wonder again.

Our own radical presence to what fascinates us elicits similar creativity to that of the hummingbird's. To allow ourselves to be drawn toward what most deeply moves us is an embrace of Eros, a desire for union with the ground of our being. This communion of one being with another gives rise to further complexification, and thus to expressions of beauty never before seen on Earth. Our human capacity to be transfixed by beauty is the same evolutionary dynamic as the draw of hummingbird to flower. Expressed through human conscious self-awareness, communion reaches an order of complexity that in a word, becomes wonder.

Often our sense of wonder, our joy, goes to sleep, or gets buried under the frantic searching of a mind that craves certainty and answers. But we can bring it back again through our breath, our attention, our heart beating. We quiet our minds, come back to ourselves, and let ourselves be sensitized to the shimmering intelligence all around us. In that place of surrender, we find the source of our wonder not only intact, but transformed.

Chapter 17

Earth, Light, Spirit

Do that which stirs you to love.
—**St. Theresa of Avila**

On the last day of the world
I would want to plant a tree.
—**W. S. Merwin**

It was a cool, blustery day, mid-morning on the beach. Billowing cloud banks played cat and mouse with the sun, dramatically shifting the light back and forth from cheerful to brooding. A stubborn shawl of fog still clung to the sandy arm of Half Moon Bay near water's edge. Walking against a stiff wind, I set out toward Maverick's Beach on Pillar Point, the outermost extreme of the Bay. Some of the largest waves in the world visited this stretch of coast. The cries of seagulls floated in and out of my consciousness as occasional bursts of ochre sunlight swirled through sporadic thinning of the fog. As I stood on the point, it felt as if the surf itself was a prophetic voice pounding again and again onto the shoreline.

It was 1994, during a time when I served on the editorial board of *EarthLight,* a magazine of ecology and spirituality that had emerged out of the Society of Friends (Quakers) community in the late 1980s. I had just left a meeting of the board, where I had been offered the position as editor when the current editor, Paul Burks, retired. I was driving back home to the Bay Area and I stopped off in Half Moon Bay to walk on the beach and consider the offer.

A swell of outrage, excitement, and fear thundered ashore, then smoothed out into a quiet spread of seawater foaming out across the sand. Outrage that my culture seemed to be under a spell of destruction driven by greed and consumerism. Excitement at the prospect of having a forum, a bully pulpit from which I might make difference. Fear that I wouldn't be up to the task. All of my teachers, encounters, and spiritual searching seemed to be converging into this single moment, offering me a vehicle for valid action in the world.

At the foundation of the magazine's mission was the realization that ecological devastation was a crisis of the human spirit. And that faith communities, scientists, policymakers, and activists could come together to address the roots of our destruction of the planet. To go to the source of the problem held out hope for authentic and profound change.

An evolving vision

EarthLight came into being out of rich Quaker values coupled with a rising concern by some in the Quaker community that the spiritual dimensions of the environmental crisis weren't being addressed, either within the faith community or the culture at large. The magazine grew organically from the Quaker values of simplicity, integrity, and non-violence. *EarthLight*'s name derived, at least in part, from a notion of the inner light, or "that of God in everyone." My own sense of it was that there is an inner light within Earth as well. That light could shine through us into a world of increasing darkness. It was the light infusing matter, the feminine principle trying to return to consciousness after centuries of suppression in Western society.

For Quakers, the primary way of accessing, opening to, and expressing the inner light was through silence and stillness. I was drawn deeply to the process of discernment that came with sitting in silence with a community dedicated to peace, social justice, and equality. For me, it was a spiritual alignment with wisdom and the spark of divinity within each of us. It was also a way of listening to the Earth. Quakers use what they call queries as a way of discerning wisdom and right action in any given circumstance. For me, *EarthLight* was an ongoing query: "What is the Earth asking of us?"

Even with this seedbed of spirituality, the magazine was, from its inception, never narrowly Quaker in its treatment of spiritual issues. It sought to be open to all faiths and spiritual traditions, to be a vessel of healing the spiritual rift between religious experience and a reverence for nature. It was energizing and renewing for many who came to it, a way to heal from within their own traditions, for finding their way back to a mystique of the Earth. For others who had long ago left their traditions behind, but who nonetheless felt a spiritual kinship to the Earth and the web of life, it was a welcoming community.

EarthLight went through an evolution of its vision over its sixteen years of publication.

The vision from the inaugural issue, articulated by founding editor Robert Schutz in 1990: "What we mean by spirit and ecology is: A vision of the Earth restored, the Earth sustained, the Earth as our mother, the Earth as a fair and beautiful place to live in, not perish in."

The vision statement in 1994, under the editorship of Paul Burks, was: "*EarthLight* addresses the environmental crisis from the awareness that at root it is a crisis of the human spirit. *EarthLight* seeks to inform, inspire, and empower individuals, congregations, and organizations toward the goal of sustainable communities and lifestyles."

The vision statement from 1996 through 2005, under my editorship read: "*EarthLight* celebrates the living Earth and our billion-years-old story of the Universe. The magazine's mission and focus is to cultivate the awareness that Earth is a sacred community to be cherished, protected, and restored, not a commodity to be exploited. We seek to catalyze the personal and global consciousness required to ensure a healthy Earth for future generations of all species."

In 1993, I wrote an essay called "A Theology of Restoration" and submitted it to the editor before me, Paul Burks. In my summation of the article, I wrote:

There is a sense of loss people feel in not knowing our natural surroundings. A new and regenerative understanding of our place in the natural world will help drive the healing of this loss. People want to take back the power over their own lives and their local communities by restoring them to health. If we feel secure in a healthy and prosperous home region through a feeling of personal and communal responsibility for local resources, systems of trade, health care, and education, we will be less likely to act out of fear, violence, and addiction and more out of love, unity, and ecological integrity. Restoration, because so much is damaged and because we as a society are adrift from the life of the spirit, should be the primary focus of our relationship to the Earth. It is both inner and outer work.

Belonging and joy

Standing on the stormy point at Half Moon Bay, I knew there was no better spiritual call I could answer. The discernment of the inner light within all of us and within the Earth. This was a new kind of wilderness to explore, a wilderness of ideas and spirit, an emergent paradigm that was only just beginning, at that time, to be articulated within the Zeitgeist. Among those ideas: our sacred relationship to animals, our kinship with all life beyond mere stewardship of the Earth, our role and place in an unfolding universe, the spiritual depths of our link to nature, a refutation of patriarchy and the Christian fall/redemption paradigm in favor of the sacred feminine, and the articulation of a new cosmology that was a unifying story for people from all faiths and backgrounds.

The spirituality at the heart of *EarthLight* was a renewed capacity to feel our deep love and connection with our fellow living beings and with each other. In this sense, I thought of *EarthLight* as a ministry from the beginning, perhaps because of my earlier idealization of my father as minister. My editorials often read more like mini-sermons. I couldn't imagine a more worthy work in the world. I had no material concerns at the time. Melinda had departed for the East Coast to complete medical school. Our divergent careers and interests had led to an amicable divorce. It was a period where I would have slept in a hut or under a tree and eaten honey and locusts to support the work. Part of my path to healing was the community that the magazine represented. My work there answered a longing within me to heal the rupture from the faith community that my family had experienced. It restored in me a new sense of connection, this time with the much larger Earth community. And with that renewed sense of belonging, joy returned. The joy is in the sharing of the personal spiritual truth of our belonging, of a deeper connection to all life. My awe and wonder at nature were magnified when shared with the community of readers, magazine staff, volunteers, and supporters.

In this sense, spirituality makes us stronger, more resilient. It insulates us from despair, hopelessness, and addiction. We are more able to cope with traumatic events in our lives. We also function better because it is a powerful antidote to depression. It activates a latent wisdom within us. The opportunity to shepherd a magazine on spirituality and ecology was an activation of the Earth Warrior energy within me, as well as the Rebel. As with any Warrior path, I needed to face fears and I needed to gain some wisdom and learn discernment. All of this would develop within me as a practice of spiritual ecology (see chapters on Spiritual Ecology). The Rebel was activated because the magazine directly questioned the foundations of consumerist industrial culture and addressed the spiritual roots of the ecological ruin we are visiting on the planet. Only then could we halt the desecration of the planet.

The magazine was an ongoing conversation, a dialogue between the inner and the outer and between human beings and the Earth. For the ten years I was editor, I dwelt in the world of words and thought. In that way it was crucial to the evolution of my own consciousness. To refer back to an earlier chapter on Matt Fox and his four spiritual paths, my time at the magazine was the *via transformativa*, a way for me to bring my own intuitions about our severance from the Earth into the realm of thought. It was also a forum for justice for the entire Earth community.

The lifeblood of the magazine, a non-profit, non-sectarian publication, was its volunteers, all of them dedicated to the exploration of sacred relationship, ecology, cosmology, and spirituality. From board members to website managers to graphic designers and envelope stuffers; from editorial advisors to writers and artists who gave freely of their time, wisdom, artwork, and writing; to donors and subscribers; a host of people gave themselves to the work with passion, dedication, and a sense of creative play. Editorial advisors included Joanna Macy, Thomas Berry, Miriam MacGillis, and Brian Swimme. As editor, I was often the public face of the magazine, but I was not the body. My personal vision rose from my passion for the topic, but the larger vision grew from the confluence of these many people and the ideas they devoted themselves to around creating a new relationship of the human to the Earth and cosmos.

The vision of Thomas Berry

My earliest memory of Thomas Berry was about a decade before I took on the *EarthLight* editorship. I had heard him speak in 1987, about the time he published his book *The Dream of the Earth*. A week later, I realized I had just finished reading what was perhaps the most important book of my life. I remember chasing Melinda around our yard in South Berkeley with a copy of the book in my hands, reading passages to her as she was trying to get some gardening done. She looked up now and then with a smile from the raised bed of baby lettuce, trowel in hand, as if to ground my unfettered enthusiasm into the body of the Earth.

Thomas's influence on me at this time is what started me in earnest writing about spirituality and ecology. This interest eventually led me to *EarthLight*. I often liked to picture the magazine and its community as a tree. If the Quaker community was the trunk, and the branches and foliage were the volunteers, readership and the larger network of spiritual centers with which *EarthLight* shared a common vision, Thomas Berry was more like the taproot. There were many other roots feeding into the magazine's vision (and my own), but the vision Thomas articulated came to carry the sap, a kind of lifeblood. That lifeblood is best expressed, in Thomas's words, as the creation of "mutually enhancing relations" between the human and the rest of the Earth community.

Thomas Berry provided the beginnings of a new lexicon as it were, a new way of articulating what felt latent within so many human souls, a language that represents a lost light shining, however dimly, in human consciousness. I saw that light grow in its intensity during my years at the magazine. A growing number of people began to realize it and express it, and it seemed that the discovery of Thomas's writings worked as a kind of watershed moment for their intuitive sense both of a deeper psycho-spiritual connection to the natural world and of an overarching alienation in the culture. Many people today continue to build on the linguistic foundations he has laid.

It was Thomas who named the source of my bewilderment as the symptom of a kind of autism in the Western world and helped me make sense of it. He identified the source of our modern alienation and and existential anxiety as a "radical discontinuity" between ourselves and the rest of the natural world. When I first discovered his writings, I began to feel less crazy, less alone, and less marginalized. In that sense he has been a part of my own healing and an inspiration for my work as a writer. And I think Thomas's writings helped give the environmental community a way of talking about the Earth in a way that could transcend the technical, political, scientific, or dry policy language that could at times be so alienating and uninspiring to the general public.

Not long after I first met Thomas, I attended a weekend retreat with him. He spoke of our living at the end of the Cenozoic Period, a "lyric" period of great grandeur and beauty on Earth. "We need the healing of a beautiful world," he said, "because we need to keep our actions authentic. We need the universe to sink in, to give us reassurance. We need to develop a mutually-enhancing manner with the Earth. It's the most difficult change the life community has faced, the most important work we have ever been called to do." Thomas also spoke at that retreat of his experience seeing lilies in a meadow when he was ten years old. "I was the brooding type," he said. "I had a choice between prison and the monastery, and I chose the latter. The meadow became a test: good economics would protect it, good politics would protect it, and so forth. The meadow became a larger dimension of my own being. The meadow wasn't just an amazing panorama, it was the determining moment of my life." He would later include an account of the meadow in his book *The Great Work*.

I finally met Thomas in a more intimate one-on-one setting toward the end of his life when he had moved back to North Carolina. It was in the fall of 2005. I began my visit the night before at the Center for Education, Imagination, and the Natural World in Whitsett, North Carolina, headed up by Carolyn Toben. Carolyn had established the Center with the mission of bringing together the inner life of the child with the beauty, wonder, and intimacy of the universe. I was staying with Herman Greene, the director for the Center for Ecozoic Studies in Chapel Hill. Herman's Center was dedicated to bringing about the realization of the Ecozoic Era envisioned by Thomas in *The Great Work* and other writings. Carolyn and Herman had organized the gathering as a brainstorming session for how to help usher in the Ecozoic. A couple dozen people, including Thomas Berry, were gathered in the meeting house in the Treehouse, a community meeting building at the Carolyn's Center. Several people were gathered in a circle around him. As I walked in the door, Thomas looked up. His face brightened with a smile, and his eyes had a warm twinkle as he gestured to me from his seat across the room.

"Hello! Hello, young man! Come, come, sit here next to me!" Part of me was stunned at the strength of his warm greeting. I was also a bit flattered to be called a young man at age 50. A warm joy spread through me as I sat next to him. On his lap was the final issue of *EarthLight Magazine*. As a tribute to him, I had placed a drawing of Thomas on the back cover. The drawing was by Catholic sister Mary Southard, someone who knew him well and followed his work. With the drawing, I had included one of my favorite excerpts from his book *Dream of the Earth*, which I had entitled: "Confidence in the Future." The book had been published in the same year I had begun my Master program at Matthew Fox's Institute in Oakland, California. Reading it and doing the program at the same time had catapulted me into a completely different spiritual orientation, one where I first began thinking of myself as a mode of the universe, not apart from its remarkable story. Placing this excerpt on the back cover was, in a sense, giving Thomas the last word in the magazine's 16-year publication. The passage is, for me, the summarizing credo of his enormous vision, which is a gift to anyone struggling to make sense of the human role in the universe. Someone had provided one page reprints of the back cover for distribution to the group. I glowed as I sat next to him, as he began to speak directly to me about the excerpt, which follows:

The basic mood of the future might well be one of confidence in the continuing revelation that takes place in and through the Earth. If the dynamics of the Universe from the beginning shaped the course of the heavens, lighted the Sun, and formed the Earth, if this same dynamism brought forth the continents and the seas and the atmosphere, if it awakened life in the pri-

mordial cell and then brought into being the unnumbered variety of living beings, and finally brought us into being and guided us safely through the turbulent centuries, there is reason to believe that this same guiding process is precisely what has awakened in us our present understanding of ourselves and our relation to this stupendous process. Sensitized to such guidance from the very structure and functioning of the Universe, we can have confidence in the future that awaits the human venture.[18]

We had scarcely begun speaking when we were called into a larger sharing circle by Herman. My moment with him had passed, at least for that day. I felt a little let down, but joyful to be there.

I went to visit Thomas at his home the next day. He greeted me with the same warmth and enthusiasm as the night before. I wish I could say that there was some profound revelation, or an amusing antidote, or something beyond the pale. The truth is, it was much simpler than that. I met him in his apartment; we chatted a while, including about a recent trip I had made to the Sonoran Desert in Southern Arizona to see the convergence of large numbers of hummingbird species that occurs there each year. He was modestly interested and patient with my story, saying at the end with a smile, "They really are magnificent, aren't they?" Then he suggested we go and get Thai food. Over dinner, he asked me a little more about myself, and then he spoke to me about Teilhard de Chardin. In the end, he emphasized, it was Teilhard's work on building a thinking Earth that was his most important contribution to our modern predicament. Teilhard had given us the notion of a time-developmental universe from which human conscious self-awareness had unfolded.

It felt a little anti-climactic to meet the man whose vision had had such an influence on me and my own work, only to just have a nice talk about Teilhard over Thai food. I had built up the visit in my mind for days ahead of time. And it turns out our interaction was some combination of pleasantries, social awkwardness, and reliving my days in the lecture hall. I would take that. It was enough. I knew the gift he had given me even if I couldn't resonate with him as deeply as I might have liked on a personal level. We chatted about Constantine and Christendom and where Western civilization took a wrong turn. But they were things I already knew from his writings. For a mind like Thomas's, this was almost on the level of small talk. I sat there, wondering: *what could I possibly say to or ask of a man whose learning was fathoms deeper and hectares broader than my own?*

I realized in the end that it didn't matter. Thomas Berry touched my soul and that was something that couldn't be put into words anyway, at least not fully. What I remember and which elicited a smile from him as I echoed it back to him that night over dinner was: "We need the healing of a beautiful world." The simple phrase he had uttered at the weekend retreat years before. Of everything that had been said over the course of the weekend, that was the mantra that has spun through my consciousness ever since. It both affirmed what I already knew and provided a simple roadmap. Preserve, protect, and cherish the living world. It was also what I knew I and so many others needed in a society that was alienated from its roots. A beautiful world gives us cause for wonder, gives us faith, gives us trust in the universe, gives us healing.

Over time, I have come to have a multi-layered understanding of the "beautiful." As complexity in evolution deepens, so too does beauty. Biodiversity of life on Earth is a kind of beauty. And the reason we need to preserve diversity, beyond the inherent right of all species to flourish, has to do with our inner life. Connecting with the interiority of the life community, of Earth process, of geologic forms, of entire landscapes, is what enhances our experience of beauty and enriches our psyches. And this is the basis for transformation and transcendence of our current limitations.

Touchstones

I have facilitated online seminars for Montessori educators on Thomas Berry's book *The Great Work* for over twenty years now for the Institute for Educational Studies. This is a visionary program of integrative learning that weaves together ecology and cosmology and was founded by educators Philip Gang and Marsha Morgan. Maria Montessori was ahead of her time in her ideas on the education of the child in a cosmological context. In those twenty years, the insights from Phil and Marsha's program just keep building out of the dialogue between the Montessori vision and Thomas's thought. One of the things from the book that has inspired the participants in these seminars is the chapter "The Meadow Across the Creek" where Thomas recounts the experience of a meadow of lilies when he was ten that I mentioned above. "This early experience," he writes, "has become normative for me throughout the entire range of my thinking. Whatever preserves and enhances this meadow in the natural cycles of its transformation is good; whatever opposes this meadow or negates it is not good. My life orientation is that simple. It is also that pervasive. It applies in economics and political orientation as well as in education and religion."[19]

I think of this as a "touchstone" experience, something that carries a significant moral imprint and guides one's decisions and behavior. When I ask the Montessori teachers to recall if they have had a touchstone experience of their own, many of them are able to identify one. Their stories are often powerful. At times, they are a general feeling of sensual encounters, the smell of the soil, the sound of birdsong, the sounds and scent of the great swell of the ocean, a shady haven beneath a large sheltering shrub where the light filters down. Some are accounts of a very specific place, a prairie, river, or forest, experiences that have never left them. Often, there is an early childhood experience or way of being in the world that is tied to a feeling of wholeness or completeness related to the natural world.

Early in my editorship, the magazine staff and I embarked on a contemplative kayaking trip in Lagunitas Creek, which empties into San Francisco Bay near China Camp. The trip was led by Kurt Hoelting, a former Alaskan and fisherman turned wilderness guide, who took corporate CEOs and Washington DC policymakers on contemplative kayaking trips in Alaska. After kayaking in silence, meditating, and sharing stories and poetry in talking circles in the evening, many of these captains of industries and politics would recount memorable experiences in nature as young people that had never left them. The contemplative nature of the kayaking was resurrecting feelings of longing and connection that had been buried under years of ambition and a corporate ethos. Kurt was connecting these high-powered people with their touchstone experiences.

My own touchstone, a day spent on a wild bend of the Des Moines River in my home state of Iowa, is recounted in the Landscape Interlude earlier in this book called "The Land Between Two Rivers." My experience that day changed me as surely as Thomas's meadow did him. It formed me in a way that led to my calling as spiritual ecologist. It was more powerful than any experience of landscape since I left the Midwest, as spectacular as they might have been. For me, it formed a deeper understanding of the sacred interplay of landscape and the human imagination.

The depth of Thomas Berry's scholarship and breadth of historical perspective have gone a long way toward affirming and authenticating my own intuitions, and those of many others, about what has gone awry in our relations with the Earth community. His spirit and wisdom help provide the energy to do the work. In his own words, "the dream drives the action."

Cathedral revisited

On Saturday, September 26, 2009, I walked through the massive front entrance of the Cathedral of St. John the Divine in New York City. *This feels like passing through a portal*, I thought as I looked up to its soaring arches and stained glass. It wasn't just the grandeur of the place. I thought back to my visit to the cathedral at Chartres in France and my attempt to internalize and feel the archetypal energy of the Virgin Mary. I thought about my desire to find a comparable modern-day edifice. What is our cathedral today? And what source might power its construction? Then I realized that Thomas Berry had been key in that search for me. And that the search had brought me to the journey of the universe itself as that source.

And so, entering the site of Thomas's memorial was a passage into sacred time as a community that was drawn and held by a common passion. The people present were the modern-day equivalent of those at Chartres in the twelfth century who had quarried rock, shaped it, transported it, and placed it; who had created the stain-glassed windows and erected the towers and portals. We were not erecting a cathedral. Now the work was a new way of being human, what Thomas called the Great Work of creating mutually-enhancing human-Earth relations. "The Earth is primary, the human derivative," he had written, and yet we had fallen into a deadly hubris that the human was the measure of all things and that the Earth was merely a store of natural resources to be exploited. Part of our way forward was to learn to see differently.

There were familiar faces of colleagues and friends from my years as editor of *EarthLight* magazine, but many more were faces I did not recognize. We were all there to honor the passage of a great elder, to celebrate his life. The program began with a processional and with dancers weaving through the crowd, trailing banners that symbolized life on Earth and the water planet. Organ strains pulsed through the cavernous space. The music of Paul Winter's alto saxophone and his ensemble swirled around the flying buttresses.

As people began to speak, a unifying theme took shape: To find the wisdom to go forward, we need to go back; back to a more primal knowledge, to the source of our identity as a species. What I noticed throughout the service, was a realization that Thomas represented an older, deeper, more primary source of wisdom, one we need so much today. He brought that out in people, gave expression to the unexpressed in so many of us, made us feel less alone, less alienated, perhaps a little less sorrowful and more hopeful about what we can do about the desecration of the planet.

A few days after I returned from the service, I was experiencing some despair over what I considered to be some key failures in my life. I was grieving lost opportunities, times when I was overcome by fear and shrank back from truly engaging with life, regretting decisions and actions that seemed shortsighted as I thought back on them. I was trying to give expression to all of this to my wife, Diana. She listened, then simply asked me, "What would Thomas tell you?" I was silent for a while, and then it came to me: go to the Earth for guidance. Trust the universe, because you are the universe trying to give birth, through you, to one more strand of its diverse expression. There is no need to be afraid.

Then Diana asked me, "And what does the Earth tell you?" After a few moments, what came was so clear. It seemed like the kind of older wisdom that so many were referring to in the memorial for Thomas. My response is the following poem:

Earth Says

...be like a tree.
Stay rooted in the dream
that breathed you here.
Give yourself fully to the seasons,
let change be change,
a strong full wind
that quickens the sky
from light to dark, and back.

Let the storms come, and pass,
and clear out what is brittle and worn.
There is a time to leaf and flower;
a time to release and be dormant.
A time to build your body from sun
and air; then give that growing back to
sustain the not-yet born.

A tree doesn't fret about
whether it is oak, or bay laurel,
or sycamore or elm; nor wonder
which bend of branch
or coiffure of canopy is in fashion;
but gives all to the sap of living.

A tree doesn't know success
or failure; they don't exist
in the mind of bark and branch,
are only concepts in the orphaned
mind, sleep walking
amidst phantoms of desire.

Earth says, be like a tree.
Stay rooted in the dream
that breathed you here.
Hold your limbs upward
to beseech the sky.
Embrace me with every searching root.

Tree of life

There was a time in my life when I struggled to endure. It was a time of great loss and spiritual exhaustion. Many of my days seemed to rise straight up from the underworld, and I felt haunted by demons of remorse and grief. I was losing my livelihood and ministry, the magazine to which I had dedicated heart and soul for nearly a decade. I had burned the candle at both ends and was depleted. In a sense, I was reliving my father's loss of his own ministry at a comparable age. The magazine was much more than a job, even more than a ministry. It had become an extended family of readers, colleagues, volunteers, kindred spirits, friends, and visionaries. For the second time in my life, I was losing the spiritual community that had sustained me. Compounding it were other losses—a relationship on the rocks; the death of my beloved cat, Rilke; some of my most cherished beliefs were on shaky ground; and I was struggling to fulfill numerous professional demands.

One morning during this time period I woke feeling more than usually groggy. I brewed a strong cup of coffee and headed to my home office to start work on the final issue of the magazine. As I approached my desk, I felt an ache in my left side near my heart. I reached up to gently massage the area, and the next thing I know I was on the floor, the room spinning around me. I lay on the floor feeling as if I was being pulled down into a dark funnel. My heart began to race wildly, and I found it difficult to breathe. I managed to get up on my knees and get to the phone to call 911. The paramedics found me face up on the floor, nearly unconscious. They rushed me to the emergency room where doctors struggled to bring down my heart rate and keep me breathing normally. After I was stabilized, they gave me test after test to determine the cause. They never found anything wrong medically. "You have the physiology of a fourteen-year-old," the ER doctor told me. "There's nothing wrong with you; your heart is strong."

My heart may have been strong, but it was broken and my spirit was adrift. There would be three more ER visits over as many weeks following my first episode, all with the same diagnosis: "nothing is wrong with you." My symptoms mimicked a heart attack. "You're having panic attacks," one doctor guessed, but wasn't sure. I refused the medication they offered. I knew that this wasn't anything that pharmaceuticals could help me manage. I was in a dark night of the soul, and my body was signaling to me the need for rest, prayer, and reflection.

It was during this time that I went on a series of self-directed spiritual retreats at the beautiful Vedanta Retreat Center. Set on more than two thousand acres of untouched forest on the edge of the Pacific Ocean, the Vedanta Society had set aside the land for spiritual contemplation only. There were modest rooms in separate buildings for both men and women. Retreats were meant to be silent and contemplative. There was a meditation room with photos of Jesus, the Buddha, and Ramakrishna, and a library with books from a wide variety of spiritual traditions. The silence and the meditation allowed me to go within and opened me to the healing of long walks on the land. The forest and the meadows there, little by little, coaxed me back to myself, quieted my ego, and calmed my anxiety. I had a deep sense of the whole of the universe story permeating the present moment. And I was a part of it, a unique emergence. The emergency room visits ceased, and I began to rebuild and restore my life. I returned to music and poetry, but only after the land had restored my heart and breathed the spirit back into me.

I made a close friend at Vedanta, and it was for her that I returned time and again to the retreat center. It was in her arms that I found myself held and healed. This friend, was for me, both a tree of life, and the Tree of Life. She was both real and mythic. She was majestic and grounded and a lover of the Earth. Compared to its magnificent cousins—the redwoods, sequoias, pines, and live oaks, the California buckeye wouldn't be considered a remarkable tree by most people. And for most of the years of my relationship to the tree, that was also the case for me. I had admired its beautiful brown chestnut in the fall. The color of the buckeye nut would be a painter's dream if it could be captured for the palette. It is a rich burnt sienna with gold undertones, the color of the Earth in alto aria. The nut is beautiful but poisonous, although not to the California ground squirrel, who has negotiated a truce with the buckeye over millennia of co-evolution. I gather the nuts in fall only to be able to ogle them on my desk.

Then, from late winter into early spring, the buckeye's budding leaves issue out into shapes and forms that rival the best sculpture. They don't resemble leaves so much as baby animals being birthed. Their red and green sepals and nascent fronds in clusters of five or six look like ceremonial headwear. The leaves unfurl slowly over a period of about two weeks, and when they reach their full expression, are about as big as your palm. There is no comparable smell to the buckeye flower in the California landscape. Walk by a blooming buckeye and be whisked away by the scent of honey and rose and freshly fallen rain all mixed into an intoxicating potion. For much of the year, most buckeyes seem like unassuming, overgrown shrubs. The tree drops its leaves to cope with the dry season, leaving a bare skeleton of twisted branches to await the rains.

At the Vedanta retreat center, I met a buckeye that was a living avatar of Earth's living community. Based on its sheer size, I estimated the tree to be upwards of three hundred years old. The great branches radiating out in perfect symmetry from the trunk were much greater in girth than the trunks of most of the smaller buckeyes I had encountered. The canopy vaulted to nearly thirty feet high and stretched out just as wide. The sun had sculpted the canopy into a perfect dome not unlike that of a jellyfish. The enormous limbs had formed elbows, each of them touching the Earth at their nadir, so they appeared to be propping the tree up. When in bloom, this buckeye was an outrageous display, a ceremonial headdress of pink, white, and green.

Part of the tree's beauty was in the diversity of life that it attracted and harbored. Honeybees swarm to her blossoms, but only native bees can withstand their poison. Birds roost in her hair at night. And more than once, as I approached the tree after an absence, her sheltering branches provided a haven for deer grazing the fertile meadow created by many seasons of fallen blossom, leaf, nut, and branch.

One extra warm afternoon I walked under the coolness of the canopy to find a perfect natural hammock on one of the massive limbs. The curve supported my back and extended legs. Letting my head descend against the limb, I directed my gaze slightly upward where I could watch the leaves, as big as my palm, gently wave, soothing me into reverie. I stayed until the stars came into view. The curvature of the universe mimicked the curve of the canopy above me. I felt held, as if nothing could harm me. I would happily be interred underneath that tree when the time comes, in order to do my part to support such splendor.

A deeper presence

"The universe is a communion of subjects, not a collection of objects," writes Thomas Berry. Out of that communion comes a new identity. I felt the inner life of that buckeye tree fused with my own, although it doesn't even feel right to make the distinction. It feels more right to simply call it love. To be present to what's there, to let it come into us, invites transformation on a bodily level. The stars, the ocean, the soaring of the hawk, the falling leaf, the sheltering canopy of the Tree of Life, all offer themselves to our awareness constantly and have the potential to heal the divide in our souls.

Why do I love the buckeye? Why do I love the plants in my native garden? Because of what happens when you pour your love into plants. You try to give them the conditions they need to thrive. You step back from that work. Something begins to happen. Sometimes they make it. Sometimes, no matter what you do, they don't. But they know how to love a place. They stay and they grow and then become the language there. A conversation develops with them and between them, a non-verbal intimacy. You hope the native flowering plant you put in the ground will flourish because you know that if it does, an entire host of pollinators and hungry birds will also flourish. And on down the line. You nourish a small piece of the living world because you know that mortality is just around the corner. But while you're still here, a seed in the ground, a seedling planted might take hold and then take the world by storm.

All it takes is an act of love to set off a chain of events that might make a difference to a far future as yet unimaginable. Did the buckeye tree, in whose arms I rested so many times, finding succor and love, grow from the act of someone in the past who placed the chestnut-brown nut in the ground, hoping for a tree? Was it a California ground squirrel stashing her future lunch in the ground? Or was it simply a random lob from the branch of a buckeye ancestor? It doesn't matter whether it is the fruit of a human hand or some other hand of nature, or if it was Earth drawing to her womb the nut from the canopy, a nut that contains within its sienna-gold all the seasons, from leafing to blooming to sleep. What matters is the draw itself of being for being, the sinking down into a promise that life always finds a way.

LANDSCAPE INTERLUDE
The Healing of a Beautiful World[20]

Nothing can be itself without being
in communion with everything else, nor
can anything truly be the other without first
acquiring a capacity for interior presence to itself.
—Thomas Berry[21]

I'm hiking a protected watershed high above Upper San Leandro Reservoir near San Francisco Bay. The day is cool and breezy. Gray-tinged clouds coast above, occasionally letting the sun through to cast the distant hills emerald. Save for the reservoir itself, there is no human habitation or artifact within sight.

Far below, I spot a familiar silhouette, one that tugs at the heart of my love for things wild. I sight in the shape with my binoculars, and a giant western pond turtle looms into my vision, the picture of dusky serenity basking on a log. Nearby, a dozen jet black cormorants pass the afternoon perched on the brittle branches of a half-submerged dead valley oak that has toppled into the water, holding their great wings out to dry like widows' capes.

My gaze follows a red-tailed hawk as it soars upward against the forested hills across the way. It spirals, drops precipitously, spirals upward again. Then, incredibly, it repeats the action. As the bird's maneuvers hold me spellbound, a question wells up within me: Is the hawk feeling joy? It's hard to think otherwise. Something in its breast akin to my own joy must be stirring. I am so totally in that moment, wedded to each drop and spiral, that my joy becomes one with the hawk's flight. The hawk and I, both borne from the Earth's travails of birth and emergence, aren't separate, so that my experience becomes flight and the flight of the hawk becomes the welling up of joy in me. It is the Earth feeling the exquisite invention of flight on a new order of complexity, in my human form, as beauty. What's more, I reflect on the history of bone and feather, talon and flesh, and what it took to refine that act of flight over eons. And so, the Earth savors its magnificence as hawk soaring.

We need the healing of a beautiful world. Living in awe of life's creative powers and the unfolding of the cosmic story moves us away from a deep-seated alienation that has permeated the western psyche, one that has created the illusion that Earth is nothing more than a storehouse of resources for human use. What is awakening in human consciousness today is the growing realization that we live in a self-organizing, self-healing, self-generative community and that this creativity courses through the human as surely as the galaxies and the panoply of life on Earth. The world lives in us; we do not live in the world. Earth's great spheres — the air, land, waters, community of life — are not just a storehouse of resources but are our identity. They are actually "generative of who we are," states evolutionary philosopher Brian Swimme. As a conscious, self-aware species, we can choose to amplify this awareness. We can embrace a life-generating role in the story.

Chapter 18
Spiritual Ecology as Practice and Story

This Earth is where you are going to find spirituality.
If you don't connect with your heart to the Earth,
you'll never really know anything.
—**Buck Ghosthorse**
  Lakota shaman

Some twenty years ago, at a Sunday morning Quaker meeting in Berkeley, I crossed paths with an unanticipated tutor. I was a regular attender at the meeting and I had volunteered to prepare the refreshments for the after-meeting social hour. Next to the community hall was a room where First Day School for young kids was held during the meeting for worship. I put the coffee on to perk, set out some ginger cookies and rice crackers, and took a breather, standing near the doorway, eavesdropping. An adult voice asked the children this question: "Do you know what brought you into the world?" A single word response came hurtling forth without hesitation from a young girl: "Joy!" Smiling, I felt a sudden shiver of recognition. Of course. What could be more true and simple? We are created from joy. We are Earth's joy, bubbling forth in awareness and speech, in music, poetry, and dance.

When we take in the magentas, vermilions, and crimsons of a sunset, and we shudder with color in our very veins, we are planet Earth shuddering. The chill we feel at the grand sweep of a forested hillside garlanded by a thin cool wisp of fog in the early morning is the Earth experiencing that chill as mystery. We are of and from the Earth, her creation. The feeling that wells up knowing that fact is the Earth feeling a deep and abiding love for her own being. It was an incredible act of risk and creativity for the Earth to bring forth a being in which celebration and joy finds a deeper awareness. As poet John Daniel wrote in his poem, "Ourselves,":

> We'll ask how it can be that we walk this ground
> and know that we walk, alive in a world
> that didn't have to be beautiful, alive
> in a world that doesn't have to be.[22]

And yet we do know that we know. And the world is beautiful. And we are, for so brief a moment, alive. Joy is the starting point of spiritual ecology. In my own life, a joyful Earth-centered spirituality has helped to restore my faith in the human prospect.

Spirituality is a vital and vivid experience of inter-connection. Some might call it mystical. When I feel that connection, the ego, which is all of the ideas and forces constituting the "me" that I see as all-important, falls away. Suddenly I remember what is truly important. And so often, because our society tends to be tantalized by titillation and focused on so much that is of lesser importance, a spiritual ecologist is a person who in our current cultural condition has a contrarian orientation to society. This is because little in the way that mainstream Western society comports itself is in harmony with what the spiritual ecologist knows in their bones to be true, with the sense of radiance that permeates the living world. That orientation has to do with a feeling of belonging in the cosmos, kinship with Earth's community of life, and a moment-to-moment awareness of relationship and interconnectedness. That feeling of connection is subjective. There are phenomena in the universe that simply cannot be explained objectively; they can only be communed with. Sentience surrounds us in all forms of life, even those we don't consider to have consciousness.

An ancient way life, re-emerging

Spiritual ecology describes a way of life that is very ancient in the sense that peoples have lived it in many times and places. It is contemporary in that it integrates the discoveries of science and a new sense of our evolutionary story. It draws both from knowledge of the ecology of the planet and from deeper sensitivities to the spiritual dimension of the Earth. As such, it forms the basis for a more comprehensive ethical code of conduct. Expanding our circle of concern to include other species, we begin to see a relationship between our spiritual condition and the planetary ecological crisis. And from this discernment, we seek to cultivate a conscious, sustainable lifestyle of simplicity and ecological integrity.

For many indigenous peoples whose cultures are relatively intact today, spiritual ecology is still a practice, although these cultures would not generally use the term to describe what for them is a way of life. While you can't really apply all practices equally to the cultures of all indigenous peoples past and present, it is possible to distinguish a consistent orientation toward spiritual ecology as a way of life within these cultures worldwide. These include a sense of kinship that extends beyond the human, a systematic observation and knowledge of plants and animals passed from generation to generation through story and myth, the notion of a living planet and of Earth as Mother, sacredness of place, humans seen as just one part of a created order, and shamanic rites which draw on the primal powers of the natural world. These are present in all of us to some extent as indigenous mind. We all come out of some lineage, some ancient culture that was, at one time, in closer alignment with the underlying dynamics of the natural world. We don't need to go back to hunting and gathering and living on the land to relive that connection. Just spending some contemplative time in the natural world can begin to awaken us from our psychological, cognitive, and spiritual sleep, opening us to the sacred wisdom that surrounds us.

Beginning of the practice

Cultivating stillness, an inner peace, is a primary step in a practice of spiritual ecology. Stillness brings us "within," where we are able to generate a center of gravity from which it becomes possible to experience the sensuous quality that is all around us. Sensuousness is spirit incarnated into matter. Stillness feeds our inner intention from which we develop the sensitivities required to receive guidance. The reason this practice begins with stillness has to do with the thinking mind. Stillness requires a quieting of the mind. The mind wants to know, but knowledge is an impediment to being present to the sensuousness surrounding us at all times. By finding our inner calm, we open ourselves to spirit. Ways I have found this calm are music, poetry, and in the still of the forest or in the clear depths of a body of water.

In a state of stillness, we let ourselves long. Longing is what will draw us to the core of who we are, to our unique gift. At that core, we find that we are Earth herself longing. To return time and again to Earth for guidance, to let the quality of stillness feed our inner intention, is to find faith in the powers that brought us into being. We awaken to the inner life of Earth and the cosmos in a way where duality ceases.

Stillness also invites the world to come into us, to know itself through us. If you sit still, especially in a more natural setting, you begin to notice that the world comes to you. There are visitations—animals, birds, insects, landforms, mountains. The green world of plants takes on a sensuous aspect where we feel the energy of photosynthesis burning as our life spirit and know that it is sacred.

Gratitude

Finding stillness is a natural doorway to gratitude. When I am still, I remember who I am. I remember my ancestors, and the long labor of stars that brought me here. In the well of this remembrance, fear and sadness are transmuted to love. Gratitude emerges from this alchemy of emotion into energy and faith. Even difficult feelings like anxiety and anger can be opportunities for gratitude. Given the right attunement, I can learn more deeply how I am co-existent with the universe, part of the long story of increasing beauty over time. The internal landscape is the mosaic through which I become an active agent building reality.

When I am confronted with thoughts or reveries that cause psychological pain (or pleasure), which can occur numerous times over the course of a day, I attempt to be immediately grateful. I try to see it as an opportunity to practice. I am reminded to be present, to observe. My awareness sharpens, then the feeling dissolves into an internal energy. In short, it presents me with a pathway to grow spiritually, even if in the moment there is psychological pain. How can this not elicit joy? Over and over again, I have a memory, or I engage in imagining something or other about a situation. I make assumptions which cause me pain and separation because of the divisive nature of thought. And then I bring my full attention to the feeling behind the thought, and just observe, attempting to suspend judgment.

Sometimes, something amazing takes place. The feeling becomes like the tule fog that steals into our neighborhood here in Northern California, but then burns off by mid-morning under the attention of the Sun. It abates, and what is left is a feeling of serenity and strength. In this sense, through the power of attention, psychological pain is effectively dealt with differently from physical pain, a kind of an aspirin for the soul. Except that the eventual release is more powerful and joyful. This moment-to-moment practice reminds me that thoughts and feelings come and go in the face of the astonishing mystery in which we live.

This wasn't always the case for me. I was largely unconscious for years, only occasionally breaking through the illusions of my own thoughts. I had to learn it as a practice over time, and it is still imperfect, always a work-in-progress. "The imperfect is our paradise," wrote the poet Wallace Stevens, but "note that in this bitterness, delight." The domain of delight is what we find if we flow with the imperfect. This is an aspect of spiritual ecology, a practice of dancing with the imperfect in a spirit of acceptance and creativity.

I describe my personal method for confronting psychological pain mostly because it is a constant, moment-to-moment practice, not one in which one sets aside twenty minutes a day amidst the busyness of the day-to-day. This is precisely the way in which we need to confront, observe, feel, and transform our cultural rupture from nature and the community of life that support us. It is a moment-to-moment imperative, in my mind, to finding the purpose and empowerment needed to embrace what Teilhard de Chardin called a zest for living. It begins within each one of us, and yet it is a profoundly communal act. "If we have a trauma-informed society," says Gabor Mate, "we have a society that looks much more compassionate."

Tending the sacred ember

It is between sets at the Bay Area jazz club Yoshi's, and I am greeted by my friend of several years, Alan. Alan is a musician who has founded a non-profit dedicated to bringing together music and ecology through an alliance of musicians dedicated to a vision of sustainability for the planet. He plays the didgeridoo, the Native huaca, the handpan, and several other less well-known percussive and wind instruments. He has asked me onto his of board of directors, so we sit together in the relative quiet of the break between sets to talk. He's wearing jeans, a Tibetan cap, and a colorful wool vest. They blend well with his ruddy complexion and kind eyes.

"In all the time I've known you, Lauren, I've never seen you without that bag," he says with the hint of a smile. "What do you carry in there? It's like you're toting a sacred ember or something, as part of some roving prehistoric clan."

The leather bag I carry is what the French call a "sacoche." It's about the size of a letter file folder, and three inches thick. It has a brass clasp on the front that secures the flap, and a leather strap that loops over the shoulder. It sits right about at my waist, hugging my torso. And Alan is right, I kept it close, constantly, right next to my body, for years, wherever I went.

"That's a fantastic image," I say. "And maybe not far from the truth."

He continues to prod with his eyes. He wants to know what's in that small appendage to my body.

"It's a writing journal. And a couple of pens," I say. "Now and then a small book or a draft piece of writing."

"Cool," he says. "Wish I could carry the didge around like that."

He is pointing up a key distinction between us as artists. His form is primarily music, mine is writing. That brief exchange with Alan cemented the image of tending a fire in my mind. I was carrying around an ember, the journal, simmering there next to me at all times. When I pulled it out to write, I began gently blowing on the ember to bring about a flame of words. Often, I only wrote notes, trying to capture some odd piece of magic that had floated into my awareness. A line of ants, branching like a tree, its singular mind heading toward some distant colony. The baritone whirr of a hummingbird's wings passing inches from my ear. The bracingly fresh smell of a cool, fog-shrouded dawn. The notes are part of the an almost daily writing practice, perhaps the most important part. There is a healing power in writing, a way to practice self-compassion and gratitude. It keeps me in dialogue with my inner self, asking questions, observing and noting down. That kind of inner discernment is part of a practice of spiritual ecology. It's not unlike learning the plants and animals and geographic forms of a landscape through direct contact with nature, not through book learning. And the writing itself brings the discernment into a healing flame.

Internal landscape

The characters you meet on the road of life—the angels, the friends, the villains, the clowns, the sages, the enemies—are all teachers, each presenting an opportunity to move toward wholeness, at least to the extent that we can be conscious of their import. Often, as with awareness around trauma, these insights don't come until some time has elapsed after the encounter occurs. Part of the spiritual work of a life is to unearth them. There are internal characters one encounters as well, the angels and demons within our own nature. And there are internal landscapes, emotional states elicited by natural encounters: I clamber over a high Sierra granite boulder tilted up by the forces of time, feeling the rough and gritty skin on the palms of my hands; I hear the clatter of tule reeds in the marshes; I feel the sting of icy wind on my face, out on the prairie in a bleak Iowa winter; I taste the salt of seawater as I fall back, blissful, into the surf of the Pacific; I shudder under the shadow of a passing vulture; or I return the gaze of a coyote and can tell by the light in her eyes that she has not mistaken me. These sensuous experiences all have an internal correspondence with my feeling self.

What I've described in the section above is the inner manifestation of a powerful tool for healing that I feel we all have at our disposal. But the practice of spiritual ecology is also a way of reconnecting to Earth's community of life, to the landscapes and geological formations and rivers and forests of our home region and beyond. While there is indescribable beauty there, what we also encounter is the equivalent of our personal psychological pain, a wounded Earth, along with our own atrophied abilities to hear her voice. And yet, with the right quality of attention and intention, we can retrieve a deeper joy in reconnecting with what is most basic to our nature as human beings. This is the heart-centered way of knowing at the core of this book.

There is an inner dimension of spiritual ecology that corresponds to sensitivity to the universe. It involves attention to one's ecosystem of emotion as much as the outer landscape. There is an honoring of intuition and the value of feeling. Fear, anger, awe, outrage, love, joy, all generate energy that can be tapped through attention. As a practice, it can help us to face the tensions of our time in creative ways.

An example of this is fear. Fear is a toxin when it is ignored or demonized. It's a natural human response to a perceived, or imagined, threat. There was a moment of crisis in Earth's history when a certain toxin threatened the future of life. That toxin was oxygen. Then came a revolutionary, irreversible act, the synergy of two microorganisms, that addressed that crisis and changed the trajectory of life on Earth. That act was the invention of respiration. One organism, passing through the cell wall of another organism, became its organelle, which shape-shifted into the mitochondrion. The mitochondrion is described as the powerhouse of the cell because it uses oxygen, once toxic to life, as food. A community of those cells gives us our body.

Fear, now, is a toxin that threatens the future of the human. It tends to paralyze us and can rob us of joy. But we need to read and understand the signs of our times and not be paralyzed, in spite of our fear. What transforms fear into usable energy? If we think about what fear drives us to—hatred, reactionary ideology, violence, desperate clinging to what deadens us in the long run—we can begin to see that conformity to a worldview that gives us all of the above robs us of the very thing that empowers us, community. Community is the opposite of conformity; it is the agent for transformation of the fear that debilitates us. And fear's energy, when transformed through a community grounded in a practice of spiritual ecology, can be a deep source of creativity.

Awareness and activation of energy

This practice is dynamic, in flux with the world, not about dogma or perfection. It's about awareness and activation of energy. This is the ultimate healing aspect of this practice. Awareness is about receptivity, presence, and listening; activation of energy, in the current form of the human being, is about an enhanced spiritual capacity to respond to the world. The sensuous experience is spirit incarnate, entering the world of matter, dissolving the illusion of separateness. Matter, spirit, and mind are all of a piece working in dynamic equilibrium. Both are about the evolution and deepening of sensitivities. One thing that has atrophied in us, especially in the Western world, is the awareness that consciousness permeates the living world; it's not exclusively human. To respect the sentience in other forms of life is to cultivate reverence. Reverence for life is one example of a deepening sensitivity. It is a frame of mind, an attitude, but it is also a new manifestation of beauty through the human as a species.

Spiritual ecology is as much an internal practice as it is external. More so, in fact for those of us who have lost touch with our indigenous past. It's easier for Western peoples to default to external, technological, solutions. Spiritual ecology is an internal orientation directed toward a rehabilitation of the conditioned mind that tells us we are separate, that allows us to objectify the world in order to exploit it. It is a reorientation in the external world toward kinship with all life and sustainable relationship. It is an approach to life, a mode of being, a way of walking. When asked by a colleague of mine what, if anything, would be the religion of his people, a Navajo elder told him: "To walk in the world ceremoniously." This religious state of mind has been characterized by some as learning to recognize the signs of the sacred within and around us. It is personified by the bow, which is both a physical act of reverence and a state of mind that gives deference to the numinous qualities within each aspect of the natural world.

The intelligence of the body

I have been greatly influenced by Gabor Mate and his work on trauma, addiction, social isolation, illness, and pathways for healing. A good deal of the recovery from trauma is balancing the prevailing influence of our head-centered culture with practices that connect us with the wisdom of the body. I have been greatly influenced as well by the work of conscious embodiment author Philip Shepherd. While not specifically based in trauma recovery, the meditations and practices he has developed quiet our head-centered selves and focus on the wisdom of the body. He states in one of his video meditations: "The more you live in the head, the more anxious you feel because you're disconnected from the grounded presence of the body. We live in self-consciousness because we live in the head. Self-consciousness is a divided state. The thing that the body most deeply understands is that it belongs to the world."[23]

Ideas are important; but the sacred intelligence of the body had a good deal more to do with my healing than ideas because it gave me back a sense of belonging. My story is the making of a spiritual ecologist out of the energy of healing the trauma wound, a spiritual rebirth that involved a balance of head intelligence and body intelligence. Another insight I gained from Philip Shepherd has particular relevance to the question coming from my family's trauma: "Is the universe a friendly place?" He distinguishes between responsiveness and reactivity, stating: "Responsiveness is a dance with the present. It is grounded in the security of your being. Reactivity is responding to the past and transposing it into the present. It is grounded in fear and the need for safety."[24] Security in my own being has to do with groundedness in the intelligence of the body. Safety is never guaranteed as embodied beings, but there is a way to feel secure in our connection to the Earth, the ground of our being.

Not long ago, listening to the intelligence of the body came home to me in a clear way. I had just had a massage and I was leaving for home, feeling pretty fine. On the narrow dirt path to the car was a fence lizard basking in the sun. They're quite common here in California. But as I slowed down to take in the lizard, I was suddenly transported back to my boyhood when I kept a lizard as a pet. I was suddenly feeling the fascination of my ten-year-old self again, feeding the lizard, holding him in my hands, feeling the smooth, cool flesh again my skin. Then, as I walked to the car, the minty smell of bay laurel took me back to the cool shade of a forest glade in summer where I played with my brothers, the earthy smell of leaves and soil inundating our hair and skin and clothes. I soon came to a guardrail alongside the parking area. The spot overlooked the athletic fields of the local high school. The baseball field and the football gridiron below were lush green and inviting. The voices of the players bantering floated up, punctuated by the crack of the bat. Again, I became my younger self, this time my baseball Little League self in eighth grade, on the pitcher's mound, feeling the excitement of the game. As I turned to walk to the car, I was struck by the deep red paint gleaming in the sun. I felt a rush of delight inside me, the same captivation I had always felt when witnessing any of the intense color spectrum of precious gems, from ruby to emerald to amethyst. It was what inspired me to collect rocks throughout my childhood.

The massage had brought me out of the head and into a purely visceral experience of my surroundings. This is the intelligence of the body, an immediacy to the world that has more to do with feeling than idea. Even as I retrieved an older sense of myself as a boy in memory, I was fully in the present, feeling the numinous radiance within everything. I was literally sensing the world with new organs of perception, seeing with untainted eyes, hearing and feeling with the purity of ears and skin that were scrubbed of thought. The obstacles of naming and symbolic consciousness had momentarily shut down and fallen away. This state of mind was not simply regression to a more innocent state. It was the retrieval of an old joy from my internal landscape. And this is important for us in our modern culture as a balance to the complexities, drivenness, and cerebral tendencies that dominate most of our waking hours.

I see body awareness, which is our intuitive nature, as an integral part of the practice of spiritual ecology. This is our way through to transformation, a new, and yet very old way, of being human that will form the basis for a new faith in the human. Qi gong, massage, a daily walk in silence, contemplative hiking, and meditation are all body prayers that have been part of my practice for encouraging the sacred intelligence of the body to come to the fore. When this happens, I am conscious, but in a much different way. I have emotional contact with myself and with the world. And with that contact, all of the naive forms of awareness the head is vulnerable to fall away. It is this constant dynamic tension between head and heart, thinking and feeling that made writing this book something of a balancing act.

For me, it is beyond naming. I recently worked for months compiling knowledge for the creation of a *Pocket Guide to Northern California Oaks*. It was only after the project of naming, cataloguing, researching, and identifying oak species in the field was finished that one day, walking on a trail in habitat where there were massive blue oaks, that I found myself, not naming, but bowing to them, just being in their presence. These elders were home to acorn woodpeckers who collectively stored acorns. They housed a hive of honeybees that hummed in the morning air. Mistletoe garlanded their crowns, where bluebirds fed and slept. Apple galls hung like dried fruit and inside them, wasp larvae that would bore their way out to freedom. The trees sheltered and fed a host of beings. I felt that I knew more about them in that one humble action of the bow than I had learned in months of data compilation. That was an opening of the heart.

There is discursive, analytic knowledge, and there is intuitive knowledge. There is what the body knows, a deeply poetic consciousness that the mystic knows best. These are all ways in which the human has deepened in sensitivity toward the phenomena of the living world. All are valid pathways evolution has found for deepening in complexity and sensitivity to its self-knowledge. But in the Western world, the intuitive heart knowledge has mostly gone quiet. This has caused an imbalance. A practice of spiritual ecology is a method for rebalancing. It is a practice of the heart, of reverence, of rightness, and so, of justice. Erotic justice in particular because it is about relationship, union as a source of generativity. "The profoundest of all sensualities / is the sense of truth / and the next deepest sensual experience / is the sense of justice," wrote D.H. Lawrence in a poem called "The Deepest Sensuality."[25] He was also naming, in his own way, the practice of spiritual ecology.

What more sensual experience is there than the bodily-felt truth of our connection to the living Earth? And what is the sensuality in Truth? Beauty, as Keats and so many others poets and philosophers have tried to drive home. What better justice is there than to be in right relationship, to maintain a balance of wisdom and compassion, in a reciprocal, generative dance with the universe? Sometimes this requires hard choices. Certainly the inner work is difficult, to cut through the conditioning and comforts of our cultural matrix, to buck the trends that keep us asleep within a consumerist dream.

Sometimes choices are difficult, not easy to get right. We need to be self-forgiving about dubious choices. It's not about perfection, but about a general attitude and intent. This came home to me recently in a very immediate and humbling way. My neighbor, Rob, decided one day to cut down a line of trees on the property line. They were trees, thirty feet or more in height, actually privet shrubs that had grown to tree size. The felling of the trees opened a gap through which the hot afternoon summer sun blasted our back yard, which was once a shaded haven along the creek. Plants which were adapted to the shady conditions withered and died under the harsh sun in one hundred-plus degree summer heat. Other plants suffered sunburned leaves. It felt like devastation. I grieved the loss of our shady haven and secretly cursed my neighbor.

But here's the thing. This devastation opened the way for unexpected healing. The trees that my neighbor cut down weren't native to the area and they actually are considered invasive. They didn't support pollinators, and the berries they produced weren't really edible to birds and animals. I quickly got busy planting water-efficient native trees and shrubs to replace the invasive privets. The flood of sunlight into the yard spurred the growth of the reintroduced native plants that wouldn't have thrived in the previously shady conditions. When the native plants blossomed in the sunlight and then went to seed in the fall, I pruned off the stalks and used them for mulch in a part of the yard that was newly flooded with sunlight. The following spring, the native seeds exploded in the area I had mulched. It was now a riot of native ceanothus, toyon, manzanita, salvia, mallow, and fuchsia that hosted a festival of pollinators. I also planted a row of native shrubs along the fence line where the trees had been cut down. They thrived and grew quickly in fertile soil which for years had been breaking down the berries and leaves from the non-native trees. The native shrubs, one of which, an island mallow, has already grown to the size of a small tree, are also drawing pollinators and birds.

So what had seemed like a traumatic and destructive act has turned out to be, in two to three years' time, an opportunity for replenishment and renewal. From cataclysm, creativity. The micro-eco-system of my back yard is the better for it. I ended up thanking my neighbor for what at first seemed like a destructive act. Perhaps reciprocity in a time such as ours, where there has been so much trauma to Earth, has a lot to do with opening up avenues for regeneration, where life can once again find a way.

This feels emblematic, to me, of our culture's bad choices, but also of the potential for creativity out of loss. The enactment of creativity out of loss is another face of spiritual ecology. There is the leaf litter of my own loss—my family's choices about how to respond to a violent event, the loss of a sense of safety, the violation of my sister, the destruction of my religious community—I've grown a psychic and emotional tree over the years through the creative response of a practice of spiritual ecology. This doesn't mean everything is magically healed, just that I feel I belong, and with that comes a certain confidence, a sure-footedness that keeps me "walking ceremoniously through the world."

The Good Story

The wild will come to you
like a good story
peopled with creatures
if you are still long enough,

like a gift of grace, a giving
that renews the marrow
and provides a home,

for those occupied with alien stories
for those distracted by the search.

Chapter 19

Spiritual Ecologist as Archetype and Person

Sensitivity holds the key not only to our understanding
of evolution, but to the understanding of ourselves.
We are bundles of quivering sensitivities.
—**Henryk Skolimowski**
 Theater of Mind

When I spend time in nature, two versions of me walk side-by-side, in dialogue with each other. I carry both a scientific mind as well as my feeling self. I am a certified citizen naturalist with the state of California, and I have been a passionate birder for nearly forty years, faithfully cataloguing what birders call my "life list" of species. That more scientific part of me always wants to assert himself. I am rarely, if ever, without a pair of binoculars and a field journal close at hand. So, in describing any given landscape in the landscape interludes in this book, I attempt to be as precise as possible in my description of the plants, animals, and natural landscapes.

The naturalist in me wants to name things, to note down, to document. The spiritual ecologist in me wants to experience, feel, to remember in my bones, not my head; to witness a river, a mountain, a wetland without words. To look honestly at my ecosystem of emotion—from anger, to grief, to regret, to joy, to love—without the content of the past. There is always this interplay throughout the landscape interludes in this book between the power of naming through symbolic consciousness and a felt, bodily experience of the natural world.

There is power in naming. To name and remember and imagine is at the root of our unique power as one species among many. As the poet Rainer Maria Rilke wrote, "Perhaps we are here in order to say: house, bridge, fountain, gate, pitcher, fruit-tree, window—at most: column, tower... *Here* is the time for the sayable, *here* is its homeland. Speak and bear witness."[26] Another of my favorite poets, Emily Dickinson, offers us this:

> *A word is dead*
> *When it is said,*
> *Some say.*
> *I say it just*
> *Begins to live*
> *That day.*[27]

And yet there is a cautionary tale in Western culture's overemphasis on naming things to the point of objectification and confusing the name with the essence of the named. Objectification creates an illusion of separation. How different would our violent world be of we could simply be in the sacred presence of each other without names and labels? My experience of the massage, bringing my body's intelligence to the fore, had brought me also into that kind of presence. As I write in the interlude, "The Kinglet at the Door," about feeling the sacred essence of a tiny bird: "I hunger, as we all do, for home and place. I feel the pangs of longing for beauty, to never shut down my inner gateway to wonder, at being stunned or terrified." To know this is to put words aside for a time and remember an older language that gives rise to what I think of as "cosmoriginal awareness" (more on this in Chapter 26). As powerful as our symbolic consciousness is, we must remember as well this primary ground of intelligence from which it has evolved. To forget that our intelligence flows out of this older wisdom would be to succumb to hubris. And as a species, we've had quite enough of that.

Archetype — a new lexicon

In order to understand the language of spiritual ecology in our time, we need to build a new lexicon. Thinking archetypically is a way to start. The language of archetypes is always larger than our individual thoughts. It unfolds in any given situation through our collective consciousness, which uses the language of the cosmos. The spiritual ecologist is the most needed archetype of our time because it is an archetype that seeks to articulate a higher, healthier vision of who we are as human beings. The spiritual ecologist understands relationship. This is true on a planetary, evolutionary, and cosmic level. The spiritual ecologist is an ascendant archetypal energy drawing from at least five great Archetypes identified by Thomas Berry in his book *The Great Work*. These are the Journey, the Tree of Life, the Sacred Center, Death-Rebirth, and the Great Mother.[28]

The Journey Archetype is the recapitulation of the universe story within the story of each individual. The creative unfolding of the universe, in both its physical and psychic aspects, is present within each of us, and finds unique expression through each of our lives.

The Tree of Life Archetype represents the interconnected web of life as integral with Earth process. We can see that each strand in the Tree is to be cherished and protected if its overall health and integrity is to be maintained. From this we develop the capacity to be present to each form of life as a sacred reality with which to commune.

The Sacred Center Archetype is the subjectivity of each being as a unique center of the universe. The greater our communion, the deeper our interiority or sense of self.

One of the current manifestations of the Death-Rebirth Archetype is the death of a materialist, consumerist, industrial worldview and the birth of a new way of being human that is more present to the sacred depths of nature. Another is that we die to our feelings of alienation and separateness into a realization that we are born from Earth, and we are part of her body, evolving into a single being that is deepening in complexity and beauty.

The Great Mother Archetype is an awakening to the realization that we are being held by an embrace of the universe from which we cannot fall out. It's our ultimate feeling of belonging. As artist and author Gwen Gordon has expressed it: "The play and experimentation of evolution can only exist within the compassionate embrace of the cosmic mother. I think the reason we are falling apart as a society and becoming literally deadly serious is because we're not feeling held."[29] This is also the power of the mother-child bond. We feel held and loved by the gaze of the universe. And so this is the way we must educate our children as well, not to see the universe as a mechanical and indifferent place, but as an event that includes their own unfolding, allowing play and experimentation within the safety of an embrace.

The spiritual ecologist as an archetypal figure is larger than any one individual who harbors a love for the Earth and seeks a deeper connection to the natural world. It is an archetypal energy that is currently ascendant, especially in Western industrial culture. It is a creative response to loss, a tendency toward wholeness, an attempt to balance out a worldview that has caused deep alienation in the human soul. The spiritual ecologist archetype is energized by the affinity of the soul for wholeness, and an affinity of the human psyche for meaning. It is the most needed archetype of our time because its energy resonates first and foremost with relationship. This is true on both planetary and evolutionary levels, because archetypes are the language of the cosmos, the way the powers of the universe manifest within us. At a time when the dominant worldview is destroying the planet, spiritual ecology is one of our most creative and healing responses. It is a tool that can help liberate us from the pervasive influence of that worldview. While spiritual ecology helps us cultivate a religious mind rooted in reverence for life, it is not a religion. It is a practice which, grounded in a deep sense of our interconnectedness, can profoundly inform and revitalize diverse faiths and cultures.

Some of the key characteristics of the spiritual ecologist archetypal figure are as follows.

Spiritual ecologist as healer

The healer works to reweave the social fabric through reverential thinking and practices that reconnect us to each other and the sacred. Regenerative agriculture is an example of such a practice. Regenerative agriculture aims to increase biodiversity and to enhance the resilience of the entire life system, including the human communities that work the land and eat the food. It sequesters carbon into the soil rather than releasing it into the atmosphere. It avoids the use of petrochemicals which deplete the soil. In other words, it produces food while regenerating the vibrancy of the system rather then drawing it down. Our relations to the other-than-human are deeply wounded and in need of healing. Healing involves developing a tenderness and sensitivity to their rights to thrive and be free of human exploitation.

Spiritual ecologist as a shamanic personality

Related to the healer is the spiritual ecologist as shaman. The sentience, subjectivity, or consciousness of species other than our own is something that we cannot know, nor ever really fully address, through reductionist science or the discursive mind. When Thomas Berry speaks of a "communion of subjects," he refers to a mode of being apart from physicalism or dualism. There is an inwardness, or subjectivity in all phenomena which cannot be fully known, only communed with. A direct experience of the spirit of another animal isn't something that can be reduced to a physical explanation. Nor can it can it be broken down dualistically into a separation of mind and body, a mental understanding of a physical reality. Listening to the voices of the other-than-human through communion is one aspect of the shamanic personality.

Mystery is difficult for the discursive mind, and yet few phenomena power the human imagination more than a sense of mystery. Mystery inspires reverence, and terror, bringing us to vitality and life through an utter feeling of awe at the forces of Earth and cosmos. The human mind—especially the Western mind—has an insatiable drive to "know," to break the mysterious into manageable and predictable parcels. But mystery forces us into a state of not knowing and humility, into living with ambiguity. This requires that we develop our atrophied capacities to trust forces beyond what our minds can understand. This is an awareness of the larger, ancient rhythms around us, of the seasons and the story which has shaped us so deeply, and a vivid experience of our inter-connection to everything else.

The shamanic personality today is a creative response to the need for transition from a death-loving paradigm to one that affirms life. The contemporary emergence of this religious personality amounts to the human imagination at work building a communal response to the paradoxes of our time. The shaman brings cosmic and primal Earth forces to bear for community healing and accentuates religious feeling (some might say faith) in transitional times. As a marginal figure standing outside secular society, the shaman is in the position to question the predominant moral authority. This is required in this time of moral vacuum. Many of our major religious traditions have become so attenuated in their ties to the mysteries of Earth and cosmos, that they no longer fulfill their function of binding us to the sacred. Another reason why this personality is needed now is that we require strength in dark times. We are faced with monumental crises—political and corporate greed, mass species extinction, a full frontal assault on the environment, climate change, terrorism and warfare, the Covid pandemic.

Author and educator Martín Prechtel, who is trained in the Tzutujil Maya shamanic tradition, relates the intense trauma he experienced in the Guatemalan village of Santiago Atitlán. The Mayan people, who were his community, were slaughtered by the hundreds at the hands of death squads and his village was destroyed. His shamanic initiation, he writes, allowed him to come through the experience with his spirituality intact, without bitterness, to actually live in, and offer healing to, the very culture that was in many respects responsible for that slaughter. Furthermore, the village shamanism survived intact. There is an indigenous soul, he writes, that is older and more durable than anything happening in our current situation, no matter how dire it seems.[30]

We are each of us indigenous to Earth, even though many of us have fallen into a profound amnesia about that reality. We each are descended from ancient peoples who practiced shamanism in some form. Understanding what the shaman is historically and what the emerging shamanic personality consists of may be profoundly helpful to our understanding of what is required of us in a time when the very future of Earth is at stake. The spiritual ecologist archetype rising within Western consciousness would seek the configuration of a new form of the shaman as a psychological and emotional healing figure. It comes back to trust—knowing we live in a profound mystery, experiencing reverence, having faith that the overarching unfolding of the Universe is benign and that we are fulfilling a unique and beautiful role in that process. This is the basis for a profound faith in ourselves and in powers we cannot understand with the rational mind. And a belief that our response, grounded in the true spirit of the shaman, will bring healing, beauty, and wisdom.

Spiritual ecologist as artist

Music, art, and ritual connect us and embed the story in our conscious-ness, using non-linear and non-rational pathways. Poetic consciousness in particular takes us into the realm of the mystic, where a heightened awareness of mystery cultivates awe and reverence. On a more down-to-Earth level, poems are attempts to capture slivers of human experience and to communicate their essence.

Creativity has a role in personal healing, as I've discussed elsewhere in this book. But the artist has a much larger ecological and moral imperative in our time of mass extinction and global environmental degradation. Author and teacher Suzi Gablik has brought this larger role of the artist in society to the fore more than any other art critic and thinker in the area of philosophy and art. In a 1987 essay, she wrote: "We have made much of the idea of art as a mirror (reflecting the times); we have had art as a hammer (social protest); we have had art as furniture (something to hang on the walls); and art as a search for the self. We need another kind of art, one which exercises its power to administrate the social dreaming through images which empower the collective unconscious. I am talking about an art which speaks to the power of connectedness and establishes bonds, art that calls us into relationship, and thus addresses our failure to grasp what it means to be actively related to the cosmos."[31]

The artist in this sense keeps alive our sense of wonder, our ability to feel, and to envision the future. The artist, through the imagina-tion, creates the future while simultaneously keeping the flame of empathy lit within us. Without empathy, without feeling, visions of the future can become overly cerebral. Teilhardian cosmology, with its emphasis on the creation of the Noosphere, or the human as a thinking layer of the Earth, requires just such a balance. The cerebralization of the planet must contain within it a feeling function to maintain a positive trajectory. The spiritual ecologist, as this new avatar of the artist, is an important force in the human psyche.

Spiritual ecologist as rebel
This is speaking truth to power, the prophetic personality, one who holds a contrarian position to the mistakes and excesses of industrial culture. The rebel subverts convention when it is destructive of life and the future, and refuses to give assent to exploitation and injustice. This can take many forms, including civil disobedience, direct action, protest, and launching a counter-narrative to violence, addiction, and mass consent to destructive power structures. The rebel sees through the naïveté of political and religious indoctrination.

Spiritual ecologist as witness
Bearing witness is not cold and detached observation of the loss and destruction taking place around us. We live in a time of the Sixth Great Extinction on planet Earth, primarily brought about by human activities, ranging from habitat destruction to fossil fuel consumption. The loss of plant and animal species is comparable to previous mass extinctions. To bear witness to this in a very real sense involves feeling the loss and "sustaining the gaze," as Joanna Macy has called it. This is a deep empathic state that keeps alive an awareness of beauty and of the value of what is being lost.

Spiritual ecologist as warrior
The warrior is fierce in devotion to the cause of life. A key ability of the warrior is discernment about what is of ultimate importance and is dedicated to its defense in a spirit of discipline and devotion. Staying informed on the issues and discerning what is right action on the side of justice and compassion is part of the warrior aspect of the spiritual

ecologist, to whom spiritual activism is a kind of sacrament.

Spiritual ecologist and the Great Mother

In the chapter "The Transformative Power of Story," I wrote about Quan Yin and the Protector of Life who represented for me the feminine face of the divine, a side of Christ that represented compassion and healing. The feminine face of the divine is strongly present in the spiritual ecologist archetype as well. I see that aspect represented by the return of the Black Madonna archetype, because this face of the sacred feminine goes all the way back to our human origins in the Earth. In addition to compassion, she represents darkness, fertility, and fierceness. The power of the dark goddess is the source of all fecundity, the depths of mystery in spiritual ecology, complementing the creativity of the masculine. Her darkness brings us beneath the surface level of our lives to the vitality of our essence. Her darkness is actually infused with light. I say more about this archetype in Chapter 24, "The Sacred Feminine and the New Cathedral."

The practice I've begun to describe in these past two chapters is essentially a practice of the heart. It builds within us a sense of place, as well as a heightened sense of the sacred within and around us. Just as crucial to our wholeness is a story that affirms one's identity within deep time. It complements the practice of spiritual ecology. And that is what the next section, "A Life-Enhancing Cosmology," explores.

Only through this story of how the universe came to be in the beginning and how it came to be as it is, does a person come to appreciate the meaning of life or to derive the psychic energy needed to deal effectively with those crisis moments that occur in the life of the individual and the life of the society.

—**Thomas Berry**, *The Dream of the Earth*

SECTION IV

A Life-Enhancing Cosmology.

Chapter 20
Radiance: The Creative Cosmos Within

The power of Radiance is an expression of the mysterious way in
which the universe cannot contain the magnificence it houses.
Instead, it is compelled to express itself in ten million different ways.
—Brian Thomas Swimme

Sometime in the late 1990s, some friends and I founded a group we
called Coco, which stands for "Celebrating Our Cosmic Origins." The
intent was to share, through story, ritual, play, and mutual support, a
simmering sense within us of the new evolutionary story and how it
was manifesting in our lives. At one meeting we decided to do what
we called a commissioning ceremony. We would each take new names
that we felt expressed our identities beyond that of family, profession,
religion, political party, or nation. What was our name as a cosmic citizen? How did it reflect our commitment to the new cosmology? We
went home from the meeting that day intent on thinking about what
those names might be.

Not long after the meeting, I had a dream in which I was being
ingested by an enormous, black spider. The spider was the size of a
large elephant and had a bulbous abdomen, not unlike that of a black
widow. No sooner had I passed into the body of the spider than I could
feel my body begin to dissolve and then pass out again as filaments of
light that spread out like a luminous web into the night sky. The feeling

of the dream was initially terror, but as I felt myself dissolve, the feeling of terror transformed into boundless energy, bliss, and expansiveness. When I woke up, I felt shaken, but energized and focused.

I returned to the commissioning ceremony the following week with a clear sense of my commission. I took the name of Earth Weaver. This felt right to me for a number of reasons. The image of the spider as the weaver of a web, and myself as a writer and poet weaving a web of words. But there was also a cosmic dimension, a generativity; and, in essence, a sense of the creative cosmos simultaneously within me and moving outward as strands of light.

The blackness of the spider is the darker side, the shadow side that is hidden, but seeks to be known. There is great generativity in darkness. It is the source of all creativity, the ground from which our lives are spun. When we are ingested and dissolved into that matrix, our lives can spin creativity out of loss. There is a certain terror in being ingested, and then again in giving the gifts that have been given to me by the universe. But then comes energy and bliss. This can only happen when there is an extinction of self. When that alchemy takes place, there is a transmutation into light that beams forth goodness, not destruction. We become part of the body of the spider, at one with the creative Earth, and with the primordial language of the universe expanding out in all directions.

Creativity out of loss

Creativity was a key avenue for me to connect again to my soul after my family's rupture with our spiritual community. This connection became my primary life ambition. I needed to express myself creatively, not because I wanted attention or fame or money, but to spin the straw of loss into gold. It was one of the ways, like immersion in nature, that connected me to spirit, to wisdom. It was either that or succumb to addiction or depression. The creative act was not unlike my attempted ascent of the small mountain at Estes Park that I wrote about in Chapter 7, full of both promise and uncertainty. And there is always a risk to creativity, a vulnerability. Calling in one's creative energies is one way of staying safe, but safety has its costs, the steepest of those being an un-lived life, one devoid of spirit.

And so, artistic efforts have been a key aspect of my spiritual path. I found that there is both wildness and domesticity in creativity; there is spontaneity and craft; the two in tension give birth to the unexpected. A poem or a melody or an image seems to come unbidden from some raw and unspoken source; or, a surprising expression takes shape from the attempt to learn the craft of a particular art form. Somewhere in the interstices of self-abandon and self-discipline is found wholeness in the psyche, and healing for the larger whole.

Beyond the conditioned self

Why are works of the imagination, especially those generated by oneself, a source of healing? The creative act in and of itself isn't the balm. It is the way in which creativity, in whatever form, tends to peel away the cultural veneer, the conditioned aspects of us, that insulate us from a higher actualization. Imagination allows us to picture in the mind, and then to *feel*, something beyond the immediate realm of the senses. It answers our longing for a connection to the divine, thus feeding the soul. To develop an imaginative capacity is also to grow in the ability to empathize, to build the muscle of compassion. It is a way to step out of the limitations of the conditioned self. The artist traverses the wilderness of the imagination and attempts to bring fresh awareness into the shared imagination of the species. This is a cosmic commission, the only real imperative driving us if we are to live a life of meaning.

The fundamental powers of the universe are constantly seeking expression through us. Or, what's within us must manifest; if it doesn't, in a very real sense, we can't thrive. I've found that if I keep it inside, or if it takes the form of pleasing the expectations of others, whether real or imagined, I suffer, and the energy turns to stress. Creativity and a sense of play are inextricably intertwined. Play is crucial to cognitive functioning, problem-solving, and avoiding depression. It's hard for me to imagine a life without some kind of creative play. This takes a unique form within each of us; and one of the unique things about human beings is that we have the ability to play beyond childhood through the power of our imagination. It's not exclusive to the artist, but inherent within each of us and uniquely manifested according to our particular gifts. And so play can be a lifelong source of healing; I've found it essential to my own.

But there is another way to think of creativity, one rooted within a cosmological context. We are evolved from planet Earth. The planet has given birth to us in a very real sense, and we are the species who has developed the power of conscious self-awareness. Thus, we are the Earth imagining, the planet aware of itself, the Earth perceiving her own beauty and woundedness. The Earth giving birth in a new way that is specific to our own strengths and weaknesses. The Earth builds the future by imagining possibility through the avenue of the human. To really think about oneself as the planet engaged in the act of imagination is to gain a profound resonance with something larger, and much deeper, than the small self. It is one of the most immediate channels, for me, of truly feeling that I am a mode of the universe giving expression to itself. And that we, as a species, do not stand outside of the unfolding, but are integral to its evolution.

This is the power of a life-enhancing cosmology. It restores a sense of the sacred that has been tragically banished in Western culture due to its roots in the secular imagination. It begins to cut through the chronic emptiness and speaks to our human need for meaning and purpose. It evokes deeper patterns that connect us to the universe.

Evolutionary philosopher and cosmologist Brian Thomas Swimme has brought this home to me more powerfully than any other teacher in my life. In the early 2000s, I attended the filming of his video series, *The Powers of the Universe*. In the series, Brian offers a captivating exploration of how the fundamental creativity inherent in the cosmos is personalized within the human. It was his creative attempt to show that our true human identity is a mode of that over-arching creative process. During the filming of these episodes, I experienced a profound understanding of Teilhard de Chardin's concept of "hominization" and the intrinsic powers that permeate both evolutionary processes and our own existence. By hominization, Teilhard was referring to the unique human expression of the fundamental powers of the universe. Brian compellingly articulated these powers, initially presenting them through the lens of science and subsequently revealing their unique emergence within the human psyche and how they tend to manifest as particular personality traits within the human.[32]

Our true identities are inseparable from the fundamental dynamics underpinning the universe's unfolding. As I explored the powers, I noticed facets of myself resonating with many of them, although some struck a more profound chord. This personal resonance was particularly pronounced for me in relation to the power of Radiance. The following is my synopsis of Brian's description of Radiance:

Radiance isn't solely a cosmic power. It is also a mode of human perception. Perceiving the universe as a mechanical construct distorts our understanding, obstructing our appreciation of the inherent beauty surrounding us. Radiance activates the profound depths of human perception—a shift in consciousness that liberates us from the delusion of viewing the universe as a mere machine.

The Sun exemplifies Radiance in its most potent form. The Sun has the remarkable capability to compress hydrogen into helium at its core, resulting in the emission of light. This light did not preexist; rather, it materialized through the fusion process taking place at the Sun's core, manifesting as particles known as photons. As these photons traverse space and reach us, we are bathed in the Sun's radiant energy. And yet, photons of light are not the Sun's sole gift to us. The Sun also emits gravitons, messenger particles that mediate gravitational interactions. These gravitons, unlike photons, penetrate deep into the Earth, generating gravitational attractions.

Human perception mirrors this duality of surface (photons) and depth (gravitons). Our perception encompasses both aspects, but in our preoccupation with machines, we have disregarded the depth of perception, erroneously equating our experiences solely with the surface level.

Radiance is the primary language of the universe—a primordial means of communication that transcends human language. We enter into relationship with Radiance through resonance and reverberation. Resonance is at the surface. But if the resonance is deep enough, it fills the being and we move to the level of reverberation. When we begin to reverberate, we are in a nondual relationship. Reverberation is finding our core identity in the midst of the voices of the universe, listening to the deep voices of the Earth and the universe. Something wakes up so powerfully within us that we become it; we discover who we are. More than any of the powers, Radiance is at the very core of who we are as human beings. People who feel the allure of the power deeply are mostly disinterested in the story of industrial culture. This is because they are sensitized to a deeper reality.[33]

I could see myself in the power the way Brian articulated it. I recognized within myself most, if not all, of the personality traits that Brian had identified as prominent in a person influenced deeply by the power of Radiance. More accurately, it felt like a mirror was held up that not only affirmed who I was and who I aspired be, but became a window for me to see more deeply into the universe.

One of those traits has to do with the tendency in a person influenced by Radiance to do the least amount of work required to survive. The reason for this, explains Brian, is to carve out the time and space to have time alone, to just be and to resonate with beauty. I was once characterized by a friend as "a least effort kind of guy." I could have been offended by this, but I recognized the truth in his statement. I had little interest in expending effort in a profession that was faithful to society's darker conventions, and thus I didn't pursue that path. On the other hand, when I eventually took on the editorship of a magazine that I felt was central to a new way of being human, I threw myself into it with body and soul. It may have appeared that I was a workaholic, but the truth is I was driven by a passion for cultivating and defending a vibrant Earth community. I wanted to let beauty shine through.

Time alone is crucial to my sanity. Solitude in nature was the beginning of healing, because I was able to be still in the presence of Radiance and to quiet the mechanistic, patriarchal, and consumerist influences that were so powerful in my society. It was a more authentic relationship, much less lonely than the forced relationships of Western industrial society. In the end, it was a marriage of my mature masculine as the creative act with the source of latent fertility that is found in the sacred feminine. These are both motivating archetypes within all of us to some degree.

Another personality trait Brian identified in a person swept up by the power of Radiance is an automatic resistance to authority. This aspect of Radiance spoke to my own disinterest in the conventional professional ambitions of most Americans and in my willingness to rebel against the mechanistic worldview and consumerist culture. I had a natural repulsion toward what I saw as the uglification of America, where vast swaths of the country were converted to a strip mall sameness and mono-cultured agricultural landscapes. I didn't want to be part of these dispiriting initiatives.

Yet another trait is a propensity to display. When I was in my teens and twenties, this took the form of clothing, jewelry, and hats, in other words, in my outward appearance. But later, this impulse was transformed into creative expression. Music, essay writing, and poetry were an attempt to connect with this aspect of the power of Radiance, to put the deeper beauty I sensed on display. Entering into relationship with Radiance was honoring the more sensitive part of my nature, my feeling for life. It was ultimately the foundation of my sense of self-worth. Now I think of the power of Radiance as the cosmos within.

In Chapter 7, I wrote about standing at the lip of a canyon in Estes Park when I was twelve, moved by what was emanating from the Earth through me to the point of writing one of my first poems. This was a deep resonance with Radiance. The poem was the outer form of a reverberation from within me, as were other experiences I've written about earlier: running with a harbor seal on a beach on the Pacific Ocean; standing on the great body of the Earth, spinning the Sun into a new day on a hill near Iowa City; and watching a hawk soar and plummet, over and over, and feeling it as joy within my own being.

The mystical experience I described in the chapter "The Transformative Power of Story" fully and suddenly opened the floodgate to Radiance permeating Reality. It was a heavy dose. My drive to express myself creatively has been my attempt to return to that splendor and to give it some kind of form that can be shared. For those readers familiar with the myth of Parsifal and the Holy Grail, it was my attempt to return to the Grail castle and ask the right question, the question that heals the Fisher King and restores wholeness to the realm. Call it beauty, or meaning; what I experienced was a luminosity that I sensed as the Reality behind our reality. For a brief period in my twenties, not long after the mystical experience, I sought to replicate it with drugs. But even LSD couldn't approximate the ineffable joy and peace that permeated me that day. As well, I didn't care for the toll that drugs took on my body and my emotions afterward, so I abandoned that particular quest.

The cosmos within

Several years ago, I began performing my solo piano pieces in public with a group of composers in my local area. My free improvisations on the piano were a particularly powerful form of reverberation with Radiance, because they were so raw and unscripted. When I play a piano improvisation in public, or when I recite a poem, I try to take a moment to remember the origin of the creative act. The movement of my hands, the melody surging up from within, the sound issuing forth from the instrument itself are all the energy of the Sun manifesting in the moment in an entirely new way. The invention of the piano, in fact, is also the labor of the Sun in a human being long before my time, as is the creation of the tonal system I use when I play. All of this creativity comes to a point in the moment of sound, all of it sourced not just from the collapsing hydrogen cloud inside a star, but all the way back to the very start of the universe. As the sound wends its way into the consciousness of the audience, it takes on yet another wave of creativity. Each person hears and feels it in their distinct way.

The fact that I know this story and can reflect on its power is the special province of my kind. The universe has found a way not just to create an image through sound in music or poetry, but to give expression to the inner life, and to have it received and amplified through others. The joy of creativity is in the sharing. To the extent I am able to share my gifts is the extent to which they take on a richness that is beyond my individual efforts and talents. It is in the larger community that they find their greatest reverberation.

Meaning, which to me is the feeling that I have a role in the divine drama of life, is something I have found for many years through the creative act. Another aspect of the creative act is its groundedness in the sensuousness of the living world, which is spirit permeating matter to the extent that there is no split between body and spirit. It is only thought which imagines them to be separate. This is the ultimate nature of the universe. The selfless creative act, done in service to beauty, connection, and meaning in human existence, pulls me out of myself in an attempt to contribute to the wholeness of the world. I believe that this is how each of us finds our role. In our self-expression we remake the world each day, bringing forth the cosmos within. We are keepers of the Sun and the Moon, tracing their arc in the sky so that future generations will have the chance to do the same.

Weaver

Weaver weaves a life,
a person, a pattern
thread by thread into cloth,
sound by sound into poem,
spun from cosmic notes
and all the accidents of a human soul.

An origin, a universe as story
to tell — billions of years to come
to this point. And we are young,
unfinished, traveling a long curve of beauty.

Weaver, keeper of the strands,
preserver of what works,
lover to stories and mystery
from whose loom as womb
stardust unfolds

Weaver, spider-mystic,
along whose web strands
the great unseen moves
giving birth through sacred vibration.

The long deliberation of stars,
the fertile simmer of soil
are carried as embers by poets
to rekindle each evening
a flame at the hearth
to light the dreamer awake.

LANDSCAPE INTERLUDE
Kinglet at the Door

Once for each thing. Just once; no more.
And we too, just once. And never again.
—**Rainer Maria Rilke**
  Ninth Elegy

This ramshackle writer's cabin works well for me. It is nestled in the hillside above the flat that empties into Tomales Bay. The area, mostly ranch land, is being returned to wetlands, I'm told. A few dairy cows are sequestered on the far side of the valley, an odd picture of domesticity against the backdrop of wild and primal Point Reyes National Seashore. The weather has been wonderfully erratic—alternating wind and rain with sun and fog, all amidst dramatic shifts of light.

There are candles mounted on the braces and struts of the cabin, heavy tools on the walls—ball peen and claw hammers, an axe, a pipe wrench, hedge clippers. These hand tools remind me that I am here to work with the tools of the word. Their solid presence makes me feel the heftiness that the craft of language carries. I feel the urge to grasp and wield, turning the fine bolt of a phrase, trimming an awkward sentence.

There is a space heater at my feet, two lamps, two pine desks, two doors opening to the south and to the west, and a balcony I can walk out onto to stretch. A wooden Adirondack chair extends its invitation to sit and contemplate amidst the coaxing of wind and encouragement of sun.

Birds swarm around the cabin like gnats to a cow. Last night, just at dusk, a Cooper's hawk perched on the railing of the balcony not five feet from me. I had ample time to take in his wild feathered beauty. Then he dropped and glided into the bramble, where moments before I had seen a salon of golden-crowned sparrows. White egrets power their way over the plain like pure thoughts, angelic and untouchable. Watching their flight distills my thinking. They light on the wetlands and the land and waters come to exquisite attention. Vultures circle over the vast green, searching for the fallen, leaving signs that the living don't want to admit to consciousness. The crows, in their iridescent black, seem the antithesis of the egrets—playful, demonic, steeped in the imperfect, tumbling in delight with Earth's constant creative surges.

I prefer the crows. They somehow occupy, live, the space between immanent and transcendent, independent and raucous in their irreverence. Their intelligence exhilarates me. I want to be part of their clan. They seem to know what's suspect and what to accept all in the same moment. They are solitary, or they flock in the hundreds, depending on what suits them. Crows talk to each other constantly, have elaborate communication systems, even on the wing. They don't worry for tomorrow. They tumble with the wind like black scarves abandoned to chance.

I stand to stretch, open the cabin door, and find a ruby-crowned kinglet dead on the doormat. Is this why the vultures have been venturing so near the cabin? I bend down to pick him up, and as I touch the kinglet, I feel irreverent. My movements seem too clumsy and too swift to impart the tenderness I feel. I can't help it—I feel the same paternal tenderness toward all animals, birds especially.

There isn't a mark on his amazingly tiny body. His head is cocked back, leading me to believe that he broke his neck flying into the window. I marvel at his lightness and at the coldness of his body, so soon after death. Most beings are heavy at death, as if they were yearning to be drawn back into the Earth.

The subtle flicker of a ruby streak on the crown of the kinglet's head flares up to a blaze underneath when I part the feathers. Ruby-crowned kinglets are nicely named, both for their color and for the royal designation. I have always been drawn to them for this reason: Kinglet, a small king. Like Rivulet, a small river. They are tiny birds—our smallest next to hummingbirds and bushtits—yet stunning and ferocious in their drab beauty. A white eye ring intensifies their gaze into a disarming curiosity.

Kinglet song is imposing for the size of its creator. The kinglet's song is Herculean, a remarkable outburst, loud and rich, peaking with a rollicking *tee-da-leet, tee-da-leet, tee-da-leet*. Kinglets revel in throwing their song to the world. In revealing themselves, questions of size or self-doubt are not in their repertoire. Kinglets are lucky to live four years.

Vultures pass shadows over the cabin endlessly. One cruises my window with a dead rodent in its beak, taunting me to distraction. Yesterday my writing wheeled around death as if to mimic the vultures. Today, I find death deposited neatly at my door in the form of a kinglet. I seem destined to face mortality on this retreat. It's as if the Earth is telling me to pay attention. Time to stop writing in circles and deliver up a package.

If I truly believed in my own death, I wouldn't waste time with doubt, I would just write. As Rilke writes in the "Ninth Elegy," "Once for each thing. Just once; no more. And we too, just once. And never again." My rough translation: "Now is my time to be Lauren."

The vultures are thickening in numbers and intensity outside the cabin. Something draws them beyond the willow thicket outside my window. They encroach and press in, the sound of their wings the music of my own dying. I try to let the fluttering leaves of the alders drown out the dour birds. But when they do, I hear the same song, even as the leaves shudder with joy. Joy sings out of the breast of death. It is the sound I am drawn to for my survival, for the marrow of my living.

"Here is the time for the sayable," wrote Rilke, "here is its homeland. Speak and bear witness."

If Ruby, as I have now come to call the kinglet on the desk in front of me, had not appeared, had not come to me in death, I may not have spoken: "Kinglet, Ruby-crowned. Too-short life abandoned."

How can my heart praise invisibly
The world as it arises within me
How can I hear the green Earth
And see the caw of the crow
And so satisfy the call of the seraphim—

Holy! Holy! Holy!

There must be some other sense
With which I can pierce the world,
Shedding my blindness
To what is so near at hand
A revelation, born of a new organ
With which to know mystery.

Each time I look at Ruby, I feel gratitude. Something wells in me that makes me feel more at home. The way Ruby was laid at my doorstep was like a gift left for a starving prisoner. In a sense I am starving. And I am a prisoner. I hunger, as we all do, for home and place. I feel the pangs of longing for beauty, to never shut down my inner gateway to wonder, at being stunned or terrified. Ruby, here beside my writing pad, makes me feel truly liberated as only *duende*, the sense of the presence of death, can.

Hunger and imprisonment are not essential to who I am. They are states of mind I induce when I forget and fear. Gratitude dissolves our forgetfulness and returns us home to Earth and each other. There are ruby-crowned kinglets. And alders, vultures, egrets, crows. Just once, and no more.

My kind is now the perpetrator of a great vanishing from the Earth. My kind also possesses a unique evolutionary heritage: to speak and bear witness. For this, I can feel fortunate to be in the world. There is no time to waste; the story strains to be heard.

Chapter 21

A New Faith in the Human

Santa Sabina Retreat Center is situated invitingly against a hillside of giant eucalyptus trees next to the shaded campus of Dominican University on the outskirts San Rafael, California. On its grounds are a straw bale hermitage, a yurt, a few live oaks with spreading canopies, towering redwoods, and a colorful assortment of flowering native shrubs. The Tudor-Gothic architecture of the Center houses a monastic chapel with stained glass, a dining hall, a library, and two large common gathering rooms on either side of the main building. The windows of these rooms vault upward and their lead-paned and beveled glass ushers in natural light, casting an appealing ambience over the wood-beamed walls and ceilings, large oak tables, and comfortable reading chairs. The second floor houses simple and sparse sleeping rooms for retreat attenders. A central courtyard opens to the sky and has arched and colonnaded porticos on all sides. At its center is a stone fountain surrounded by flowering plants and small trees.

Encircling the courtyard is a walkway onto which a series of stones of various shapes and sizes has been placed. Many of them are lit by candles. Painted onto the surface of each stone is a major transition or emergence point in the story of the universe. You can walk the periphery of the courtyard, alone and in silence, letting the stones speak, or with a companion, with whom you converse quietly, stopping at each station of the cosmic story marked by the stones at your feet. Every year, for nearly ten years, a pilgrimage of sorts was made to Santa Sabina in the form of three-day weekend retreats. I was part of many of these weekends, and they were observed in silence in order to encourage contemplation and a deepening of interiority.

The placement of these stones around a courtyard at the heart of a Catholic retreat center was a departure of sorts from the long-simmering antagonism in the larger culture between religion and scientific cosmology. Instead of stations of the cross, the stones marked stations of the cosmos, a kind of walking meditation centering on key points of emergence in evolution. Different stones, painted in white letters, represented the birth of the universe; the emergence of elementary particles; the transformation of atoms into stars and galaxies; the birth of our Sun and its planets; Earth's shapeshifting from a rocky planet to a living planet; then the planet's four-billion year passion play, from the emergence of prokaryotic cells (the most primitive and ancient form of life), the rise of eukaryotes (cells with DNA inside a nucleus), of sex, and plants, and animals and fungi, into the emergence of the human being; of hunting and gathering, then villages; and then of symbolic consciousness in the human that birthed language and societies, religious traditions, science and technology, agriculture and cities; and now a human- generated global nervous system, a sphere of mind, a new layer called the Noosphere, on par with the earlier layers of geological formation and oceans and rivers and the biosphere.

Just down the hall from the courtyard is a library where one can reflect on the words of Thomas Aquinas, St. John, Teilhard de Chardin, Thomas Merton, and Bede Griffiths and on back to the medieval Rhineland mystics Hildegarde of Bingen, Julien of Norwich and Meister Eckhart. Poets like Walt Whitman, William Wordsworth, Mary Oliver, William Stafford, and Rumi invite deeper contemplation. There are writings of Aurobindo, Vivikananda, Krishnamurti, and Buddhist authors like Thich Nhat Han, the Dalai Lama, Dogen Zenji, and others. The library also houses a collection of natural history and ecology writers, as well as the works of a number of scientists, cosmologists, and evolutionary philosophers. You can explore the synergy of science and religion in the library, then cap it off with a walk around the circle of cosmic stones in the courtyard.

A life-enhancing cosmology

I go into some detail to set the scene at Santa Sabina because there was an important incubation happening during these weekends. This was an incubation not only of ideas, but of energy and creativity. But the setting's offering of a synthesis of the insights from religious figures, evolutionary thinkers, and nature essayists was only a backdrop to something more momentous. For me and for my friends and colleagues, it was a kind of nursery and breeding ground where Brian Thomas Swimme (introduced in the previous chapter) would, through a series of inspiring weekends, unwrap, float, and refine his insights over a period of several years. These weekends ranged from one entitled "The Sacred Depths of the Cosmos," to literary and cosmological explorations of Dante's *Inferno,* to the philosophy of Alfred North Whitehead, to a taping of Brian's video *Earth's Imagination,* and finally, a scientific exploration into the fundamental "powers of the universe" that would culminate in Brian's video series by that name.

On one particular weekend, the focal point was the life and work of French Jesuit priest and paleontologist Teilhard de Chardin. Brian combined his own science-based insights as a cosmologist and evolutionary philosopher with the spiritual vision and scientific scholarship of Teilhard's writings. The intellectual and spiritual synergy between the two brought me to a turning point in my thinking about the human in an evolving universe. The contemplative atmosphere of the retreats at Santa Sabina provided a crucible for deep reflection and synthesis, and it did so within the cell-like structure of a community. The sense of a universe that had grown more complex over time, the emergence of human consciousness from within that unfolding, and Teilhard's notion of zest for life all pointed the way to a new sense of the human. As human beings, we are not just a blight or cancer on the planet, as many in the environmental movement believed. We are self-aware participants in an epic evolutionary unfolding. As such, we have the power of choice about the direction that unfolding might take, including a more compassionate orientation toward the community of life on Earth.

It was a vision that effectively washed away whatever lingering misanthropic residue remained within me. I grew up under a general cultural disenchantment with the natural world in favor of a consumerist orientation. It was the dominant earmark of growing up American in the postwar Industrial Age. It was also a view that went largely unquestioned by that culture's religious and educational institutions. Education was scrubbed of spirit and religion was mainly relegated to weekend piety.

This new cosmology called that into question and laid the foundation for a new faith in the human. Brian was pointing the way to a life-enhancing cosmology, and the way he presented it — with deep love for the universe and unflagging, contagious enthusiasm for its unfolding mystery, combined with impeccable scientific knowledge — made me feel happy to be alive. I felt proud to be a human being. His key insights into cosmology and evolution and the role of the human relit the torch of belonging within me. The feeling was akin to the one within my seven-year-old breast when I strode into the church sanctuary singing a hymn, surrounded by my human community; only now, my community was the universe. Belonging was returned to me in a more mature form, grounded in a story of my true evolutionary origins. My sense of self grew beyond all of the smaller associations down through my life: minister's kid, Protestant, white American male, Democrat, magazine editor, brother, son, uncle, and so many lesser personae. None of these mattered so much when held up to the larger identity with the

Earth community and the magnificent ancestry of the stars that was all of ours to cherish.

On the first day of the retreat, after a shared dinner, the group waits quietly in the common room. The required silence of the event lathers on an additional coat of anticipation. Other than subdued coughs and occasional whispers, the carpeted room is quiet. People mill about and greet each other with silent nods or an occasional hug, eventually taking seats. Brian enters and saunters slowly to the front of the room. At about six and a half feet tall, lanky and graceful, he naturally draws our attention. He is wearing dark pants and a thin maroon cardigan over a gray dress shirt. His thick, dark hair, with streaks of gray, frames a wide, slightly ruddy face that imparts kindness and boyish enthusiasm at the same time. He takes a seat beside a flowering quince branch placed into a tall vase by Harriet Hope and Suzannah Malarkey, the retreat managers and organizers of the weekend. He faces the group with an expectant smile and a warm twinkle in his eyes. The glow in his face reflects back the feeling of anticipation in the group. Settling into his chair, he turns to gaze at Susannah and Harriet with an almost playful look of "okay, are we ready to get into this?"

Many of us have been here before, in this room, bathed in the allure and excitement of leading edge ideas, energized by keen curiosity and a mutual feeling of connection to the cosmos and concern for the planet. There are a few more moments of silence, some welcoming words, and then a poem from Rumi, the thirteenth-century Persian poet, to set a contemplative tone:

> *Out beyond ideas of wrongdoing and rightdoing,*
> *there is a field. I'll meet you there.*
> *When the soul lies down in that grass,*
> *the world is too full to talk about.*
> *Ideas, language, even the phrase each other*
> *doesn't make any sense.*[34]

Brian begins to share his insights on Teilhard, first highlighting key aspects of his life and the significance of his thought. Then he begins to lay out the essence of Teilhard's ideas on the importance of relationship in the universe. The following are the key ideas that stuck with me and initiated my own exploration of Teilhard's writing.

Fuller being is closer union

"Teilhard's deep insight and a summation of his thought," states Brian, "can be found in his phrase 'fuller being is closer union'. This refers to the affinity of being for being. This affinity for deeper intimacy results in greater complexification in evolution. For Teilhard, the act of relationship is also the act of self-actualization. We deepen into intimacy and become more ourselves at the same time. They happen simultaneously." Brian gives the example of atoms which are initially repelled but ultimately cannot resist being joined together by what is deepest in themselves. "We have all these dormant affinities," he adds, "we're profoundly drawn toward communion. And yet, there are also all these tensions. The universe transforms itself through the deepening relationships of the beings themselves."

My journal reflections: drawn to what we love

As an American, I grew up in a hyper-individualistic culture where self-reliance and independence were seen as the supreme values of personal identity. Self-reliance was a high virtue, dependence on others a weakness. Freedom was defined as a kind of cowboy isolationism that was antagonistic to connection to others. Responsibility, instead of a "response-ability" with others in a kind of dialogue that ultimately brought forth something greater, was about being true to one's own interests, values, and opinions. As I wrote in an earlier chapter, our educational system has largely shut down our inborn capacity for deeper communion, and encouraged individualism and competition instead.

My experience of transcendent awareness that I wrote about in the chapter "The Transformational Power of Story" told me a different story. We are connected in a field of consciousness with other beings. This is the very essence of spirituality, and the foundation for creating a new way of being human. The experience came for me at a time when I was unable to think of it in terms of how I could be of greater service. And so, at that time, while I experienced a state of bliss, it didn't have the power to heal the trauma in my life. It would take many years and encounters with teachers before I could understand it as a source of healing, as an experience of profound communion.

For Teilhard, it is communion, not individualism, that is the basis for creativity. Individuation was important, but finding our genius, the unique mode of creativity that we have to offer as a gift to the larger community, is enhanced and drawn out by union. Letting ourselves be deeply drawn to what we love, in a state of self-forgetting, brings forth a new depth of expression We become what we love most deeply. Both relationship and differentiation are important. Fuller being, for me, is that unique genius within each of us, magnified by communion. We become more fully ourselves in our relationship to others, including other species in the web of life, not in isolation. It is also the foundation of a spirituality that has restored my faith in life, given me a sense of belonging, and nurtured my capacity for joy.

Zest for life

Brian continues with Teilhard's emphasis on what is needed to activate psychic energy in the human in our current age. "Relationship energizes what Teilhard held was the primary spiritual challenge of our times—the evocation of zest. Teilhard defines zest as 'the spiritual disposition, at once intellectual and affective, by virtue of which the Earth and action seem to us luminous, interesting, and fascinating.'"

"The zest for living," Brian elaborates, "is the energy which impels evolution along its axis of creativity, and thus complexity. Another way to see this complexification of forms is a deepening of beauty."

My journal reflections: activation of energy

The foundation of a zest for life is joy; underneath that is our capacity for wonder and gratitude. When I use the phrase "spiritual ecology," I often think of the word spiritual as describing the animating dynamic we feel in the web of relationships that is ecology. It is our capacity to feel the sensuousness aspects of nature as joy and wonder. "The spiritual ecologist in me wants to experience and feel," I wrote in the Introduction, whereas the naturalist in me wants to understand, to be amazed by ideas, to revel in the discoveries brought to us by the human intellect in its exploration of our world. Both of these aspects of my nature ignite zest. Zest is the animation of the whole person in response to the universe.

In the chapter "Creativity, Loss, and Risk," I wrote about my feelings of tenderness and respect for all life, the energizing impact of beauty, and a resonance with the radiant and spontaneous energies of the natural world. These all generate a feeling of zest within me. Radiance was the resonance I felt when fixed by the gaze of the harbor seal ("Gaze of the Other," end of this chapter). Zest was the energy I felt on the prairie running with the Rottweiler, then feeling the surge of prairie life beneath my body ("Prairie Heart," Chapter 10). Zest could also be pent-up, as with the caged lion in the Oakland zoo roaring out his wild essence in protest at the indignity of containment ("Wildness and Domesticity," Chapter 8).

Creativity and the human

Another central idea from Teilhard, for Brian, was concerning the nature of creativity. "Teilhard believed the human to be at the center of the universe," he states. For many, this centration is all too redolent of anthropocentrism in Teilhard's thinking. But Brian explains that it can also be seen as a way of claiming our unique creative role in evolution: "We're at the center of the construction taking place in the known universe," he says, "Much of Teilhard's work was to try to convince us that the human is actually at the center of creativity." Brian clarifies what this means for the human being in the context of evolution: "Every place in the universe is a center, but also every species that's here is evolving and is central in some way. Given all that, there is a way in which the human is central in a way that other species are not. As humans, we have a different challenge from the bacteria or the antelopes or the whales. Our challenge is the feeding and development of zest. To some degree, this is our responsibility."

My journal reflections: our unique expression

Human creativity is the way nature manifests through us. As our unique expression of the divine manifests, we add to the richness, depth, and beauty (complexity) of the universe. In other forms of life, nature manifests differently. Throughout my life, I had felt a drive to create, primarily through music, writing, and poetry. I had been drawn to books on the nature of creativity and beauty. My piano improvisations were raw in-the-moment expressions of the zest for life. The raw play of improvisation was the most immediate way into a deeper aliveness. But it was always in the presence of others that this aliveness became zest.

As part of the graduate program at Matthew Fox's school, I took a course called "Artist as Spiritual Voyager," taught by the painter and dancer Robert Rice. For a class presentation, Robert encouraged me to play a piano improvisation for the class. In the campus chapel, we gathered in a circle and joined hands, chanting the sacred "ohm" for a few minutes before I rose to play. I felt a rhythm, a fiery motif that beat at the heart of the universe; and with it, a palpable connection with those present. When I touched the keys, my hands moved of their own accord and resulted in some of the richest and most surprising music I've ever played. The music felt like it was coming from a connection in all of those present to something larger than ourselves. Unrepeatable, unique to that moment only, it was an experience of complete relationship. Of fuller being, and utter joy.

The brief summary above only touches lightly on the richness of ideas from Teilhard that Brian presented at the three-day workshop. But my three main takeaways — unitive experience, the zest for life, and the centrality of creativity in the universe — would stay with me and marinate over time. The experience of the weekend sparked my own closer reading of Teilhard de Chardin's master work *The Human Phenomenon*, his autobiographical book-length essay *The Heart of Matter*, and others of his works. A new translation of *The Human Phenomenon* by Sarah Appleton-Weber, published in 1999, coupled with a conference at the Sophia Center at Holy Names University on Teilhard's life and work, further deepened my exploration. I was Executive Editor of *EarthLight* magazine when the new translation appeared, and the culmination of the book and the conference would comprise an issue of the magazine focused on Teilhard in the Fall of 2000. The title of the issue, "The Fire of a New Faith: Living the Great Story," laid out the basis for a new faith in the human. In my editorial, "Keeping a Flame for the Unborn," I wrote:

What motivates us? Where do we get the psychic drive to get up each morning and live our lives, to be creative, to engage life when we are faced with the destructive fires of climate change, war, epidemics of addiction and violence, species extinction, and the decimation of Earth's life-support systems? A cosmology, a story for our moment, orients us to a new source of psychic energy, and even more importantly, a human role in the cosmos that not only gives our lives meaning, but makes us indispensable to the evolution of the living Earth. Such a cosmology can be a source of enormous energy. A functional story is a primary source of energy that will pull us back from psychic depletion and despair. It's a story that shows us that we are forged from the stars and that our very emergence has been contingent on many transformational moments in the 13-billion-year universe story. Thomas Berry calls these moments of grace, inflection points where creativity emerged from crisis. At so many points in the story, things might not have gone our way, or the conditions not been met such that life could emerge or continue. It's not just that we develop a sense of the magnificence of this unfolding of life, but also of the miraculous nature of its enfolding, or "folding in." This "folding in" of the complexifying universe on itself created a depth of interiority and awareness that makes the human a way in which the universe reflects on its own beauty and mystery. What arises from within this human capacity to be the universe reflecting on itself is a zest for life, and a deep faith that empowers us to persevere, even in times of doubt, chaos, and destruction.

Teilhard understood the fire of divine love from his mystical visions and his devotion to both science and religion. He also knew the destructive aspect of fire from his time in the WWII trenches as a stretcher-bearer. It's this profound understanding that prompted Teilhardian scholar Ursula King to write the following about the prominence of love in his vision of evolution: "Teilhard loved the Earth and its peoples. He loved his church and his order. And he was filled with the fire of love for the ever-great Christ. For him, the symbol of fire meant the warmth and radiance of love and light, the energy used to fuse and transform everything. But fire... can destroy as *well as transform. In Teilhard's understanding, it is the transforming power of the energies of love which alone can create a truly humane community and provide it with its strongest points. Thus, the fire of divine love may be the only energy capable of extinguishing the threat of another fire, namely that of universal conflagration and destruction."*[35]

It is in our trans-genetic coding, a gift from the story of the universe itself, to be more than a destructive conflagration on Earth. We can burn with divine love for all Creation.

On one of the evenings during the weekend on the Powers of the Universe, we are gathered in the common room. One of the powers we explored was Radiance. Brian walks in and settles into a chair at the front facing us. He is holding a copy of *EarthLight* magazine. He opens it and begins to read from my essay "The Kinglet at the Door": *"If I truly believed in my own death, I wouldn't waste time with doubt, I would just write. As Rilke writes in the "Ninth Elegy," 'Once for each thing. Just once; no more. And we too, just once. And never again.' My rough translation: 'Now is my time to be Lauren.'"*

"This," he says to the group, "is Radiance."

I can barely contain the glow within me. This is not just a random affirmation. It is a convergence of my four healing pathways of connection I wrote about in the Introduction: There I am in my human community; interacting with a man who had mentored me into a new story of the universe; he is reading from my own work; and it is an essay about a luminous interaction with the natural world. A profound moment in my healing journey.

Radiance

In the darkness below,
a fountain in the courtyard,
and candles, each illuminating a stone
that speaks a moment of emergence
in the long tale still being told.

Flicker of water, trickle of fire,
bright star radiating coolly overhead.
Starlight circling, flickering, trickling.
running warm through hands joined,

Flicker of touch, trickle of memory.
Dance of flesh, and thought,
and flame, and stone.
Song of light, burn within us,
flare into night, bring us home.

LANDSCAPE INTERLUDE
Gaze of the Other

One does not meet oneself until one catches
the reflection from an eye other than human.
—**Loren Eiseley,**
  The Ghost Continent

Limantour Spit dangles in the waters of the Pacific Ocean, an oddly tattered and fragile-looking appendage to the Point Reyes Peninsula. It is shaped somewhat like the lower, ragged jaw of a beached and fossilized ocean dinosaur. The Peninsula itself is not actually a part of the North American continental plate to which it appears attached. It forms the far eastern edge of the Pacific plate, which is chafing in a northwesterly direction, inch-by-inch, against the vast North American plate. The fault between the two plates, part of the San Andreas fault, creates a unique biome and geologic zone. Ninety miles beneath your feet, as you stand on Limantour, magma noses upward from the Earth's mantle, then spreads out underneath the planet's crust. This action floats the Pacific Plate ever northward in a slow but steady migration. Sixteen million years ago the Point Reyes Peninsula would have been found hovering in the vicinity of modern day Monterey Bay, over 110 miles to the south as the brown pelican flies.

When I visit the Peninsula with this geologic perspective in mind, I sometimes have a sense of precariousness in my body, with the slightly uneasy realization that I am balanced on a very thin shaving of land at the edge of the enormous body of the North American continent, which stretches so far east as to include Greenland. I imagine that shaving, jostled loose by a sudden tectonic shift and floating away to rendezvous with the Farallone Islands, which can be seen far offshore on a clear day.

It's summer of the year 2000. I am in the midst of my editorship of *EarthLight*. It's a Tuesday, a day I renamed "Museday," a day I habitually took off work to recharge my Muse by spending unstructured time, dreaming, usually in a natural area. On this day I am at Point Reyes National Seashore and I'm on my favorite trail near the Limantour Spit. As I walk the thin trail north on the seam of the two plates, with the ocean on my left and the estuary on my right, I balance on the boundary of two worlds. Flocks of white pelicans garland the eastern estuary shore. A large flock of mergansers churns the water in a choreographed dance across the shallows, while on the opposite side of the trail, the sea-beach surf thunders onto the sand in regular pulses. I'm surrounded by a great tangle of various green shades: dark cypress trees, haggard-looking, wind-swept, but strong and persistent in their watchfulness; sage green waves of bush lupine; and sunlit emerald stands of coyote bush and chaparral harbor a riot of life underneath their rough cloak.

Today, slowed by the raw rhythms of rock and wind and weather-hardened plants here, I walk silently absorbing the sights and sounds at play around me. My quiet footfalls and slow progress are soon rewarded by a small drama. A rabbit spurts out from beneath the branches of a coyote bush and onto the path, taking the opportunity of freedom from obstruction to quicken its flight. It is being pursued. An instant after the rabbit disappears around path's bend, a long-tailed weasel bursts out in hot pursuit. But as he reaches the path, he abruptly halts and sits upright, his snout in the air and his paws pulled in close to his slender body. He is facing away from me and upwind, so even though the weasel is only several paces away, he is unaware of me for several long seconds, enough time for me to fully take in his black-tipped tail, white-tipped paws, and ochre body. When he does see me, he fixes me with a piercing gaze. His brown face is daubed with white beneath the pert ears and between the eyes. And then he is gone, bounding energetically in the direction of the rabbit's disappearance.

It's rare to see a weasel here. I realize that the thick, rough coverlet of green between myself and the estuary houses a fiesta of life beneath its placid mask. Often a landscape can appear devoid of animals. Here, wrentits and white-crowned sparrows flit furtively across the low shrubs. A lizard occasionally skitters across the path. But wait long enough in the company of your own silence, and respectful attention and a hidden richness of life begins to come into view here. When it does, there is nothing so arresting as a gaze.

The gaze of an animal, even as diminutive as a weasel,

elicits a re-cognition within me, an inscrutable remembering. It subtly disrobes me of domesticity, bringing me from my restless, thinking mind to my naked, animal body. More than once, I have encountered a lone coyote on the path while out hiking at Point Reyes. There is always a moment of uncertainty when our gazes meet. Will I be seen as friend or foe? When the moment passes, I feel a certain recognition in the disinterest as the coyote goes about her day, ignoring me. She has not mistaken me for either threat or prey.

Once, out on Limantour, barefoot, walking the firm wet sand at ocean's edge, I was disarmed by another wild gaze. Lost in thought as I walked, I looked up to see the bobbing head of a harbor seal in the swell of a wave. The seal's dark eyes were cast in my direction. I'd seen harbor seals here before. Sometimes they were pulled out, basking in the sun. But this one was very near and seemed unusually curious. I ventured a wave in the seal's direction, as if hailing a neighbor with a "hi-ya there." Then, as the seal began to swim parallel to the shore, the urge to begin running came over me. The open sprawl of beach ahead lured me on, slowly at first, then in an exuberant burst down the flat pallet of sand. As I ran, I was surprised to see the seal's shining, dark head bob above the surface again, still even with me, and eyes in my direction. Then the seal dove, out of sight for several long seconds, and surfaced, dove and surfaced, in a rhythm that I could almost anticipate. I ran a mile or two down-beach, then slowed, hands on my knees, catching my breath. And there was the seal, stopped, gazing. Delighted and a bit puzzled, I laughed.

I turned to run up-beach, again thinking I'd leave the seal behind. At first this seemed to be the case. But then, the smooth dome of the seal's head appeared, glistening under the late afternoon sun. It seemed the seal had turned to follow me. I reached my beach towel, and slowed to a walk. After a time, I collapsed onto the towel, facing the sea, legs bent, my arms resting on my knees. There, the seal had stopped and was drifting on the quiet swell of seawater. The dark gaze met mine one last time, and then the seal was gone in a quick blip beneath the crest of a wave. I felt tired and exhilarated. I dropped my head between my folded legs, the mystery of that gaze still in my mind's eye.

What was this? I felt that tenuous feeling of being on a minuscule sliver of land between two plates on the edge of a continent. It felt fragile, just as fragile as my own and my kind's connection to the living world. Both rare experiences on the liminal zone of continent and sea, the borderland of our human heart and the wide green world. We are a ragged crumb away from a radical severance from the world that birthed us, precariously balanced on the edge of disaster. For a moment the seal seemed to offer me remembrance of a sacred unity, the gaze of the other bringing me home. Running brought me into my body, drawing up relationship into a moment of zest and beauty. The gaze brought me out of my thinking self, without ideas of "seal." A moment of no division, no conflict, selfless. Beyond ideas of memory, belief, dogma.

My Seal of Memory

You swam, keeping pace in the surf
while I ran barefoot
down miles of firm brine-wet sand.
You plunged, surfaced, and then
you were gone, submerged.

What world might I imagine
beneath the vast silver Pacific?—
your sleek mottled body,
flipper-vaulting, tail-ruddering
through paths of kelp forest.

Surfacing again,
wet gleaming head bobbing,
black eyes trained toward me
as I ran
fleeing the bodiless life...

... I know I did not imagine that gaze,
which saw me for who I am.
There is no greater humbling wonder
than the gaze of an exotic other.

I ran. You swam, more fleet than fear,
right into this poem,
my seal of memory.

Chapter 22
Cell and Membrane

These weekends transformed Santa Sabina into a kind of organic cell, and its walls were a membrane that held the community within a protective ambit of contemplative awareness. There wasn't merely a desire in the participants to escape into comforting ideas and spiritual platitudes. It was a mature symbiosis of people who cared deeply for the planet and the human future, and sought to achieve a renewed union with each other and the cosmos. Over the course of a weekend we danced with each other like organelles in a living cell. In the common room on the final day, we verbally exchanged the energy and nourishment of ideas. There was the expansion of ideas, but it was contained within the cell of the community. Some kind of gestation took place, but what was being born was inscrutable and would only show up later in the far-flung places and activities of our separate lives. The fifty or so people gathered here were from many walks of life, to mention a few: artists, religious leaders, scientists, writers, a high school teacher working with at-risk youth, a corporate CEO, an engineer from a water utility, a biology teacher, a clinical psychologist, professors, a magazine editor, the dean of a college, a yoga instructor, a Jungian therapist, the director of a charitable foundation, storytellers, college students, and more.

The nourishment of Teilhard's philosophy in synergy with Brian's invigorating and thought-provoking perspective as an evolutionary philosopher osmosed through the membrane and into our consciousness. A doorway opened to seeing more deeply, and seeing more deeply is the portal to a new way of being human.

The cell image is aptly Teilhardian. He uses the cell as an example of the way evolution turned inward to develop interiority in a process called enfoldment. Seeing more deeply was also a unique aspect of his thought. Interiority for Teilhard was the "folding in" of the exterior of the evolutionary process on itself. The result was a parallel interiority that intensified and deepened through time. The interiority of a cell was a similar inward-folding process as human conscious self-aware-ness, but the latter took place at a different point of emergence and on a new order of magnitude in evolution. The result was more depth in seeing and complexity in thought. This intensification of evolutionary unfolding in the human is what Teilhard referred to as "hominization" of the powers of the universe.

Discernment

After the Saturday afternoon session on Teilhard, a group of us are huddled in the library near some lead-paned windows that vault to the ceiling, letting in shafts of honeyed light that inundate the dark carpet and heavy armchairs arranged around a central fireplace. Two great live-oak trees lean in toward the windows, eavesdropping just outside, the wind moving their leaves in subtle resonance with the energy of the group. We are having trouble maintaining the retreat's code of silence. The life-blood of the ideas just wants to explode into conversation.

"Did you get that part about hominization?" whispers the engineer.

"Yeah. I mean, no. Not quite," whispers back the clinical psy-chologist.

"That the human transforms previously existing processes and functions of the Earth through the phenomenon of thought and sym-bolic consciousness…" chimes in the high school teacher.

"Through the power of the imagination," adds the yoga instructor.

"And it just explodes over the planet in the decisions we make," rounds out the engineer in a voice elevated slightly above a whisper.

"So hominization is the human form of the basic powers of evolution unfolding in a unique way. And we're having an impact on the level of the other great spheres of the planet," rephrases the clinical psychologist.

"Yes, on par with the hydrosphere, bathysphere, atmosphere, lithosphere!" says the biologist, in a voice verging on impertinence.

"And," blurts out the magazine editor a little too loudly, "human decision, the choices we make, have overtaken or usurped natural selection as the major force driving evolution!"

"How am I going to explain that to my students?" muses the high school teacher.

"How am I going to explain that to my *husband!?*" exclaims the engineer.

"Yeah, I know," commiserates the yoga instructor, "I don't think I have a yoga move that..."

She is cut short, because Suzannah is bearing down on us quickly from across the library. Soon, having broken the stern code of silence, we are gently banished to the grounds outside the retreat center to continue our conversation. There were these occasional minor transgressions of the ritual of silence at the retreats. Sometimes, there was just no containing the energy of the ideas. This came in the form of whispered hallway conversations, pairs huddled in the corner of the common room by the fireplace, and occasional groups of all-out insurrectionists breaking out of the membrane of Santa Sabina's walls to hike the eucalyptus groves and golden hills beyond. There, people could chatter with impunity outside the earshot of others. The library, the sleeping rooms, the art room in the basement of the administrative building were also lairs of temptation where many of us succumbed to rebellion.

We ate in silence too, even though dinner and conversation are two of the most difficult human activities to segregate. Even if it's just to say "pass the salt" or "thumbs up on the veggie lasagne this year," what better place to be convivial than the dinner table? And yet, while it was hardest to be silent in the dining hall, ironically it was where we most faithfully observed the ritual silence. There was peer pressure there. No one relished a stern glare from above a bowl of minestrone across the table.

More often than not, I preferred the silence, the opportunity to quietly reflect and marinate the ideas. There is a general discomfort with silence in our culture, especially in extended doses. For me, the silence was food; for a culture built on speed and busyness, it can rise to the level of medicine. I think that what we found on these weekend retreats was that the silence fed us in ways that food could not. It fed a spaciousness that comes from putting the restless mind on hold; having a thought, then observing it and letting it sink in. And then another thought, and another, until you find yourself in a clear, cool glade of awareness, instead of the thicket of noise in which we live most of the time. When we did return to interaction with each other over lunch in the dining room on the final day, we each brought that more refined awareness to each other. And then, often, there would be an explosion of pent-up energy from three days of relative silence. The final communion of ideas, charged by the depth within each of us, produced a new synergy, one that we could feel was only just finding its way into a new form.

The silence served another purpose. It slowed down and in many ways deepened our responses to the ideas. In a way, it was too tempting to reach for easy answers as to how to apply this new cosmology in day-to-day life. It wasn't something that could be answered immediately through the intellect. It wasn't even something that could come immediately from the heart, because this new perspective needed time to marinate and seep into the depths of my own interiority as well as that of my friends and colleagues. Two processes were happening simultaneously: deepening interiority and the synergy of ideas and feelings. Within the protective crucible of the retreat setting, a discernment was taking place. We were folding back on ourselves, just as Teilhard had characterized the cell and the young Earth, attempting to internalize a cosmology that, while more fully articulated by science with time, isn't yet ripe within the wider culture. Science is uncovering the details; we were part of the process at Santa Sabina of interpreting it into a usable cultural story, a cosmology that would move human beings forward. I learned that it was necessary to keep the ideas in front of me as much as possible and to feel my way, to grope forward into making the word flesh, into finding some sort of everyday embodiment of ideas that were overturning my own cultural conditioning and early landscape of identity formation.

Mandala on the Birth of the Universe

I'm gazing into the looking glass of deep time
through the portal of a womb
the mirror that reaches back to the birth of stars.

In the center, primordial figures gestate:
magma, embryo, seed, prokaryote.
If this is a promise, it is as old as the galaxies.

The membrane of the womb is a border
and a gateway; it protects and discerns,
keeps out, lets through.

One segment, unlike the larger circle,
seamless with the membrane,
but distinct. The entire ring eternal, inevitable.

Chapter 23

A Dynamic Tension

He felt pity for those who take fright at the span of a century or whose love is bounded by the frontiers of a nation.
—**Pierre Teilhard de Chardin**
  The Heart of Matter

I rejoice that there are owls.
—**Henry David Thoreau**
  Walden

Despite these profound influences on my thinking, there was a lot in Teilhard that didn't square well with my readings and reflections on natural history and deep ecology. They didn't immediately find common ground with the sensuous experiences of the Earth that I describe in many of the landscape interludes in this book. In particular, much of what resonated with me in Henry David Thoreau's writings seemed to contrast sharply with that of Teilhard's. Thoreau's challenge to the power structures in society in "Civil Disobedience," his skepticism about technology as a panacea, and his desire to commune more directly with the natural world were missing in Teilhard. Thoreau loved the swarming, luscious Earth; Teilhard managed a love as big as the cosmos. I resonated with Thoreau's rebellion against authority, and yet I admired Teilhard's obedience to a greater good. Thoreau was immersed in the flesh and blood of nature; Teilhard embodied an evolutionary, futuristic vision of a new way of being human as a thinking layer of the planet that he and others called the Noosphere. Thoreau's attention was to the local and a specific place; Teilhard focused on deep time and the whole of the universe.

Although Teilhard saw spirit at the heart of matter and his notion of zest was an affirmation of life, his spirituality seemed mostly cerebral, disembodied, theologized, technologized, and cut off from any visceral connection to the natural community of life. This was despite his work as a paleontologist, working with rocks, the flesh of the Earth.

Contrast that to Thoreau's *Walden*. One chapter alone, "The Ponds," is a veritable feast of the sensuous. Thoreau is swimming in communion. He describes Walden Pond using all the senses. The world of nature is immediate and palpable, not merely an abstraction or an earlier form that gave rise to the human, but a sensual experience continually arising around and within us.

In one of *Walden's* most reflective passages, Thoreau seems to lose a sense of the small self and fully belong to his surroundings to the point where he no longer craves human companionship. He also offers his own answer to my persistent questions about the friendliness or unfriendliness of the universe. He speaks to the benefits of solitude I had experienced many times over. Many of these I have shared in this book in the form of landscape interludes. In this passage, I feel a spirit kindred to my own:

I have never felt lonesome, or in the least oppressed by a sense of solitude… But once, a few weeks after I came to the woods, for an hour, I doubted whether the near neighborhood of man was not essential to a serene and healthy life. To be alone was somewhat unpleasant. But I was at the same time conscious of a slight insanity in my mood, and seemed to foresee my recovery. In the midst of a gentle rain, while these thoughts prevailed, I was suddenly sensible of such sweet and beneficent society in Nature, in the very pattering of the drops, and in every sight and sound around my house, an infinite and unaccountable friendliness all at once, like an atmosphere, sustaining me, as made the fancied advantages of human neighborhood insignificant, and I have never thought of them since. Every little pine needle expanded and swelled with sympathy and befriended me. I was so distinctly made aware of the presence of something kindred to me, even in scenes which we are accustomed to call wild and dreary... that I thought no place could ever be strange to me again.[36]

Thoreau "rejoices in owls," and in all the plants and animals the woods of Walden Pond present, but also the birch logs sunk to the bottom of the pond and the cold clarity of its waters. This sensual connection to nature was more in line with my experience in the prairies, woodlands, and riparian habitats of the Midwest, Canada, and the Pacific Coast. This was the transformation I experienced surrounded by ebony jewel-winged damselflies in an Iowa forest ("Magic in the Glade", Chapter 5), and on the floor of the prairie, face-to-face with the visages of wildflowers and nose down in the smell of the rich, dark soil ("Prairie Heart", Chapter 10).

In many respects, Teilhard and Thoreau are representative of my contrasting experiences of the domesticity of Europe and the American Midwest and the wildness of the Canadian provinces. But I was seeking to move beyond thinking in dualisms of wild and domestic, the raw and the cooked, nature and culture. Teilhard and Thoreau represented a dialogue within me that sought not so much a resolution as a dynamic equilibrium.

I use Thoreau's writing as a counterpoint to Teilhard because it has a special resonance for me. But his work is but one example of the necessary diversity of thought that can enrich the dialogue about the human relationship to nature. Teilhard and Thoreau were not creatures of the same time and place; Thoreau lived in the mid-nineteenth century; Teilhard was born about twenty years after Thoreau's death and lived until 1955. Thoreau lived at a time when the American imagination was grappling with how to relate to a still mostly wild continent and how to define freedom from the Crown within such a setting. Teilhard lived in a Europe where the natural world had long been subdued, tamed, and sequestered and which would see two brutal world wars during his lifetime. Both thinkers offer their unique wisdom tempered as much by their historical circumstances as by their individual genius.

Teilhard put much emphasis on the development of an ultra-human beyond our earthly origins, and had an undying faith in technology as a key part of the spiritual force that would move humankind forward. Unlike Thoreau's challenges to power, Teilhard was obedient to the church and didn't challenge the idea of unlimited progress or the unchecked exploitation of natural resources that were ascendent in his time. He didn't seem to have a concern for the limits of Earth's bio-systems to absorb the impact of human activities, and he accepted the dogmas of industrial culture all too easily. He was enamored of atomic energy, and rather than seeing the destructive aspects of the splitting of the atom, he felt that it would not only heighten human progress and unlock unlimited energy, but would serve to make war obsolete. His fealty to church patriarchy and to technology, even if it potentially led to ecocide, were two aspects of a fundamental defect in Western thought. Teilhard died in 1955, seven years before Rachel Carson would write her seminal ecological work *Silent Spring*. The full industrial assault on the planet had not yet reached its peak in Teilhard's time. And so, he seemed blind to the consequences of ecological overshoot. We should acknowledge these shortcomings in Teilhard, states Thomas Berry, but still embrace him as foundational to our understanding of a time-developmental universe. He ushered in a revolution in how we view ourselves, from inhabitants of a fixed and cyclical cosmos to participants in a dynamic cosmogenesis, an unfolding story in time.[37]

Play of opposites

Both Thoreau and Teilhard live within me in a dynamic tension and ultimately I saw no reason to reject one in favor of the other. It was a consummation of sorts, coming out of the marriage of Cosmos and Gaia. What I was learning was that cosmology can be the basis for a rebirth of wonder. But it had to be cosmology embedded in an understanding that we are integrally connected to the community of life. A sense of an evolving cosmos gives us a story based on an emergent universe; a sense of Gaia, or Earth, gives us a sense of place. The former connects us in time, the latter in space.

As a child, I was steeped in a Christian cosmology that God made me, and all the rest of the world. That seemed good enough for me at the time. But if one's faith in God is challenged, as it was for me in the trauma of my sister Kristin's kidnapping and my family's subsequent break with the church, new questions rear up. If God didn't make me, or indeed, if there wasn't even a Creator to make me, where did I come from?

My first step away from a deistic understanding of my origins was the theory of evolution. My exposure to it was pretty basic in terms of my grade and high school education—humans were primates, descended from apes. Some mysterious but seemingly random force down through time drove natural selection and gave rise to me. The next step away from deism was that we were stardust, according to cosmologists like Carl Sagan and others. The elements in our bodies were forged from stars that went supernova, spewing the basic constituents of all life on Earth out into the void. These elements coalesced into, well, everything we know, from algae to walleyed pike to tigers. This felt somewhat more scintillating and more definite at the same time. It seemed more immediate, easier to imagine. And yet, while fascinating to contemplate, it still seemed depersonalized and cold. The final step away from deism was a return of sorts. My origins, human origins, were in the very primordial flaring forth,[38] the birth of the universe itself. The human is integral to the universe, not only in space, but in deep time.

This was a return in two senses; the first being a return to the very birth of time and space, the ultimate mystery; the second being a return to a sense of the divine within everything. In a word, my ultimate step away from deism was a return, not to deism, but to the ineffable, because the one really big question just hangs there: What was there before the birth of the universe? Could anything actually "be" prior to time and space? Was there a primary cause, mover, force, energy, presence in the pre-existence of everything? In essence, a mystery. Scientists haven't been able to answer that question yet, and it may be the primordial mystery that will never be solved, the void that cannot be known.

Teilhard saw a psycho-spiritual component to the universe from its very inception. This means that my own awareness, my own spirit, had to have had its origins in the very birth of the cosmos. That is one reason for awe. But then there is the sheer wonder at emergence itself. That anything should exist and have come to be at all out of what seems to have been nothingness. If the universe was creative from the very beginning, and not merely random or directed, then who, or what, out of that nothingness, was behind the original creative impulse? Back to God. And faith. It requires a leap to embrace that there was something *a priori*.

On the other hand, one can derive faith from observing the evolutionary dynamics that brought us forth, because they were a series of creative responses to crises that arose as the universe unfolded. Life found a way to arise; as did consciousness. They arose and complexified together. They seemed to be psychically hard-wired into the evolution of the Universe from the beginning. Knowing the grand sweep of that story can engender wonder as the basis for faith. And the spiritual practice that goes with it? A deepening of one's sensitivities to the universe, of one's depth of seeing. Depth of seeing is depth of being. The essence of the spiritual ecologist archetypal energy. The more one is attuned to the universe, the more one is truly oneself.

ψ

Groping was a favored concept of Teilhard's, and one of the least understood, especially for those looking for certainty in their reading of his work. This is one of the ways the divine enters into us and transfigures us in ways we don't expect. The divine manifests of its own accord, or it grows organically from our own interiority in interaction with our world. Or we are de-sensitized or distracted and fail to see it. In the same way, an experience of the luminous qualities of the natural world comes to us when we let down the defenses of our thinking mind, open ourselves to listening, grope with every pore of our being. Then we begin to see truly.

It was when I was able to integrate my transcendent experiences with the sensuous quality of my experience in nature that I would combine Teilhard's evolutionary and Christic vision with the writings of Thoreau and others. "Our own age," wrote Teilhard, "seems primarily to need a rejuvenation of supernatural forces to be effected by driving roots deeply into the nutritious energies of the Earth. Because it is not sufficiently moved by a truly human compassion, because it is not exalted by a sufficiently passionate admiration of the universe, our religion is becoming enfeebled."[39]

Many of Jesus's teachings were profoundly feminine. He preached love for one's neighbor. He was a healer. And his death was the ultimate act of surrender and sacrifice. Compassion was one of the key teachings of Jesus, one embedded within me as a boy. I couldn't deny it even as I rejected the fall-redemption framework of the Calvinist religion. Teilhard's vision of the Christic dimension in all matter and throughout evolution helped to activate within me the capacity for a comprehensive compassion, one which could encircle all of life. The unifying principle for me was compassion born out of a resonance with both the beauty and the suffering of the Earth, as well as wonderment at the magnificence of the universe. The religion of my youth, having become "enfeebled," created the imperative within me to cultivate a more religious mind. And a religious mind contributed greatly to my overall psychological health.

Depth of seeing

Little by little, I felt I began to see. Even more, I began to feel and to live more deeply. I was migrating toward a more open heart and a deeper faith. I came to understand myself differently within the context of the new story that was emerging, Feeling that I was part of the creative adventure as old as the beginning of the universe began to work its way into my moment-to-moment awareness. But it took work; and it took a practice. Time spent in nature and spiritual readings were part of it. Connection to a community exploring the new cosmology was also key. To be in a shared mental space kept me from falling into isolation, and the collective enhanced what I could do individually. But creativity was also crucial because it was taking action and involved the body and the senses. To some extent, I was able to let the feeling come through me in music and poetry. I composed piano pieces based on improvisations. Many of them began with the unforced movement of my hands on the keys, and action without thought, that started as a movement within. And the raw creation would always be more exhilarating and energetic, a more pure form of that movement, than a finished composition. The improvisation connected me to a larger harmony with life, and the music of the cosmos. When it was no longer an improvisation, it was no longer fully of the moment. It was like a snapshot of the moment that fades with time and only captures what is contained within a border. Then it was time to begin again with a new improvisation.

Similarly, a poem would occasionally come out of a heightened sensitivity with that same primal energy. At the end of one of these sessions on Teilhard, we took some time to silently walk the grounds of Santa Sabina in reflection on our dialogues. I stood in the presence of the live oaks, my awareness churning with the enormity of Teilhard's vision, with its fire and music; and it was as if the trees grew luminous from within. And my response at the time was the poem on the following page.

A Budding Sense

With only silence for company
I began to see. And what I saw
were trees aflame with music
in rhythm with the broad-arced sky,
each enamored with the churning Earth.

Nothing made sense, but didn't need to.
Inside, a stillness roared through
and in the ancient shrine of rock around,
in whose fire all great stories burn,
I wandered, my awareness a newly burning star
among old stars and younger trees aflame.

I breathed and waited and turned to stillness,
until the wind came back
and I felt a budding sense, a new flame,
which was my clue to the heart of hearts
which was our deeper pulse, our brighter flame.

LANDSCAPE INTERLUDE
Moods of a Mountain

This week the first heavy rains came to the Bay Area. This causes a stir of anticipation in me as I think about our local mountain. When the rains bring back the grasses, Mount Diablo begins to don a rich green shawl. The dormancy of summer ends this time of year and the transformation happens almost imperceptibly, a slow emerald spread across the flanks of the mountain. At its peak, in the clear, cool light of winter sunshine, the slow flare of green creeping across the mountain is magnificent.

When I first saw Mount Diablo in the fall of 1988, this fine green shawl was not yet thrown over her shoulders. My landing area in California was in the East Bay hills near Mount Diablo in Orinda Village. I lived in a former monastery. Outside the window of my room loomed a golden hillside. As fall surrendered to winter, my wife and I witnessed the slow verdant transformation of the hillside brought by the rains. It was evocative of the more subtly rolling hills of my native Midwest in spring. Except that here in California, the rains come in winter.

Across San Francisco Bay is Mount Diablo's sister mountain, Mount Tamalpais. The two mountains are a study in contrasts. Mount Diablo is drier, lighter, more open, and hot in summer. The habitat is primarily oak scrubland interspersed with coyote bush, chaparral, manzanita, and the remnants of grazing land. Mount Tam is dark, moist, cool, often fogbound, and shrouded with pine and towering coast redwoods. Gray whales can be spotted migrating twice each year past Mount Tam, and humpbacks can be seen breaching off her coast. Descend through giant redwoods on Mount Tam's western slope and end up on the Pacific Ocean. Descend through live oak woodlands on Mt. Diablo's northern slope and end up in the marshes of Suisun Bay.

The two mountains could not be more different in temperament and personality. I'm often tempted to see them as two aspects of the same Hindu goddess: Parvati, who embodies nourishment, harmony, love, beauty, and motherhood; and Kali, the fierce, dark goddess who destroys evil in order to protect the innocent. These two sentinels flank the San Francisco Bay estuary, standing guard over its rich community of life. No wonder the Bay Area is seen by some as a mecca, a portal to the spiritual world.

I've been getting to know the temperament of both mountains over the past thirty-odd years after hours spent on their trails. But the changing moods of Mt. Diablo hold a special place in my heart. Time on the trails is up close and personal. My sensitivity to those moods took a different turn for me during the several years I commuted on the BART train between Oakland and Walnut Creek. When I stepped onto the platform at the beginning and end of each day, I was greeted by a clear view of the mountain from a slight distance. What I began to notice was that each day brought a unique hue, a changed aspect to the mountain. I began to realize that as stationary and permanent as mountains seem in contrast to our rushed and harried lives, they are anything but static and unchanging. They shape-shift in an unending dance of light, rock, plants, clouds, rain, and wind.

I came to look forward each day to being greeted by Mt. Diablo's subtle shapeshifting. It was a little like rising each morning to my wife. One morning rowdy, another melancholy. One evening ebullient, the next quietly reflective. The humorous eddies of light on her summit could bring up a smile; the brooding furrow of a tankard gray cloud-head could elicit foreboding. A honey-blood wash of light in a winter's early evening cast her in radiance. A wash of light gray sky and she was aloof, distant, unreachable. The mountain, her weather, her unending dialogue with sky and light conjured a personality. At times, apart from her, I day-dreamed about past encounters, and longed for the next. How would I be greeted as I stepped onto the platform each morning and evening? Each day a new face, another mood.

The color green reflects just one of Mount Diablo's many moods. The range seems to span the spectrum of a painter's palette, melancholy indigo and jubilant gold; angry thunderhead gray and glowing amber; sullen, fog-bound cerulean and the washed ochre of summer; forest green cast in blueish light; menacing dragon asleep on a pillow of fog; innocent white snowcaps left by a winter storm; orange rain at sunset and dappled humps of twenty shades of green across the north slope. The emerald green of Mount Diablo is also the most ephemeral and brief of colors; its mood doesn't last long. But it wasn't always so.

Before cattle ranching overran the mountain, the green endured for much of the year. The native peoples, the Miwok and Ohlone, who saw the mountain as sacred, the origin of Creation, would have experienced a very different mountain, one that stayed green throughout much more of the year. This is because the native grasses that populated Diablo's flanks in pre-European times were well-adapted to the semi-arid climate. They had roots that grew far into the soil, and so they retained their verdancy into the hot, dry summer. The grasses introduced by cattle ranchers grew fast and abundantly but had shallow root systems. Largely dominant on the mountain today, these invasive plants quickly dry up and go dormant in the summer heat. Mount Diablo and her companion hills throughout the range turn golden brown.

But this was all from a distance of the train station. It was on the trails that things got intimate. Up close, on the miles of trails, was bird-rich, riparian habitat, soaring granite cliffs of Castle Rock, swaths and ribbons of live oaks; hidden waterfalls, fields of spring wildflowers and bluebirds; poorwills, owls, scorpions, and tarantulas at night; soaring hawks, plummeting peregrines, cruising vultures, and much more.

Now, I'm perched high up on Sugarloaf, one of two ridges cradling my home on San Crainte Creek. On one side, Las Trampas Wilderness; on the other, Shell Ridge, a foothill to Mount Diablo. Above, on the ridge, I can make out a line of residual shells from when the area was an ancient sea. Below me, is the valley in which I live. I trace the line of valley oaks that shade the creek as it flows into San Ramon Creek, then into Walnut Creek which flows for over twelve miles into Suisun Bay in the Grizzly Island Wildlife Refuge, just to the east of the San Pablo Bay estuary.

I look to the ground at my feet and see that the rain is already summoning forth the first tender blades from their summer sleep. To the east, Mount Diablo seems to simmer in anticipation, mirroring my own mood. Faint necklaces of emerald are beginning to glimmer on her flank. The season, however short, is imminent, and I'll be here to witness its passage. Summer dormancy is an odd thing for a native midwesterner like myself. Winter is the dormant season in the Midwest, not summer. The dead grasses of summer in California lie down on the hills like the cover of snow across the plains of an Iowa winter. Plants go dormant here in order to endure the searing heat and dry air, instead of waiting out the bone-biting cold of a Midwest winter. In winter here, the rains coax the grasses from their slumber. In the Midwest, the rains do their conjuring in spring. To get some semblance of a snowy Midwest winter, you have to go to the higher altitudes in California. The body knows what it knows and adjusts accordingly, eventually. But not without some longing for what it has known.

Mount Diablo is not a tall mountain, but that doesn't make her diminutive. The view from the summit (at 3,850 ft) is one of the most expansive in California due to the mountain's unique geographical situation. Mount Diablo sits on the edge of the Central Valley. The snow-capped peaks of the Sierras are visible to the east, the Golden Gate Bridge and Pacific Ocean to the west. Mount Shasta, far to the north, is visible on the clearest of days. Forty of California's fifty-five counties are visible from

Mount Diablo's 360 degree panorama.

This sacred mountain, more than anything, has taught me lessons in seeing. There is the middle distance view of her weather-formed, light-tinged mood shifts through the seasons. Then the close and intimate view of her hills, her manzanitas and oaks, her riots of wildflowers in spring to keep me joyous, snow peak in winter to keep me fresh, tarantulas and rattlesnakes at my feet to keep me on my toes.

Mount Diablo is a living being profoundly vibrant in temperament, color, and movement. There is seasonal movement, yes, but movement in time as well. If we could fast-forward time like a film, we would see her gallop across the face of the Earth. All the while, the smallest particles comprising her body arise and fall away on the quantum level. She bursts into and out of being again and again like a wave foaming onto shore. The view afforded from her peak is broad, an unparalleled panorama in California. To see far and to see widely, perhaps, is only a degree of separation from seeing more deeply. More deeply into time, into ourselves. The two feed each other, a dialogue of inner and outer, from which a brighter mood of reverence slowly winds its way.

Chapter 24

The Sacred Feminine and the New Cathedral

The world is just hurtling to destruction
without the feminine principle. And the Goddess
is not going to let that happen.[40]
—**Marion Woodman**

As I was writing this section on cosmology, I had a dream. I am seated in a dimly-lit room and I am bleeding from a wound on the top of my head. A woman with long, dark hair and dark complexion approaches me. She has a male companion, who walks behind her. She touches the top of my head lightly, then looks at her companion. They nod to each other in some kind of agreement, then he recedes into the background. Towering over me, she places both hands on the wound, pressing lightly with her fingertips. At her touch, I slip into a state of bliss. I can also feel her body against mine, and I feel held by a maternal energy. Her touch feels very soothing, healing.

This dream came as I was trying to reconcile a tension within me. The simple articulation of ideas in this chapter was in some sense limiting my ability to impart how cosmology had become a healing force for me. My approach was head-centered, cerebral. The dream helped me to realize that it wasn't the ideas that were healing, although they played a huge role in shifting my worldview. It was something much more ineffable, a mystery beneath the surface, a felt sense of my place in the universe. I was the universe reconciling pairs of opposites through self-healing.

I was bleeding from my crown chakra, representing the center of my spiritual soul, consciousness, wisdom, and prophetic thought. This was a hemorrhaging of a mystical connection, my transcendent awareness, my divinity. The Universe as Mother Goddess in the form of the Black Madonna was touching me in profound ways, first with healing hands on my crown chakra, but also with her very body. This contact put me in a state of profound bliss. I achieved an equilibrium as I accepted my body's intelligence every bit as much as my cerebral self. An integration, a sense of balance, a wholeness, permeated me as I contemplated the dream.

Resolving the tension between the cerebral and the sensuous wasn't enough. There had to be a healing of what Jungian scholars call the feeling function within me. Joanna Macy's work, which I mentioned in an earlier chapter, represented a path forward in this regard. She provided powerful rituals for grieving and for developing an empathy with all of life on Earth, back through deep time. There had to be an embodiment within me of the sacred feminine. The return of the sacred, conscious feminine is a realization that matter everywhere is suffused with light. There is no distinction between inner and outer. The field of light contains them both simultaneously, complements to each other, but unified.

The healing of trauma is found precisely in this greater realization of the unified nature of all things. And it is through ritual and telling the story that this realization is enacted. The self finds both individuation and completion. To expand on Marion Woodman's epigraph at the head of this chapter, she states that a balance is needed between the masculine and feminine principles within men and women. "Sophia, the goddess of wisdom," she says, "is the bridge that connects the head and the heart."[41] The rainbow, often associated with Sophia, is a symbol of that bridge.

The Black Madonna came to me in a dream to remind me to grieve. I continue to grieve my family's loss—the loss of innocence, the loss of community, and of a sense of safety. This grief also encompasses my culture's severance from the natural world. The Madonna, according to Marion Woodman, represents groundedness, the shadow side coming to light, the fertility of the Earth, the lust for life. "When she comes in a dream," states Woodman, "she is saying: 'I can take you to the feminine side.'"[42] For me, she assists me in metabolizing my grief into creativity. She creates a space within me for the birth of a new faith. I felt like Kristin's adoption of the ten-foot-tall, dark-skinned Indian woman dressed in blue was the Black Madonna infusing her with courage and wisdom, giving her the will to survive a horrible situation. This is the same kind of strength she offers us in her return to Western consciousness.

Teilhard and the sacred feminine

Over time, I came to realize that there are a number of ways in which Teilhard's vision affirms the power of the sacred feminine. He was both a scientist and a mystic. I came to see the mystical in Teilhard as a feminine infusion of sacred love into the masculine creativity of his thought. This is love as the fundamental transformative power of the universe.

Teilhardian cosmology overthrew, for me, the notion of inert, crass matter in the universe. Matter is not just inert, but has a radiant intelligibility, a psycho-spiritual as well as a physical component. Spirit has been present at the very heart of matter throughout the entire unfolding of evolution. There is an interior progression in evolution (a deepening) as well as an exterior one. And so there has been a progressive emergence of ascending forms of consciousness. Consciousness in the human has folded back on itself, become the universe reflecting on itself. This overturned the materialist mindset of the industrial culture within which I was raised. Matter wasn't merely an object to be exploited and manipulated to human ends. There was a divine spirit, a psycho-spiritual essence within everything from the beginning.

My mistaken notion that the human is separate from the emergent universe was also overthrown. The human is integral to the universe, not just in space, but in time, all the way back to the fireball that began the emergence. We are one with the body of the cosmos.

Finally, Teilhard saw that love is primary as the transforming power in the Universe, writing that "everything we experience and even everything that we see displays a singular 'bias' for *transforming itself* into love." The power of what Teilhard called "amorization" personalizes cosmogenesis, or the unfolding universe, and it is the avenue through which we see more deeply. "A current of love is released, to spread over the whole breadth and depth of the World," he writes.[43] The conscious, sacred feminine is the meaning infusing scientific cosmology, just as the Black Madonna represents the light in all matter, the energizing force that animates love-in-action.

All three of these insights from Teilhard felt to me like a return to the sacred feminine, not simply as an unarticulated, unconscious force, but as a light-filled and fully aware way of healing our rupture with the field of consciousness we share with all life. Teilhard might not have characterized this as the sacred feminine. But my inner image of "God" went from a male sky deity when I was a boy to the universe as Mother Goddess. I believe that the articulation of a new cosmology must take place within this realization, and not as a reiteration of masculine scientific cosmology of the past.

The creativity that has gone into the scientific enterprise is immense. It has given us remarkable insight into the universe. That creativity is in large part the masculine principle at work in the human psyche. Now, an infusion of the light in matter from the Black Madonna is required to take that scientific knowledge and transform it into a meaningful cultural cosmology. This is the masculine and feminine principles in convergence. The return of the sacred feminine is in a more conscious form from that of previous centuries, an intentional cultivation of its principles.

I realized that there was that of the sensuous in Teilhard. It was in the form of the divine feminine. His notion of closer union as fuller being is our unified consciousness. His enamorment with matter was a draw to the light within matter. His notion of amorization was the embrace of the universe as Mother Goddess. What earthy, grounded immediacy was lacking in Teilhard, but that I found in Thoreau, was resolved in the sacred feminine aspects of his thinking.

In a passage on the spiritual power of matter in "The Heart of Matter," Teilhard writes: "I tell you: even though, like the Sage of sages, you carried in your memory the image of all the beings that people the Earth or swim in the seas, still all that knowledge would be as nothing for your soul, for all abstract knowledge is only a faded reality: this is because to understand the world knowledge is not enough, you must see it, touch it, live in its presence and drink the vital heat of existence in the very heart of reality."[44]

Abstract scientific knowledge is given embodiment and infused with meaning by the sacred feminine principle returning in a conscious way. The Black Madonna represents the energy in all matter, the energizing force that animates love-in-action. Fundamental to the Madonna are groundedness, wisdom, fecundity, bounty of the Earth, Eros, and a fierce determination to save the planet. "There is a wisdom in matter that is taking us into a healing process," states Jungian analyst Marion Woodman, "into a blossoming that our conscious ego knows nothing about."[45]

The new cathedral and a new question

There is a collective creativity, that which Thomas Berry characterized as the Great Work of our generation that subsumes and transcends individual creativity: "the heart of hearts, our deeper pulse, our brighter flame," to use an image from my poem above, "A Budding Sense." In an earlier chapter, I wrote about my visit to the medieval cathedrals of France, puzzling over what our modern cathedral might be, and what might drive its construction. The way I have come to think of it is that our task today isn't to build some kind of new physical edifice nor even to simply design a green city rising from the Midwest plain, as alluring as that might sound. It is a much grander task, even more difficult, and yet closer to home. It is an internal reconfiguration that ignites an outer transformation, a fundamental shift in the shape and contours of the human. It is individual work, but inextricably collective. The task is to build a new kind of human.

The modern-day equivalent of the medieval cathedral is based in communion, a sensitized human who consciously participates in the mystery of evolution. Perhaps the Virgin Mary is reconfiguring herself as well as the encircling curvature of the universe itself, personalized, a story that could unite all people and religions. In this moment, as many people are recognizing, she is returning as the Black Madonna, her darkness representing the shadow side, or that which is not yet manifest in our collective consciousness. Matthew Fox writes, "A cathedral by definition meant the throne where the goddess sits ruling the universe with compassion and justice for the poor."[46] A functional cosmology, permeated with the wisdom of the sacred feminine, is the new Mary, driving our psychic energies. The Black Madonna is the return of the Virgin in conscious form, determined to save the Earth, bringing with her the energy of love-in-action, and the power of unitive experience.

I think I've come to see that the question "is the universe a friendly place?" is not precisely the right question. It's more: "How does the universe live within us and manifest as love?" It's not: "is the universe friendly to me?" so much as: "How can I bring my own creative powers to bear in the service of love, thus building a new reality?" For me, it was through the power of Radiance most strongly, but other powers were there within me as well. I'm still learning to recognize them.

The collective task of quarrying rock, transporting it, shaping it, and erecting it into a cathedral was now the task of retrieving lost wisdom traditions, and interpreting, shaping, and internalizing aspects of the Great Story. In that sense, we are each blocks quarried, transported, chiseled, and placed; or we are the rose and cobalt and amber shards of stain-glassed windows; or we are candles lit and quivering in the naves, dedicated to stations of the cosmos. Through the stories of our lives, an edifice begins to take shape, its larger contours unclear, but affording glimpses now and then through the example of a life, a compassionate action taken, a greater wisdom gained and shared. The new cathedral is the new human, thinking, feeling, and acting, fully integrated and whole, generating the future, with faith in the powers of the evolving cosmos, always nascent within and around us.

Chapter 25
Cosmic Citizen[47]

Planet Earth, turning and turning, transmutes the rays of the Sun into a dazzling multiplicity of form and expression, an alchemy of tassel and leaf, fin and feather, eye and bone; all are progeny of a planet in reverie. And the dream becomes life in its full tapestry.

The human, born from millennia of Earth's invention, trial, creativity, struggle, and increasing complexity, is the ultimate dream animal. Of all Earth's species, we are the lucid dreamer, the dreamer who watches the dream. Through the profound mystery of conscious self-awareness, the human reaches a depth of seeing never before achieved in the history of life; and depth of seeing is depth of being. Our gaze is Earth's gaze. It is a gaze into the mirror at the planet's beauty and diversity of life, but also to destruction and loss at human hands. The gaze is also an outward gaze, one that penetrates to the stars from which we've been created, and to the beginnings of time itself. Instruments of technology have become a kind of extension of our eyes. With the James Webb telescope, which became operational in 2022, we can now peer further back in time than ever before, 13.5 billions years in fact, far enough to witness the very early formation of stars and galaxies. Back on Earth, webcams set up in the nests of raptors and other birds bring us into their world in a way never before possible.

When I was an undergraduate, I took up birdwatching. Birds were on my radar as I grew up. I knew the common species. However, I had never actively and systematically sought them out. Every break from the books found me out in the fields and forests for hours in search of new species to add to what birders refer to as the "life list." I quantified, categorized, and made notes as any dutiful student of the natural world would.

One summer afternoon I headed for one of my favorite spots, a pristine stretch of creek that ran aboveground for several miles. The creek was shrouded by mixed deciduous woodlands for the entire stretch. I made my way for some time through this green arcade until I reached a small sandy area underneath an embankment along the creek. A weathered and sun-drenched log was the perfect spot for a rest.

The log warmed my back. Although it was a nearly windless day, the leaves began to move in a fantastic, sunlit dance. I felt the embrace of birch, elm, and willow as their sway and flutter came alive within me. The landscape seemed to radiate from within. The creek, following its natural course, was as alive in its relationship to its stony bed as the juncos were to the elm branch on the bank opposite me.

In my total absorption, the arrival of a night heron seemed natural, a perfect enhancement of the vivid dance. Her graceful glide and landing created a quiet joy within me. The heron fished, stalked the bank, and groomed herself in the shade of creek-side willows. I slipped beyond an awareness of time.

Heading home toward dusk I realized that the yellow-crowned night heron was a new bird on my list. But somehow that felt secondary. I had internalized a more primary knowledge, a seeing beyond intellect, a total immersion in the vitality of another being. That afternoon ruined me for birding in the way I had been accustomed. On subsequent birding trips, I was less absorbed in my "life list," and more in the unique presence of individual birds, whatever the species.

To feel internally the heron foraging, or the fronds of birch swaying, or the hawk soaring, or the salmon driving upstream, is to be freed momentarily from the blindness of a more conditioned self. In this freedom, there is a deepened capacity to see, to *discern*. Something that stirs in the breast of a hawk soaring has its equivalent in human joy. Something in the body of a salmon knifing upstream has its equivalent as human intent. And the heron foraging? Perhaps something as yet unnamed.

Discernment

"One could say that the whole of life lies in seeing—if not ultimately, at least essentially," Teilhard wrote. "The history of the living world can be reduced to the elaboration of ever more perfect eyes at the heart of a cosmos where it is always possible to discern more."[48] Discerning more, for the human, is seeing outside the confinements of the conditioned self. Doing so brings us into a relationship with a reality that is beyond the limitations of symbols and abstraction. It opens the door to beauty and thus, wonder. It brings us into the richness and fullness of the present.

I was once tutored on the importance of discernment by a trout. I was hiking the contours of an eastern Sierra stream not far from Tuolumne Meadows near Yosemite National Park and had stopped to lunch stream-side on a large, flat boulder. In the stream was a trout, nosing into the current, and yet at the same time suspended, as if on a string. I watched for some time as the trout rose periodically to feed on hatching flies. Although there was a good amount of leaves, twigs, and other debris carried on the stream's surface, not once did the trout rise to a false meal. There was within the trout a practiced discernment of when and when not to expend energy. When up against a human predator, the fly fisherman, this discernment can mean life or death. In a sense, the challenge of the fly fisherman is to break through the discernment of the trout with the irresistible offering. The fisherman must attempt to see as the trout sees.

I also once experienced discernment in a flock of goldeneyes and pintail ducks. The birds were gathered in large numbers, feeding in Drake's Bay, an estuary of Point Reyes National Seashore. From a cliff high above, I watched as the entire body of birds suddenly shot into the sky in response to the silhouette of an eagle slipping silently over the lip of the cliff. Moments before, I had mistaken the eagle for a turkey vulture, but the water birds had an instant and ancient recognition of the eagle's dark shape against the sky. Vultures passing overhead, although a similar shape and size to the eagle, hadn't triggered the same response. It takes energy to flee. Do it too often, when there is no danger, and you may well perish from exhaustion or hunger.

"To try to see more and to see better is not... just a fantasy, curiosity, or a luxury," Teilhard continued, "See or perish. This is the situation imposed on every element of the universe by the mysterious gift of existence. And thus, to a higher degree, this is the human condition."[49] He saw an increase of consciousness, of vision, as an imperative. The levels of discernment found in the trout and the duck, in all of life, have their equivalent in the human. In the trajectory of evolution, depth of seeing has complexified in the human being into conscious self-awareness. In the human, sight has become insight, the planet perceiving and reflecting on her own depths.

Reveries and landscape

Increased depth of seeing in the human serves to bring to light our unconscious allegiances. Those allegiances—whether they be to ideology, power, money, success, fame, or some ideal of physical beauty or immortality—shackle us to constant desire, to a sense of lack. They form a kind of central dream of our life which is often not apparent to us. One of the most powerful unconscious allegiances of our time is anthropocentrism. Its mystique has such a powerful hold on us precisely because—in the Western mind at least—it remains largely unconscious and automatic. Even for the well-meaning and aware citizen, this mystique is difficult to overcome.

These allegiances are very powerful because they come out of our landscape of formation. They have their source in our earliest experiences and create what Argentinian philosopher Silo (Mario Luis Rodriguez Cobos) identified as the "primary reveries" of our lives.[50] Our primary reveries are largely subconscious catalysts for our actions and decisions. They rarely operate on the level of everyday awareness. They may slip through to our awareness in moments of dropping off to sleep or waking, but they remain hidden to us most of the time. And yet they determine to a very great extent how we view the world, and often they blind us not only to valid action, but to the truth, even when we are confronted with it. Once we become aware of our primary reveries and the "reverie nucleus" (central daydream) guiding our decisions and our emotional orientation to the world, we can find more freedom in our actions. The term nucleus is apt because the nucleus of the cell is not only central and internal to a cell, it regulates the cell's activities. Silo posits that the reverie nucleus normally changes as a human being matures, but it can get lodged in an earlier life stage and cause a person to repeat beliefs and patterns of behavior that haven't evolved with a constantly changing world.

My primary reveries

A very powerful reverie, from early in my life was a felt need to redeem my family. I have come to see this as my reverie nucleus. It came out of a combination of the fall-redemption religion of my youth combined with the trauma-inducing events of my sister's kidnapping and my family's subsequent departure from the religions community. These had all been a key part of my landscape of formation. I needed to prove our worthiness, to rescue us from the shame of being the black sheep in our circle of family and friends. We had "sinned and fallen short of the glory of God." With this came the primary reverie of a drive toward perfectionism within me. Thus, everything I put out in the world had to be polished and flawless, otherwise I would risk shame all over again. With perfectionism came a fear of risk. I could be exposed as a fraud. This was a second primary reverie, the need to feel safe (is the universe a friendly place?). I wanted to be seen, but I feared the limelight. I sought connection and affirmation, but I couldn't allow myself to be vulnerable. Compounding these fears was a feeling within me, a third primary reverie, that people couldn't be trusted. The only people I kept close to me were those I knew to be trustworthy. I had to learn over time how this reverie operated, the distance it created between me and others. Eventually, I was able to feel more freedom to be spontaneous and vulnerable with others. I found this enacted in the way I performed on the piano. To risk improvisation was to be vulnerable. So it became one of the ways I found to heal the effects of trauma in my life.

To see myself as an embodiment of the creative universe played a key role in changing my reverie nucleus from that of fall/redemption to self-realization as a blessing in the universe. Polish writer and philosophy professor Henryk Skolimowski, who was deeply influenced by the work of Teilhard de Chardin, wrote about creativity as the essence of everything in the universe:

> *Why do we create?*
> *Because the universe creates.*
> *Why does the universe create?*
> *Because it is in its continuous*
> *Journey of unfolding.*
> *Why is it unfolding?*
> *Because it wants to make something of itself.*[51]

To see myself as part of a creative unfolding pulled me out of the small self concerned with appearances and my family's standing (and redemption) in the community and toward a more generous, expansive orientation in life.

Cultural reveries

In the Western world, we have difficulty seeing the mutuality of our relationship to the rest of the world because of the way we are brought up, our landscape of formation. The establishment of our primary reveries and the reverie nucleus makes it difficult for us to see things differently. To be in mutually beneficial relations with the non-human is an alien feeling for us. So, for example, in terms of climate change, even when faced with stark facts, if they don't resonate with a primary cultural reverie of a prosperous wonder-world, unlimited growth, and unfettered capitalism, they may not feel particularly real. Anthropogenic causes of climate change won't register as important, or register at all. Climate denial may not be so much willful as being stuck in maladaptive repetitions of belief and behavior.

A reverie nucleus won't change simply through intellectual discernment. It has to change through efforts that transform the basic psychological and emotional climate of an individual. There are two points in time when a reverie nucleus might change. The first is during the time of a major developmental transition in life, for example, from childhood to adolescence. This underscores the importance of rites of initiation for boys and girls as they approach adolescence. If a child is brought up to form an inner life that has resonance with the natural forms and primary relationships around him or her, an initiation will ripen a sense of interconnection throughout adolescence and into adulthood. The second impetus for change is through a significant shock, an event or life change where the reverie nucleus destabilizes and reforms in response to a powerful experience that changes one's worldview.

Writing about the importance of the natural world in the transition from childhood to adolescence, the professor of natural philosophy and human ecology, Paul Shepard, observed: "In the West, it is the failure of the adolescent's religious mentors . . . to translate his [/her] confidence in people and the Earth into a more conscious, more cosmic view, in which he [/she] broadens his [/her] buoyant faith to include the universe."[52] If we don't have an eco-cosmological basis within our landscape of formation, and if our unconscious allegiances—the things that we "worship"—are self-oriented, then we will fail to recognize that our actions are connected in any tangible sense to the wider world. We become alienated when we begin to believe the fiction provided by the dominant cultural reverie: that maturity means to "grow up" and acknowledge that the natural world is essentially without value unless for human use or as constituted by human consciousness. Everything outside human value feels like an abstraction, and our behavior follows suit. When something feels like an abstraction, no matter how soundly reasoned, it has much less persuasive energy around it. The Latin origin of the word abstraction is "to draw away from." When we abstract the natural world, the next step is to objectification. It is much easier to give one's assent to the destruction of something abstracted to the point of being an object. A living redwood becomes board feet of lumber, a living community of prairie becomes an acre of production.

Children and a sense of communion

A primary reverie, whether personal or cultural, is essentially an unconscious attempt to make up for a deficiency in the fulfillment of a particular need. It could be something more basic like the need for food, health, safety, or shelter, but it could also be the need for acceptance or approval by a social, familial, or religious group. One way to break through a dominant cultural reverie is to develop the capacity for really seeing our unconscious allegiances for what they are and realizing how they constrict our larger freedom as human beings. Shedding light on the hidden parts of ourselves that keep us captive within a realm of secondary concerns is the first step toward deeper seeing—which is a more refined discernment, and which becomes wisdom when internalized. This can be a lifelong process of maturation. The best starting point for greater discernment is with children. Their context—a maternal bond where they feel held and thus safe to explore, direct contact with natural forms, and the power of story grounded in evolutionary cosmology— allows them to build their interiority upon a landscape of formation that will connect them to something transcending the self.

The most powerful way to break through abstraction and denial is through direct contact with the tangible, ordinary reality of the natural world. This contact gives children a felt sense that they are not only on Earth, but that they *are* Earth, and that the planet is self-aware through their own senses and consciousness. If a relationship isn't felt, it atrophies. Without that felt sense, an assumption begins to take root that the only way to know the planet, a tree, an animal, another human being, is through the mind. Conscious self-awareness, as the deepest level of seeing yet to emerge in the evolution of the Earth community, cuts through that kind of objectification. You are not simply a subject *perceiving* the beauty and grandeur of the planet, you *are* the planet *feeling* its own beauty and grandeur. Through this kind of felt relationship, children can grow into an ever-expanding communion over the course of a lifetime, becoming adults who are more deeply initiated over time into the mysteries of ecological citizenship. This is the basis for the cosmic citizen, the truly mature human, the human of the future. It is also the basis for trust, which is key to a child's feeling secure in their existence. A child initiated into the mysteries of the universe and the powers and graces of the natural world can build confidence in the future and her role in it.

Ecological grounding gives children a sense of where they are, of place, of how they are related to the other-than-human. Cosmological grounding gives the child a sense of *when* they are, and how they are related to the creative arc of the universe through time. In the Western world, we went from a sense of time as cyclical—connected to the seasons and the movement of heavenly bodies—to a sense of time in the Industrial Age that is linear and tied to the hands of the clock. Evolutionary science and cosmology is presenting us with a sense of time as developmental, unfolding, and creative. "We can begin to reflect on the way in which time, in a cosmological sense, is the creativity of the universe itself," write Swimme and Tucker in *Journey of the Universe*. "There was a time for bringing forth hydrogen atoms. There was a time for bringing forth galaxies. There was a time when Earth became ignited with life. These are not indicated by anything mechanical, but by the deepest processes of the universe itself. There was likewise a time for the universe to bring forth the human species."[53] A whole constellation of discoveries coming in from physics and astronomy will need to be transitioned from scientific cosmology into a cultural cosmology—a story that meaningfully portrays us as creative participants in an expanding universe and evolving cosmos.

Both ecological and cosmological grounding are necessary, and they are deeply interrelated. Divorcing them has given us such false dichotomies as that between ecological and social justice. Both groundings are part of a continuum of the human maturing beyond a limited parochial perspective; they are not separate concerns. The ecological/social justice dichotomy is especially crippling for a society that aspires to democracy in any meaningful sense, and it is one of the key reasons democracy is failing in America in the early years of the 21st century. The very faltering of the Western democratic tradition is due to its failure from the start to draw on the foundations of ecology and cosmology. A false dichotomy between human rights and rights for all nature is the result. You can have one but not the other, we grow up to believe; but when you feel yourself within an eco-cosmological reality, you can't have one without the other.

The failure of our educational and religious institutions to initiate children into the mysteries of the planet and the universe is a key driver of this false dichotomy. Children who grow up not only with a sense of place, but of *story* (participating in a creative, time-developmental universe) will understand the connection innately. They will realize that to be informed citizens is to be part of a *biocracy* where rights extend to non-human species, landscapes, and watersheds. To afford these rights expands the overall potential of the whole to thrive. While there is no guarantee that any individual child will grow into a more mature, ecological citizen with a broader, expanded circle of concern, it is nevertheless necessary in order to provide a background reverie and formative landscape from which extra-human empathy has the potential to evolve. The acquisition of new, ever-deepening sensitivities in the human person is a refinement of seeing, an impulse that helps drive evolution forward. Chief among these new sensitivities is reverence for life.

This is why contact with nature is so crucial for children during their formative years. If a child hasn't been brought into proper relationship to the Earth, or even his or her own mother's embrace, how will he/ she ever feel the larger maternal embrace of the universe? My own early experiences in the natural world, and the fact that they continued throughout my life, served to form an ecology within me that helped me to withstand the debilitating effects of trauma.

The diversity of the planet enriches the interiority and the potential of the human, and it is through deepening communion as we age that we are brought into an ever-widening circle of freedom. That's what creates meaning as we grow. The formative connections of our childhood season and deepen. The ultimate source of meaning for the mature human is liberty from limiting identifications that fall short of our potential as individuals and as a species. Ecological citizenship finds its most mature expression in the cosmic citizen.

Discernment

The trout hangs, nosing up-current in the flow.
The stream's surface a vast membrane
carrying mountain slough,
pine jetsam, the hapless and fallen.

Stillness of trout, an old discernment:
Twig or damselfly, leaf or mayfly?
Food or danger, rise or stay?
Recognition from an old brain
spurs thrust of fin, flip of tail.

Succession of eyes down through time,
seeing ever more perfectly. Deeper
seeing, fuller being. To see is to live.

A person walks in the flow of the landscape,
stops. Around her, the lives of trees are told
in the angle and curve of the branch.
The land undulates with stories.

.

She sees for the first time what is written there,
and rising to the membrane of memory,
is nourished from within time,
flip of tail, her wave of recognition;
thrust of fin her power of intent.

The Mine and the Rainbow

A gray veil hung loosely across the face of the land. It was dawn, and dark phantoms of small trees and large shrubs were stirring underneath the quilt of mist hung over their shoulders. Now and then small dervishes of golden light pirouetted through, swirling away as quickly as they appeared. Dawn birds cast their first tentative songs into the quiet morning. My wife, Diana, and I were making our way silently through a nature reserve toward the San Pedro River. As we neared the river, a small glowing red orb appeared, swimming through the mist. Its flight undulated evenly, then settled onto the tip of a mesquite shrub. The little orb shuddered lightly as if to throw off the dew, then settled into stillness. After a short time, a second bright orb, then a third one settled onto the crown of a shrub. The three orbs sat apart, as if respectful of an agreed upon distance, occasionally looping out from their perches, and back again.

Vermilion flycatchers, our first sighting. I had ogled them in the pages of field guides for years. I thought: *What better way to make an entrance than through a gradually dissolving curtain of mist among swirling golden wraiths of light? Flying out of the obscurity of a book to become real.* We watched the flycatchers with delight as they swooped from their perches: out and back, out and back.

This flyway following the San Pedro River Valley was once the site of unparalleled biodiversity. The San Pedro is a major winter corridor and stopover for hundreds of migratory bird species. The river valley supports nearly two-thirds of the overall bird diversity in the continental U.S. More than 100 species of birds breed along the river. At least eighty species of mammals, including coatimundis, bats, beaver, mountain lion, and the extremely rare jaguar, call the San Pedro watershed home, as do more than 65 species of reptiles and amphibians, and the highest diversity of moths and butterflies on the continent. The whole of the region lies at the confluence of the Chihuahua and Sonora deserts, as well as two major southern ranges of the Sierra Madre mountains, thus accounting for its high diversity of plants and animals. People have been living and traveling along the river for at least 10,000 years, most of that time in small bands and villages that had minimal impact on the natural wonders of the area.

We would discover on this visit how the convergence of weather, distinct biomes, geographical and topographical complexity, and the plants and animals that thrived in its matrix would also generate a visual feast. The vermilion of the flycatcher was an early taste of the smorgasbord of color in store for us.

Deluge
After our hike on the San Pedro, we headed south. We were in a

bit of a rush, trying to outrun a monsoon that was speeding our way. Dark thunderheads pursued us as we drove, looming ever-closer in the rear view mirror. To complicate things, in order to get to our destination, Bisbee, Arizona, we had to double back at one point. This drew us directly into the storm's front edge, and the monsoon hit us full force, just before we reached Bisbee. The windshield wipers couldn't cope with the curtain of hard rain, so we pulled over, driving completely blind. The car tires crunching on the gravel shoulder were our only guide to a safe landing. Gusts of wind and water rocked the car, in a series of assaults. To help us wait out the deluge, Diana slid Keb Mo's country blues into the CD player, but we had to crank it up to counter the roar of the rains against the roof of the van.

Twenty minutes later, the rain and noise let up, and we drove into Bisbee under a bright sun that threw a sparkling seine of water droplets over everything. Approaching town from the west, we rounded a long curve. Reddish cliffs towered on our right. Opposite the cliffs was a vast open pit—the Copper Queen mine. Left out in the sun like an abandoned sandbox, the mine is the last trace of a desert mountain. But it is a mountain inverted, gouged-out, as if the extractive economy had smacked the Earth like an angry fist. There are before-photos of what was once a desert mountain at the future site of Bisbee. The after-photo depicts a yawning chasm, a mirror image of the mountain dug into the flesh of the planet. Its sheer size is mind-boggling. Even before the open pit mine was dug in a last ditch effort to find more copper, over 2,000 miles of tunnels bored into the Earth around Bisbee, descending as far as 3,000 feet. The open pit itself is 900 feet deep and spans 300 acres,. Now, at the nadir of the pit, acid mine drainage seeps into fissures in and through the rock. To stand at the lip of the Queen Mine at Bisbee and to really take it in is to take in the power of a story, one that literally moved mountains with its rapacious vision of limitless growth, wealth, and prosperity.

A new covenant

On the way up to our rental house, we are blasted by a second wave of rain. We dash inside, laughing and shivering, then dry off with thick towels provided by our hosts. When the monsoon eases up again, we look out over Bisbee from an upstairs balcony. A brilliant rainbow spans the sun-washed town from end to end. One end of the rainbow's arc touches down precisely onto a rock spire just above the Copper Queen.

"Wow! Cinematic!" Diana says.

"Even biblical," I add. *Begging a different promise from that of the Old Testament God that there would never be another deluge,* I think, *perhaps a new covenant the human has yet to make with Earth's larger community of life.*

The next day we descend 1,500 feet into the mine on a tour. It is a constant 53 degrees, damp, the smell of earth penetrating and close. There is scarcely a foot of clearance on each side of the trolley and above our hardhats. As we move deeper into the shaft, rough rock flows past like the flesh of a birth canal. I have conflicting feelings of claustrophobia and being held. I feel myself moving along the veins of a wound. We stop at a small cavity in the rock where an elevator once ferried miners to the surface. To tamp down my terror of tight places, I focus on the guide's voice, a former miner here: "When the veins began to dry up, miners dug the open pit mine you saw at the surface, searching for more copper. Instead of copper ore, they stumbled across turquoise, thought of as the 'rare blue lady.' They call it Bisbee Blue. Dazzling as peacock feathers." He held up a piece as big as his hand. "You can't find any turquoise with as deep a hue," he continues, "They gave each of us a chunk like this on the final day, before they closed the Queen. Me and the men I worked with were sitting in the lunchroom after work, each of us with a piece as big as this one. I look at it now and it reminds me of how the mine fed us all those years, my family, and so many other people."

Watching and listening, our guide's enthusiasm for the story of the mine ignites my own passion. I think of a new story, one of a benign human presence on a vital Earth with flourishing species. One where we see ourselves as part of a vast interconnected universe, not merely as pursuers of wealth, power, and consumer goods. I sense its power and promise, realizing that this could be the miner's guiding story too, and that of his grandkids and ancestors. I struggle to hold the incongruity of the two stories as the shuttle takes us to the surface. I take off my hardhat and safety vest and go to thank him for the tour and the story.

Color of consciousness

Looking at the deep hue of the turquoise in the miner's hands made me consider yet another experience of color we had while in the area. We had come there in the first place because of hummingbirds. Thousands of the famed feathered jewels grace the forested canyons of the Chiracahua and Huachuca Mountains. There is a concentration of hummingbird species in southeastern Arizona, more than anywhere else in North America. Their plumage refracts light into purple, chartreuse, tangerine, crimson, magenta, turquoise, and cobalt. And seeing them bends sunlight into our consciousness in the form of a rainbow.

There are at least three different ways we receive the gift of color from nature. There is the pigment in the feathers of the vermilion flycatcher; there is the refraction of light in a rainbow or a hummingbird gorget; and then the there is oxidation of minerals by water to give us gems like turquoise and azurite streaking the flesh of a mountain. The colors are rendered, the eye evolves to see them, the brain learns how to differentiate the hues, and the sensitivity develops within us to feel them as beautiful. This is what the Earth has wrought through the human, a being through whom the planet knows consciously her own splendor.

And then, there is the rainbow. Sophia, the goddess of wisdom, is often associated with the rainbow. The rainbow reconciles, connects and unifies in a dazzling arc of light and water that mirrors the curvature of the universe itself. Sophia reconciles Heaven and Earth; head and heart; human and all other living things. She is the conscious feminine come to restore balance to a world gone mad with destruction.

This year, because of a very wet winter, there was a super-bloom of wildflowers in my state of California. People were drawn from all over to witness it. Beyond the spectacle, we were also swept into awe by an idea—the super-bloom was so huge, it could be seen from space. The human isn't the only animal drawn to color. Pollinators, for example, are drawn in as well. The fascination of the peahen draws out the outrageous magnificence of the peacock's plumes. We don't know exactly what their experience of color is. But we do feel within us the stirring of the planet's heart at beholding the shades of blue called turquoise spun out of the dance of water with zinc and copper; and again when we take in the whole spectrum of iridescence blaring out from sunlight bent within a matrix of feathers. Or again, when we witness the color vermilion burning on a branch in the gray dawn from the encounter of carotenoid and a gene cached within the DNA of a tiny flycatcher.

This is the promise of the planet's rainbow display of colors, from flowers to geodes and gems, to feathers, sunsets and the aurora borealis. We stand as the Earth, transfixed by her own exquisite drama of play and toil down through the ages. There is so much more promise in this realization than in the stunted human aims of industrial plunder. The mine left standing in the open like an inverted monument at Bisbee has within it a potential blessing. We see the wound, but we can sense the healing.

While human beings created the story that flattened a mountain, human beings can also fashion another story, one with even greater power and holding out a better prospect for all life on Earth. Under the sway of a new story, one rooted in the lessons of past longings, the desire for wholeness, and the crucible of loss, we might do more than merely take. We might shake off the sadness, embrace joy, take comfort from a new covenant of gratitude and reciprocity.

Chapter 26

The Great Enamorment

*We would win, I thought steadily, if not in human guise
then in another, for love was something that life in its infinite
prodigality could afford. It was the failures who had always won,
but by the time they won they had come to be called successes.
This is the final paradox, which men call evolution.*
—**Loren Eiseley**
  The Inner Galaxy[54]

When I visited my ancestor's grave in Blije, Netherlands, many years
before my encounter with a new cosmic story, I did as we all tend to do.
The first impulse is to look into our human past, searching for a direct
line to the famous, the spectacular, and the noble, wanting to claim a
pedigree of accomplishment or beauty or power. We all want to feel
special. We want to know where we come from. But far beyond our
human ancestry, we already have a direct line to a spectacular ancestry,
one with a magnificent pedigree. It has the specialness of an incredible
story, one of feats and adventures way beyond quests and rescues and
the slaying of dragons. It has riveting tales of crisis and creativity, dramatic reversals, leaps forward, and harrowing escapes. And all human
beings share in that story.

Feats such as the invention of photosynthesis by unicellular organ-
isms who learned to snare photons from the sun as food. Plants burst
out across Earth and changed everything. With each meal and contemplation of a flower, I can remember those ancestors.

Feats such as the invention of respiration which started when a cyanobacteria, about two billion years into the story of life on Earth, began to produce oxygen in copious amounts, feeding off the limitless energy of the sun. Oxygen was toxic to life at the time; nevertheless, one of our bacterial ancestors evolved into the mitochondria which processes oxygen in the cells. This was an enormous new source of energy, and it would evolve into aerobic breathing that would drive the advance of multicellular life. With each draw of breath into my lungs, I can remember those ancestors.

Feats like the human hand, a marvel that can shape and nurture as well as destroy. I gaze at my hand and contemplate how it came to be that such a masterpiece exists. This hand can cultivate the future by sowing native plants in my little plot of Earth that will sustain pollinators and a host of other life. The same hand can move words onto the page that might live beyond the limits of a lifetime. Or this hand can hold another's in comfort and solidarity in life, or companionship in death. It can strike and destroy, or heal and build. When our ancestors stood on two legs, the hand was freed to become more than a means of locomotion. It could grasp, gesture, communicate, create, and feel the world in ways that would evolve into speech and supercharge human evolution.

And feats like the furnace of stars that forged the elements, then went supernova and sallied forth into blood, bone, flesh, and eventually self-organized into mind and consciousness. Those stars burn brightly in our consciousness, for those very stars became the early churning planet Earth, and the seas, the rock, the atmosphere, then the rudimentary consciousness that grew into a species that is the universe reflecting on its very existence. This is our amazing pedigree, a lineage to the stars themselves, also our ancestors.

So, as time passed, as I began to think of what I have been bequeathed from this evolutionary story, I have begun to consider not so much who my human ancestors were, but what kind of ancestor am I? How will I continue this lineage? What will I leave for future generations? Can I forge the care and compassion that will shape a future that builds on the "journeywork of stars," to use Walt Whitman's apt phrase?

One of the key reasons I changed my name from Smith to de Boer was that I sought a connection to the land. What could I as a Boer, a farmer, cultivate in the inner landscape? What could I help build through a love of and attention to the present? The self we cultivate and the actions that live beyond us are the pedigree that surpasses mere physical heredity. What we pass on to the future is no longer simply genetic but a trans-genetic legacy, that which, as ancestors to the future, we safeguard and generate.

In reverse-time, the twig of a human life pulls into branch; branch pulls into trunk, back to sapling, down into root, seed, soil, rain, mineral, humus, Earth, star; and we realize that this is a constellation of the self, our deeper identity. Clues to our identity may not lay solely in the past, but as much in the present, in awareness of the infinite spaces within. All of this constitutes a self. All of time and all of the ancestors are there.

Whose ancestor am I right now in this moment of awareness? What issues forth from me like the elements from a star? What is my unique constellation of the adventure of the elements, of argon and carbon and helium and iron?

Not long ago, my niece, Ember, asked me to take de Boer for her artistic name. She does compelling sculpture in the area of arts and ecology, work that celebrates the ancestors in its own way, using the ancient to hold the contemporary up to scrutiny. Her self, her unique constellation, is still rising within the matrix of that work. But she is already an ancestor at the ripe old age of twenty-something, cultivating the present for the future.

Perhaps one day "ancestor" will become a verb: *to ancestor*, meaning "to cultivate the ground of the self for the future." The eternal ancestor of the present, always generating. What we receive from the past we can give to the future. And yet, what we give to the future we are also giving back. Reciprocity is a re-creation of our origins, an act wherein you have to acknowledge that you are both back there and that you are here, creating the future with every action.

The tornado that swept through my family's life took a wrecking ball to my childhood faith, as formative and reassuring as it had been. The citadel of faith in a certain kind of God crashed down. My heart broke, my world fell apart, and my family and I entered a dark spiritual night that was characterized by the search for a new community and a groping toward a new faith. But on a cultural level, the religion of my youth had left me bereft in spirit because it had severed itself from our planetary home and the universe. In fact, it was generally antagonistic to the body, nature, the Earth, except perhaps as a reason to praise the Creator God. God was a deity above and Spirit was separate from matter and nature, which were seen as degraded forms of existence.

In spite of this cataclysmic breakdown in values and belief, I still carried within me the seeds of faith. Having known faith as a child, I set out on a search to find some semblance of it again as a young man. That seed of faith was looking for more fertile ground. Although I was unaware of it at the time, it was the pivot point where I began the process of finding true faith, a more mature faith, the fire of a new faith. Teilhard and the new cosmology that has come out of his lineage from various thinkers helped me form this new faith in the human. Combined with my love of nature, deep empathy for plants and animals, and an inborn zest for the community of life, I did find more fertile ground. Without the initial loss, I may have never availed myself of the creativity of the universe in so transformative a fashion. But without the discovery of a scientific cosmology that supported that creative reconfiguration in my life, I may have stagnated or regressed or fallen into addiction. The temptation to fall into addiction was always there, just over my shoulder.

Three concepts from Teilhard began to generate the psychic energy within me to deal with the "crisis moment" of my family trauma and the larger crisis of my society, which Berry has described as "a radical discontinuity between the Earth and the human."

First, is the interiority of all things. The psychic "enfolding" of the universe as complementary to its actual physical unfolding is key to Teilhard's thought. This interiority bound me to the world in a way that a dualistic Cartesian cosmology did not. The interiority that is present from the very beginning in the universe didn't simply give rise to my own; it is co-existent with my own.

The second concept is the capacity of the human for seeing more deeply and the power of reflexive consciousness. We only have to see more deeply the remarkable emergence around us to understand that the same powers that brought this into being exist within and around us, supporting us. As a basis for faith, it is both tangible and mysterious. We can reach out and touch the rough trunk of an oak with a sense of wonder. We can feel an affinity and love for the tree and wonder at the mystery behind that capacity, that it should exist within us at all. That the self-organizing dynamics of the universe could bring this power of contemplation into existence is a source of amazement in itself.

Rabbi Abraham Joshua Heschel wrote that faith is impossible without awe. "Awe precedes faith; it is at the root of faith. We must grow in awe in order to reach faith. We must be guided by awe to be worthy of faith." This is more than mere belief because is comes not out of concepts but from a sensual experience and feeling of amazement at the world. Beliefs can keep us tethered to fear because what we believe in is ultimately transient and thus subject to loss. Faith is also beyond simple hope for a better future, what some call "hopium;" it is an internal state born from a connection to the dynamics of the universe. Hope keeps us tethered to longing and what is not yet. We are drawn into an idealized future, and thus pulled out of the eternal present. Optimism is similarly bound to an ideal. Faith goes deeper than optimism because it forms the basis for valid action in the world. Optimism can make us feel absolved of taking action when it assumes that things will somehow right themselves.

Faith, on the other hand, awakens us to the time-developmental process of the universe. We begin to see that evolution complexifies over time and through that process makes the divine more and more explicit. Faith is permeated by a sense of a focal point in the future that draws us energetically forward but is also intensely present. This focal point in the future is what Teilhard referred to as the Omega Center. Omega is both a focal point of convergence toward which the evolution of consciousness moves, but it also "already exists and is at work right here and now in the deepest part of the thinking mass..."[55]

The third concept is the omni-presence of love-in-action, the "amorization" that personalizes everything in the universe. I came to see how this permeating love enriched my own creativity. My own creative energies couldn't be separated from a universe that is fundamentally creative. Fuller being is closer union. That which binds me to all makes me more deeply who I am.

Love-in-action

Driven by forces of love, the fragments of the world
are seeking one another so the world may come to be.
This is no metaphor—and far more than poetry.[56]
—**Teilhard de Chardin**

Every living thing, but one, is fluent
in the language of the Great Heart.
—Deena Metzger
 Ruin and Beauty

Our interiority, the inwardness that makes us capable of contemplation and reflection, is rooted in our kinship with nature. This is not just some vague affinity for the beauty of the natural world or the grandeur of scenic vistas or inspiring landscapes. It goes to the heart of our desire for relationship, what I see as the "great enamorment," something that pervades the universe throughout time and space. Teilhard writes in *The Human Phenomenon*: "If some internal propensity to unite did not exist, even in the molecule, in probably some incredibly rudimentary yet already nascent state, it would be physically impossible for love to appear higher up, in ourselves, in the homonized state. Since we have observed its presence with certainty in ourselves, we have every reason to suppose that, at least inchoately, it is present in everything that exists."[57] (p. 188, Human Phenomenon)

Our culture has largely shut down "the language of the Great Heart," as Deena Metzger writes in the epigraph in this section. The Great Heart is our unitive consciousness, the spiritual awareness where we feel a deep love and connection with all life on Earth, including each other. Relationship is the basis of the ecology of life on Earth, and is what drives the fitness of species. The notion of fitness in evolution has been misunderstood as simply competition, that nature is "red in tooth and claw" and only the strongest survive. But "fitness is relational," states Francis Heylighen, a Belgian cyberneticist known for his investigations into the emergence and evolution of intelligent organization. He explains that fitness is actually found in the capacity to form relationships. This is expressed best through the concept of synergy, meaning that "together you can do more than alone. Fitness is about minimizing conflict and friction and maximizing synergy."[58] Cooperation, in other words, is more of a driver of evolution than competition. In this light, Social Darwinism, the concept that only the fit will survive competition in a socio-economic setting, is not only pernicious, but wrong.

Our sensitivities to this relational nature, of our fundamental kinship with life, even with the most rudimentary particle in the universe, results in both an attitude of reverence (a feeling of respect for the divine inward nature of all life) but even more crucially, a sense of wonder. Wonder is energization of relationship. To feel amazement at the ground of our existence, the planet, the still unfolding evolutionary journey and our role in it, is to develop an unshakable faith. Not faith in "God," but faith in the becomingness of the Universe. If God is the term we use, it is God as verb. Wonder opens our hearts and allows us to deeply see the magnificence around us, and that is in constant supply. We live in an ocean of beauty. A regular practice of spiritual ecology helps to reawaken that great enamorment, keeping it central to our actions.

Why fight to preserve the beauty and integrity of the Earth? Because to diminish it is to diminish the ground of our faith. Sometimes a natural wonder can bring us into awe; sometimes music or a work of art incites the imagination; sometimes the beauty and elegance of an idea energizes us. These are all ways to awe. But then, there is a point where we enter pure presence, when all of these images and ideas fall away and we enter a state of emptiness, of stillness, that contains all things, the whole universe. And then we have found the freedom to be the universe as our most profound and aspirational selves.

This is a state of deep trust. The friendliness or unfriendliness of the universe can be measured in the extent to which we feel at home in a place, the Earth, the universe. Do we feel loved by a place, by the universe, not only in the fullness of our lives, but even in death? In this sense, the universe is not only supporting of our actions, but based in love. Teilhard makes a remarkable statement: "A love that embraces the entire universe is not only something psychologically possible; it is also the only complete and final way in which we can love."[59] I would add that it is the only complete and final way we can be loved.

To understand his statement, you have to understand what he means by the inwardness of things, how the universe not only diverges and evolves outward, but converges on itself in deepening interiority, driving beings toward affinity for each other. This convergence is the love of the universe pressing in on us at all times. And this affinity for each other is what drives the universe forward, not only into deeper interiority, but into greater complexity. Or, in a word, beauty. "Love alone is capable of completing our beings in themselves as it unites them," he writes, "for the good reason that love alone takes them and joins them by their very depths—this is a fact of daily experience. For actually is not the moment when two lovers say they are lost in each other the moment when they come into the most complete possession of themselves?"[60]

Caring deeply for another is finding one's own depths of meaning. We become fluent in the language of the Great Heart.

Chapter 27

Sacred Earth, Rising Within

"Earth, isn't this what you want: to arise within us, invisible?
Isn't your dream to be wholly invisible someday? —O Earth: invisible!
What, if not transformation, is your urgent command?"[61]
—**Rainer Maria Rilke**

We live in a cosmos that is evolving. This evolution deepens in complexity over time. This is the unfolding nature of evolution. Evolution also folds in on itself, deepening interiority. Complexity has given rise to consciousness. This consciousness turned inward, folding back on itself, as Teilhard characterized it, has given rise in the human to conscious self-awareness — we know, but we also *know* that we know. Thus, we are the species through whom Earth has become self-aware. The planet is aware of her evolution and place in the evolving cosmos through us.

We don't live in a dead and objectified cosmos. Every living being, each stone at our feet, every landscape, every mountain, every star flaring forth, has a story to tell. We become energized and our intelligence is activated through a sense of our kinship, our common story with all of life. Our intent becomes luminous through a basic trust built out of an awareness that there are shaping forces in the universe that can guide us if we open ourselves to their influence. We need only remember how evolutionary forces from the very inception of the universe have given birth to the phenomenon of galaxies, the birth of stars, geological formations, and a fluorescence of life on Earth to know that there are shaping forces in the universe in our favor.

Our deepest intelligence is activated through what I call "cosmoriginal awareness." Cosmoriginal is a word I coined to refer to something arising from the depth of wholeness, out of depth of seeing, of awareness. This is our intuitive connection to the sacred Earth. It's related to the word *aboriginal*, or "having existed from the beginning." The philosopher Pythagoras first used the term "cosmos" for the order of the universe. Geographer Alexander von Humboldt excavated the word in the nineteenth century, using it as the title of his five-volume treatise, *Kosmos*, a work which contributed to a conception of the universe as one interacting entity. The word "original" comes from the early sixteenth century: from French *origine*, from Latin *origo, origin-*, from *oriri* 'to rise.'

The cosmos, the sacred Earth, rise within us.

This is an awareness beyond mere discursive thought and deeper than human language can fully express. Aligning ourselves with the profundity of the universe ignites our unique genius. This genius, as it finds expression, becomes a strong center that collaborates with other centers (the genius of others) and finds synergy. This process of synergy activates evolution toward deeper complexity, more pervading beauty, and divine expression. We find purpose through self-expression in synergy with others. It gives us a sense of the future.

Story is inherently ecological. Just as nature has created the tapestry of green and ochre and blue that is our planet, the human being has woven a tapestry of stories. Story and nature are in a constant dance. Our creation of story comes out of a sense of place and explores relationship on many levels. Traditionally, story works within a cyclical reality — the changing of the seasons, the migrations of animals, the rhythms of germination, blossoming, ripening, and decay, dissolution, and return. The emerging story begging to be told in our time is that of the development through deep time of an ever-complexifying universe.

Cyclical reality is contained within that story, circles within a spiral. The data coming to us from the sciences about the universe is being increasingly interpreted through the lens of psychology, religion, and the arts and humanities in a collective effort to create a meaningful cultural cosmology. What this cosmology would look like would be in part a reintegration, a return to our sense of kinship with all life. But even more so, it will have the aspect of a ripening and a fulfillment. We will have reached a new level of complexity in the evolution of life on Earth.

Self as universe

It was 2017 and we were coming out of a long period of drought conditions in California. There was so much water that year from the winter rains, that they were calling it a one-hundred-year event. Standing at the base of Yosemite Falls, in the looming presence of granite, and the waters just bursting out without end, booming over and through the land, I had a visceral feeling of the presence of our planet. I could just feel the immensity and power of Earth, water flowing like blood through her veins, inundating her crust. And the light... at certain times of the day, the falls of Yosemite Valley were misted and festooned with iridescent gold, luminescent formations of spray, and shimmering rainbows.

It got me to thinking about John Muir and his use of the word "glorious." It's not a word used much anymore, but it was one of his favorites, especially when he was referring to the Sierras, which he called the Range of Light. Muir had an almost ecstatic sense of nature. He was North America's premier nature mystic, and few, if any writers since approach his sense and articulation of the sublime. For him, the natural world was often suffused with the divine. The word "glorious" has connotations of magnificence, beauty, splendor, and delight. But also an older sense of "bliss," or the "bliss of heaven."

How do we approach this kind of ecstatic sense today? I think that it is latent and buried within us, and that it is largely connected to the body. Today we are suffering from a disease of dislocation in time and disembodiment in space. Ideas can be inspiring, they can intrigue us with their power. But can they bring lasting transformation, a new way of being human, without a grounding in the wisdom of the body, without an infusion of the ecstatic?

We are primarily embodied beings; and we do live in time and space. So perhaps our way there is through an awareness of *where we are* — a fullness of presence to our place as a way of re-instilling bliss, awe, and wonder. But in addition, an awareness of *when we are*, our part in the story of the universe, an event in which we are participants, gives us a sense of meaning and purpose.

Muir was often out rambling in the mountains; he was in his body a lot. He sensed in this way the radiance of the mountains and the pines. But in a very real sense, I think, we have an additional tool at our disposal that he didn't. We have both an awareness of place and of a unifying story. Our story of the universe is more comprehensive than in his time. And this emergent process of the universe has resulted in something really quite remarkable: the appearance of a being through which the universe reflects on its own magnificence. The human is the way through which the universe feels the glory in a sunrise, a pine forest, or the light in the Sierras. My wife Diana and I have returned many times to those mountains because of that radiance of light, sensing the glorious within it.

Along with a renewed sense of place and of time, I think a third sense is needed — a connection to what artist Agnes Martin has called our "unconditioned self," to a lexicon that is more fundamental than human language. Presence to story and place helps us open to this self. The unconditioned self is a place and a capacity within us for stillness and patience that moves us beyond our social conditioning, beyond thought, beyond ideas, beyond words, a pure and embodied presence to everything around us. We wait in readiness for a deepening state of self-awareness, a mind that is connected to the larger ecological Self. I believe this third sense is the most basic. The purpose of life, to me, might even be seen as getting to know the true unconditioned self. This part of us is what can swim in the "glorious," truly feel it as a part of our identity. It's always an unfinished practice, but a practice is what embeds meaning into human existence.

This is cosmoriginal awareness. To be *cosmoriginal* means, to me, to feel a mystical union with all that is, to feel that in both space and time. It also means a return in one's thinking, to draw on the energies of primal knowledge. However, it also indicates a capacity, in the present, to dive deeply into the language of the Earth and the universe for a richness that is still only nascent in human symbolic consciousness.

Essentially, cosmoriginal awareness is a remembrance of our essential nature. As real as living in our bodies might seem, and thinking with minds that appear to be independent of the world, we are not separate bodies, and our minds are linked to a larger consciousness. Our senses, feelings, and mental formations are temporary manifestations. And so, the practice of cosmoriginal awareness, liberates us from fear. It is the ultimate security, the only real source of peace. We know that even death is only a phantom arising from our thinking mind. We are the universe; that is our true identity, the only ultimate reality, and death delivers us back home. I have come to realize that in my own story; it is this internal sense of our origins that has held the most profound healing for me. It is a healing from the trauma of radical severance from the sacred essence, one that is constantly reshaping me and supporting my actions.

Invisible Earth

Earth invisible, rising within us. We cease to see the planet as other. The feeling sense of our being embedded is so deep that objectification isn't possible. The "urgent command" of transformation Rilke writes of. It's what I felt when, after many months of identifying and writing about native oak trees in my region to create a *Pocket Guide to Northern California Oaks*, one day I felt all of the names drop away, and I realized that I was *feeling* the oaks as an ineffable presence. Each oak I encountered, even those just emerging from the acorn at my feet, seemed alive in a new way within me. The easy part was learning the names. The more subtle and sensitive way was learning the way of oaks, getting a sense of their essence which can only happen in wordlessness. And the way of oaks participates in and supports a whole panoply of life, from fungal networks to acorn woodpeckers, each with a nameless numinous quality. Their power might not rest in a name, but that doesn't mean they don't speak to us through their presence.

I was thinking of the term "cosmoriginal" as I watched surf scoters diving not long ago on the shoreline of Point Reyes National Seashore. Surf scoters are masters of the waves. They hover at the lips of the waves, dancing precariously. As a large wave approaches, you think it will completely decimate the bird. But then, just before the wave crashes, the scoter blips out of view like a particle becoming a wave. It dives and swims underwater in search of nourishment. And then, if you wait for it, the bird bobs up from the depths to ride the surface of the waves again. I've seen scoters ride waves cresting to well over ten feet, waiting until the last minute to disappear into the body of the wave just as the crest turns to foam.

The cosmoriginal human is a human being who ideally navigates depth and surface with equal fluidity, and by doing so becomes someone who is deeply actualized as a unique expression of the universe. The cosmoriginal human is someone who has become better at being the universe through a sacred and primordial alignment with its dynamics. This is both an actualization and a return. We must align ourselves with the living cosmos, align ourselves with Earth process. To the greatest extent possible, work with Earth process to regenerate and preserve biodiversity. There may be great destruction ahead, but there will also be the birth of something new that we can't yet ascertain in the evolution of planet Earth.

In much the same way as the hero's journey sees the hero individuate from the community from which s/he developed and grew, and then ultimately return to the community in a more mature aspect bearing gifts, the human race is also attempting a return. Western culture took a hard break from its origins through Cartesian dualism in Western thought and fall/redemption theology in religion. Original sin and the attendant need for salvation was ultimately a loss of connection, and an atrophy of the capacity for gratitude and wonder for the world of nature from which we evolved. We lost touch with the paradise from which we originated, expelled by our discursive, analytic mind, but our basic need for belonging and purpose was never fully addressed. We fall into addiction and violence because our very nature has been violated, a rupture has taken place between us and the root of our being.

Part of the return involves a more mature outlook based in the reality that we are born not in sin, but as active agents in a universe blessed with creativity and beauty. Rather than fallen, we are integral to the unfolding process of evolution and inextricably connected to the world. To the extent that we retrieve that awareness we expand our capacity for joy. We reach joy through a deepening of intent, just as the salmon driving upstream contains a zest within to reach the pool high in the mountain where it dies and whose body returns to the river and feeds the continuing saga of future salmon. The salmon's existence as an individual fish in the stream dissolves back into the larger story of what it means to be Salmon within the greater community of life. The life of the salmon and the life of the river and the sea cannot be separated in that enactment. Nor can the human; and that is when Earth "rises within us, invisible."

As a species our egotism has given rise to a profound divisiveness and has been so destructive of our world. We have seen the implications of an ego-driven world. Love is a choice, but it is a choice we can make only when we can set aside the ego demands of our conditioned self. Now we must move beyond hubris and embrace our greater destiny as cosmic citizens. It begins with the building of a planetary identity, one where we truly see ourselves as Earth dreaming and giving birth to her own future. This is our new story, the tale still being told.

Chapter 28

Awakening into a Sense of Future

Humankind is being led along an evolving course,
through this migration of intelligences,
and though we seem to be sleeping,
there is an inner wakefulness
that directs the dream,
and that will eventually startle us back
to the truth of who we are.[62]
—**Rumi**

We live in a dream, and yet we are unaware we are dreaming. Education, a human life, the process of individuation are all potential paths for awakening. Taking in the depth and mystery of the universe story awakens us from the slumber of consumerism, individualism, and tribalism into a greater sense of the human as an active agent in the evolving universe.

The prospect of awakening to greater freedom and to a more meaningful role for the human is a familiar motif that has surfaced in film in recent years. Films such as *Dark City*, *The Thirteenth Floor*, *The Matrix*, and the *Truman Show* have borrowed from a theme from Gnostic literature of a populace inhabiting a dark city (a state of being unaware), and gradually waking up to its true situation. The latter film speaks more directly than the others to the mystique of consumerism and the fabrication of an idyllic wonder-world that is so characteristic of the

Western industrialist worldview. Truman Burbank, the main character, lives within an artificial and manufactured world, the town of Seahaven, which is, unbeknownst to Truman, a vast movie set built within a dome so huge it is visible from space. Every moment of Truman's everyday life is broadcast as "The Truman Show" to billions of people around the globe, completely without his awareness. Truman's clothing, the food he eats, the car he drives, as well as those of the Hollywood actors who are his fellow townspeople are consumer products that can be purchased by viewers. The advertising of consumer products becomes one and the same with Truman's day-to-day use of them in an eerie depiction of human identity as consumer. As Truman slowly wakes up to his situation, the film's narrative shifts from its predictable ground to his dramatic efforts to escape to a greater freedom outside the safe bubble of Seahaven. This ancient Gnostic theme calls us to break through the mystique, the predominate Dream of material consumer culture, and to awaken to our larger spiritual nature. This Dream, in American culture, one that is reinforced on all sides by social media, the corporate media, and advertising, has been largely based on the rape plunder of the Earth, an assault on the body of our planet.

But what are we waking up to? In an early chapter I wrote about what seemed like miraculous occurrences that saved my sister's life. What I've come to realize about the miraculous since then is that it is all around us constantly. You could even say that it is what has brought us into existence. We are here in spite of overwhelming odds against our emergence. When you consider, for instance, that the rate of expansion of the universe is just optimal for anything on Earth to exist. At an infinitesimally faster rate, the galaxies wouldn't have formed. Infinitesimally slower and the universe would have collapsed.[63] Any closer to the sun and the Earth would be molten; further away, the temperature would be too icy for life to survive. At an evolutionary moment when a new toxin appears, an organism learns to use it as food, and respiration becomes the breath.[64] Life finds a way. These were breathtaking "edge of the knife" moments where the conditions for life and consciousness to continue to emerge and complexify had to be "just right." These "Goldilocks" moments meant that either the miraculous was inherent to creativity, or that there was an overall guiding presence to the process. The cosmic story is full of such "moments of grace," as Thomas Berry has named them, and he identifies our current moment as one of them: "There are cosmological moments of grace as well as religious moments of grace. The present is one of those moments of transformation that can be considered as a cosmological, as well as a historical and a religious moment of grace."[65]

Our personal lives are a mirror of the universe in its unfolding. When we peer into the details of our stories, we see the cosmos gazing back. This is true of moments of grace as well as cataclysm. In fact, moments of grace often come out of crises. Alongside the personal sense of trauma from my family history was a growing sense within me of loss and grieving over the destruction, and the despoiling of our beautiful garden planet, of the irreversibility of species extinction. In a sense, it felt like I was losing my newly-found community to the destructive side of human nature, just as I had lost my boyhood community of believers due to the violence against my family by the perpetrator. My kind was now the perpetrator of a great vanishing of species, a radical diminishment of Earth's life support systems. What should have been inviolable and protected in my sister also should have been inviolable and protected in the Earth as well. And yes, I was the product of a culture that was largely and willfully blind to its own rape and plunder. Something sacred was being violated, and the grief was almost unbearable.

If I had gone along without cosmology, spiritually adrift, a person without a functional story, I might well have fallen into a state of irreparable despair. I might have found other spiritual paths, for instance, but none of the paths that I encountered were anything more than newly minted experiments under a New Age rubric or under older, tried and true traditions, but without a meaningful understanding of their wisdom. While these traditions were certainly powerful, and germane to people down through the ages, they no longer seem sufficient to the task of defining who we are as a species on planet Earth, and what our future might hold in the evolutionary process. A scientific cosmology, now being interpreted by evolutionary philosophers like Brian Swimme into a usable, cultural cosmology that is relevant to the current stage of human evolution, offers the potential to unite the power and beauty of the world's religious and spiritual traditions with a new sense of the human within the universe.

Had I remained within the bubble of the fundamental Calvinist spiritual beliefs into my adulthood, I might never have extricated myself from this particular form of conditioning. I might never have taken off with my young wife in a somewhat beaten-up, powder blue Plymouth Valiant down a path that led me to a new vision of what it means to be human. To feel myself as part of a creative cosmos in which divinity is deepening through complexification, has given me the impetus to find meaning in my life. In a word, it has given me a new faith in the human as an active, creative agent in the future.

In a certain sense, Teilhardian cosmology brought my concern for the Earth into a new order of expression and intensity. It cast each species as a unique emergence, as unprecedented expressions of complexity, strands in a story as grand as the universe. This view rescued me from the despair, pessimism, and the inevitable personal depletion of energy that occurs in a meaningless and purposeless universe. There was a change in my consciousness. What I had to come to see was that the human had come from within the evolutionary process, and was not a mere addendum, anomaly, or a mistake. What I had learned to love in the Earth had come from my direct experience of being held within the embrace of the natural world as a boy who had lost his spiritual community.

The story of original sin and the human born into a fallen state seemed quaint and powerless in the face of a new story: that we are a blessing, not a curse, and the human, far from a desecration of the planet, was a shooting star lighting the darkness with conscious self-awareness. It was one thing to stand on the Earth at dawn, to feel her great curvature, feel her turning. But to stand there, and know that I am the planet aware of herself, feeling the beauty and the birth pangs in the poignancy of death giving birth to life was to awaken to a sense of the future. Curve of Earth, curve of cosmic mind. In myself and all of *Homo sapiens*. We are the universe aware of itself, standing in a state of wonder.

Ultimately, the contradictions I felt between the Romantics, American Transcendentalists, nature writers and Teilhardian cosmology dissipated, and I came to see them as powerful worldviews in dialogue, not in conflict. I could hold them both, and in that container, my soul grew. There was both intimacy and individuation, self and Self, immanence and transcendence, Gaia and Cosmos. What I felt on that hill outside of Iowa City was now given a new depth as well as an outward expansion. The planet turned, not as an isolated "blue marble," but as part of a story in a universe that was still being completed. And humans not only had a role, but were indispensable in a key way. Our self-reflective consciousness was the latest unfoldment that complemented, and was nested within, the unfolding of the cosmos. The Earth has its own spirit, its own spirituality, with an interiority in and of itself that was commensurate with, but independent, of my own. The "within" of the Earth was both integral to the within of myself, and of its own genre and expression. Within the Earth's membrane, I was both an interdependent organelle, but also vital to the larger cell of the planet.

As are we all. We each have our unique constellation of gifts, and it is through giving them that we each become indispensable to the whole.

But there was something even more powerful than all of these. Watching Earth roll the Sun into view from the crest of the hill, with the stars still visible but fading slowly from view, our own daystar drowning out their glow with its own light, was a mind-blowing event. I was seeing the stars that actually gave birth to me and my kind. I *was* the planet looking to her origins, knowing through my self-reflective awareness that she was the creation of those very stars. And so, I was the stars, looking at the stars, aware of their own beauty, aware that even they too will die one day and be transmuted to countless other forms. And finally, that I embodied Earth's awareness of the evolutionary miracle that brought us here. Healing, as the Universe, is an expanding process, not finished, not perfect, but always complexifying into greater beauty.

This is what gave me a sense of the future. The fact that we have a choice is empowering. It gives us a feeling of relevance and a celebration of relationship, and in a way, it is what makes us indispensable. Our arrival was inevitable as the universe deepening in beauty and complexity. And we are not simply individuals striving toward private ends, but a community moving into the future. I would venture to say, that the energy compelling us, Rumi's "inner wakefulness that directs the dream," is love. Here is Teilhard, in *The Human Phenomenon*:

"In its present state, the world would be unintelligible, the presence of the reflective within it would be inexplicable, unless we suppose there to be a secret complicity between the immense and the infinitesimal to warm, nourish, and sustain to the very end, through the use of chances, contingencies, and freedoms, the consciousness between them both. It is this complicity we must bank on. *The human is irreplaceable.* Therefore, however unlikely the perspective may seem, *humankind has to succeed,* probably not necessarily, but infallibly."[66]

As I was completing this book, my wife Diana and I attended a ceremony, a celebration of the unfolding of the cosmos, at Grace Cathedral in San Francisco. It was an experience that brings us full circle to the balancing act I wrote about in the Introduction. The sacred intelligence of the body, the intellects of our gut and heart, must be brought into dialogue with that of our head. Practices and rituals that embed within us a felt sense that we *are* the universe unfolding are as important as the ideas of the new cosmology. These ceremonies can integrate the best parts of us—the artist, the scientist, the philosopher, the lover, and the spiritual ecologist to form the basis for a transformation in the way we perceive ourselves and the universe. When the whole of our intelligence comes into contact with the present moment, we are truly embodied. Then we are the universe fully aware of its unfolding.

The event took place fittingly in the soaring cavern of a cathedral, reminiscent in a way of the stone caves of our ancient ancestors. In fact, Brian Swimme spoke briefly that night about ancient humans going deep underground to caves where they would come to paint the first symbols of animals on the walls. They were etching their memory of real animals into the pores of rock, an act that may have marked the very beginnings of symbolic consciousness.

A hundred or so of us were positioned in a circle around an ancient labyrinth etched into the floor of the cathedral. A length of white rope had been laid in a spiral over the surface of her labyrinth to represent the unfolding universe. Our ceremony began with conscious breathing and a settling into our bodies. Then we began a slow rhythmic movement originating in the pelvic floor. Acoustic flute and handbell music bathed our ears. A young woman walked the spiral in dancelike, graceful movements as our emissary from the cosmos. She lit a candle for each point of transformation of the universe story, as the voices of

Brian Swimme and Kacey Carmichael resonated through the cavernous space, naming each evolutionary emergence. After each lighting of the candle, there was a call and response as we put our folded hands first over our hearts and then outward into the space before us:

In this Emergence
We see with awe and wonder
The Universe shines forth

When the walk of the cosmic spiral was finished, we all held a beeswax candle, looking around to see over a hundred points of light illuminating the faces of the other people there with us. It created a profound sense that the experience was communal, that it unified us in a world torn apart by war, addiction, and alienation. The fire in each hand called us back to the caves and forward into the future. But it also made us profoundly present.

The combination of words, movement of our bodies, and nonverbal expression were the balancing act. Just what we need now as we feel our way into a new way of being human, embedding this awareness more deeply into our beings.

Afterword
A Return to the Fold

I feel like I've returned to the fold, but it is the Fold, a much higher integration of spiritual community than that of my boyhood. It was a movement beyond herd mentality and certainty to adventure and flux, a more cosmic perspective. This book has been an attempt to chronicle that movement.

My father returned to the pulpit after over thirty years, when he was in his late seventies and early eighties. The minister of his local Unity Church pounced once he found out my father had been a preacher, inviting him to share his insights and life experience. These sermons were informed by his spiritual growth in the years since he left the ministry. One of them was a reimagining of the Lord's Prayer in a more cosmological way. He passed in 2018.

My mother survived him by a little over two years. Kristin and her husband, Lynn, gave her a dignified death by taking her into their home for those two years. My mother had spent her last two or three decades in a group, reading and discussing spiritual ideas that expanded her notion of the sacred. The expansion of her spiritual views never stopped her from treasuring many of the hymns that gave her comfort when she was younger and Christian. These were played at her memorial, as well as some more contemporary music.

My sister's story is more open-ended. Healing from trauma is a lifetime of work. She continues to this day as her life unfolds beautifully into courage and wisdom. She went into a healing profession, working as a hospice nurse for many years. Another part of that unfolding has been the raising of a beautiful and creative daughter. My brothers each raised two children, who in turn surrounded my parents with grand children and great grand children as they aged. My own progeny have been of a less biological type.

A big part of my culture's story has been a collusion in a great secret, a period of silence about the true condition of our existence. That best-kept secret has been our belonging to the community of life, that we are not just inextricably embedded in the universe, but that the universe lives within us, that we *are* the universe weaving a great story. And that we are held in that web of connection and cannot fall out. As with all secrets, it begins to fester under the weight of silence. But there is a turn back toward the sacred in the culture, even in the midst of more and more challenging crises. The universe wants to know itself within us in every moment. Gaia wants to be known again as the sacredness in the world, and she is a formidable force who will not be silenced.

Author's Note

This Fable came to me in a dream as I was in the throes of writing the book. I wrote it from start to finish in one sitting of two or three hours. I consider it a communication from my subconscious. Dreams and their images can be a commentary about life, an exploration of our time that comes from our deep time origins. In that way, they can help us look toward the future. It is a different kind of writing, meant to convey images from the inner landscape, not appeal to the discursive mind.

POSTLUDE
A Cosmic Fable

There was once a boy who lived with his clan on an island. He fished the waters surrounding the island almost every day. The waters were at the convergence of the sea and the rivers flowing from the north. One day, when he was quite young, he was told by his father never to venture near the land mass to the south. "Long ago our ancestors fled those dark tree-filled places to a better life here, where we want for nothing," he told the boy, "to go ashore there is to die." Then as a reminder, he gave the boy a knife. "Wear this always on your belt for protection. You will now be able to find food for the village. It is also good for cleaning fish."

As the boy grew into a young man, he learned the language and customs of his clan. But he also grew to know the currents of the waters that circled around and nearby the island better than almost anyone else in the clan. And he knew the fish living in the currents. He knew which currents would sweep him in the direction of the southern lands, so that, heeding his fathers' advice, he kept his distance.

There came a time when the clan was no longer flourishing. The waters grew toxic, animals scarce, the land grew sterile, and crops failed. One day, very early, while the others slept, he took a boat out around the southern tip of the island. He took a burlap bag of dried fruit and a canteen of pomegranate juice his mother had prepared for him for his next fishing expedition. Just as the sun rose and stretched bright fingers across the still surface, the boy looked into the clear waters and saw several large dark shapes pass beneath the boat.

"They move slowly," he said to the wind, "with your breath in the sails and my effort with the till and the oars, we will keep pace and the village will be fed with the bodies of these great fish."

He set himself in pursuit, keeping pace with the dark shadows beneath the surface, forgetting time and himself in the process. Soon, the shadows dove deeper and out of sight. The boy found himself far from the island. Having forgotten the currents, he found himself swept toward the southern lands. The boat moved swiftly and as he approached the shore, it ran violently upon a shoal of rocks and was splintered to pieces. The boy managed to grab the bag as he was thrown overboard, but the canteen was lost to the waves. He fought the pounding surf which tried to pull him to his death until, exhausted, he pulled out on a beach. He was bruised and bloody from the rocks, but he managed to stand and walk into the forest. There, he sat, bleeding and weak, beneath a large oak with sheltering branches.

As day fell into dusk, the boy heard the voice of a young woman, "what do you carry in the bag?"

"Dried pears and apples from my mother's orchard," he

replied, looking around him, "who is it that asks me this?"

The young woman jumped from the branches of the oak and snatched the bag from his weakened grasp. Opening it, she said, "they are soaked through with water and salt," she said, reaching inside, "but the bears, my friends, will eat them. They can eat anything. The fruit will put me in good stead with them. Trade me this bag of ruined fruit for these two oranges I have."

The boy saw that the dried fruit, now soaked with seawater, would not sustain him. He gazed at the young woman and was struck by her beauty. And in his reverie, he relinquished the bag, trading it for the oranges.

"I warn you," said the young woman, "one is bitter, but the other is sweet. You will not be able to tell which is which. If you are of good heart, your hand will guide you to the healing orange. It will heal your wounds and you can be on your way."

The orange he chose was indeed bitter, but he was famished and delirious from his wounds, and so he fell to devouring it. As he swallowed, the bitterness brought tears to his eyes. They streamed down and fell to his bruises and cuts. To his surprise, the wounds began to heal before his eyes. Weary, he fell asleep beneath the tree.

In the morning he saw that his wounds had healed and that he felt strong enough to be on his way. He looked up into the tree for the young woman, but she was nowhere to be seen. A cloud of sadness passed over his heart. But he gathered himself and followed a footpath into the forest, walking for some distance until the ocean was no longer near to him and all he could hear was silence.

"This is indeed a strange country," he whispered to the silence, and he remembered his father's words of warning that to enter here was to die. "But the trees are speaking in a language that is familiar," he said to reassure himself, "even though I do not know the meaning of their words. And these deep pools in the streams, so clear that I can see down to the gravelly bed, shelter fish that I, versed in the ways of fish, do not know."

Soon he came to a juncture of the main path and a wooden bridge that led over a creek that was full to the brim with dark, fast, roiling water.

"Since I am in a strange land and do not know what lies in either direction, I do not know how to choose," he thought. As if to answer him, a fish crow flew and perched on the bridge railing, calling three times.

"Fish crows have been helpful to me in finding fish in my native land. But what is this crow doing so far from the sea? In any case, I will follow the crow."

The young man began to pass over the bridge.

"Do not look into the obsidian waters, croaked the crow, "Keep your gaze to the path."

"How is it that you speak?" asked the young man, "crows caw, but they do not speak where I come from." But the black bird was already gone to the wind.

The sound of the dark waters lured him, but since crows had never steered him wrong, the boy kept his eyes to the wooden slats of the bridge, even though they were slick with the dark water splashing from below. At the far end of the bridge was a very narrow path. He followed it, but it soon trailed off into nothing but leaf litter and ferns. There were no prints to follow, neither of hoof nor paw nor shoe. The young man grew fearful and was about to turn back to the main path, when he caught sight of a golden glow through the dark trunks of the trees. He was drawn toward the light. When he neared the source of the light, he saw a straw hut in a clearing.

"This will be a good place to rest for the night," he thought, but as he approached the hut to announce himself to anyone who might be inside, a deep growl issued from the edge of the forest:

"Stop!"

The young man turned to see a large bear.

"You are the one who carried the bag of fruit," growled the bear, "Eating the fruit made me and my cubs very ill. Tell me why I should not kill and devour you on the spot?"

"Because the sea runs in my veins," replied the young man cleverly, "and the salt of the sea is what made you ill."

"What is that on your belt?" asked the mother bear. The young man put his hand to the large knife in its leather sheath on his belt. "My father made this knife for me in the year of my birth. He gave it to me in the year of my learning to use words. It has killed and cleaned many fish and helped to feed my village." The knife had been a useful tool for the young man throughout his boyhood, and on occasion protected him from harm as a weapon.

"Give me the knife and I will give you your life," said the bear, "the only way to save yourself is to enter the hut. The knife is your passage."

The young man thought to himself, "if I kill this bear, I can both keep the knife and enter the hut." And he unsheathed the knife slowly, meaning to kill the bear. When he lunged forward, the bear moved quickly aside and raked the young man's thigh with her claws. However, the juice of the bitter orange still flowed in his veins, and so the wound was not fatal. On the ground, the bear loomed above him. The pain of his wound and the juice in his veins caused his eyes to see more deeply into the essence of the bear. In the eyes of the bear, the young man saw, as if in a mirror, an image of the young woman who had dropped from the tree. In his astonishment, he rose to his knees, then laid the knife on the ground at the bear's feet. The bear took the knife into her mouth, turned and headed into the trees. From the dark green of the forest, the young man heard the voice of the bear: "Because of your insolence, I have taken your voice. Search the land beneath this land and if you are lucky, you may retrieve it." The young man attempted to ask the direction of this land, but found that no words would come to his lips.

The young man was alone and cold, and so he entered the hut. His long journey and encounter with the bear left him very hungry. His wound pulsed with pain. He remembered the second orange in his coat pocket, which he peeled and began to eat. The orange was very sweet and delicious, so much so, that he could not stop until he had completely consumed its flesh. As he ate, he heard a voice whispering a name that seemed to be his own, but the sound of it was much older, and it beckoned to him. The voice came from beneath his feet, where he had dropped the peels of the orange. As he looked down, he saw a widening hole, and in the hole, a stairway. Feeling renewed and healed by the sweetness of the orange, he couldn't resist following the stairway down toward the sound of his name. At the very nadir of the stairway, he arrived at a precipice that overlooked a landscape that seemed to stretch without end to the horizon and beyond.

"I am so far from home," he thought, "that I am forgetting

the land of my birth." He tried to say to himself, "I should turn back," but the words would not come to his lips.

As he turned, he saw that the hole from which he had come had vanished. Disoriented, he descended into the broad valley in search of his voice. He climbed its rolling hills, forded rivers, and groped his way through dark forests. Many times he saw wonders, and tried to speak, but the words would not come. Many plants and animals sustained him, but he could not thank them, except with a bow. The pain of his wound from the mother bear came and went, but would not heal.

Late one day, seeking shelter from the cold for the night, the young man climbed up to a cave he had spotted from far below in the valley. As he approached the mouth of the cave, a shadowed figure with an enormous misshapen head appeared, barring his way. As the young man tried to push his way through into the cave the figure threw him to the ground. A furious struggle ensued between them, but after some hours, the young man stood, victorious above the figure, now prone before him on the cave floor. As the light of the setting sun illumined the cave, he saw not a menacing figure but an old man who appeared weak and malnourished. The young man, looking around, saw that there were few provisions, and that a fire that the old man had been tending was sputtering out. He rekindled the fire and gave the man what was left of his food.

"You have questions in your eyes, but it seems that you cannot speak," said the old man weakly, "so I do not know where you come from. I would make you go on your way, but you have shown me kindness. Rest here for the night."

In the morning, as the young man set out again, the old

man took the cloak from around his own shoulders and placed it around the shoulders of the young man. In the pockets of the cloak were seeds.

"Each of these seeds contains a kernel of an old language most have forgotten. It is a language the animals and stones and plants are still speaking. When you learn to speak again, throw the seeds on barren soil and a story will grow."

The young man went on his way thinking that the old man was a little odd, and what use did he have for stories anyway? He soon forgot the encounter as he continued his trek. Finally, many seasons later, feeling tired and despairing that his search would never stop going in circles, he stopped by a boulder larger than himself on the bank of a stream. The pain from his wound made him delirious, but the murmuring of the stream soon soothed him and made him drowsy. The murmur seemed to him like a story he couldn't quite recall. He noticed that it mimicked the beating of his heart. He fell fast asleep leaning against the boulder, and had a dream in which he was a salmon nosing upstream. The current was strong and the swirling eddies buffeted him. But the entire body of the salmon was as a single mind striving upstream. And so, after many moons had come and gone, with one final fierce push, he reached a quiet pool high in the mountains.

In the calm of the high deep pool, the salmon was finally free of the struggle of the current. But after the upstream journey, the salmon felt tired. He slept and dreamt that he had become a hawk soaring over the pool. The hawk circled and soared, spiraling higher and higher. She dropped swiftly, then rose again in a high spiral. From the skies she could see over the vast landscape below. As the moon rose, the hawk plunged to Earth once more and came to rest on a high crag above the pool. She felt tired from her flight. She slept and dreamt that she was a luminous distant star reflecting in the surface of the pool.

The star poured forth light, giving her dark body over, time and again, to fire. But after the passing of time, the star grew tired from the labor of her fiery sacrifice, and she pulled into herself and slept. The star dreamt that she was free of the struggle of fire. The dream became her body flaring outward one final time into countless sparks and particles of light that spread far and wide. The dream of the star traveled far and became stream, hawk, pool, salmon, human, and all forms that have their being.

The man woke on the bank of the stream. Above, in the half-light of dawn, was a star shining steadily. Something like the dance of feathers and wind stirred in him, and he felt it as joy. Something like the play of fin and water surged in him and he knew it to be clarity of intent. The man's feet began to move of their own accord. Each step was a breath born of the marriage of joy and intent. For the first time in his long journey the wound in his thigh gave him no pain.

The man walked and walked, following the stream, until he found himself on the shore of the southern land again. There, he met the woman who had traded him oranges for dried fruit. But he saw that she was no longer young, but ageless. She held out the canteen he had lost long ago.

"Drink," she said.

He drank long and deep. When he finished, he was astonished to hear himself speak again, and when he spoke, his first words were: "What is your name?"

She responded, "I have no name, but I am the name of

everything."

She led him to a boat and the south winds blew and ferried him to an island. Although his eyes were not the eyes of his youth, he slowly came to see that he had come to the place of his birth. The villagers did not recognize him, but they found his stories useful and amusing. Little by little, as the stories were passed from mouth to mouth, the fertility of his homeland grew and the waters flowed cleanly. And so they welcomed him, and he made the village his home until the end of his days. He told stories harvested from his garden where he had planted the old man's seeds, on nights when the distant star grew brightest in the sky.

The Small Song

That stone path you can see from the road,
the one that leads to the wooden bridge,
the one crossing the creek
to where there are no more wars
and even nomads stop wandering;
take a left there
and go until you come to a straw hut
that breathes steadily in the yellow dusk.

It will whisper a small song
that might carry into the next valley;
it might be your older name, the one mountains know.

To enter the hut is to hold your face
next to the warm Earth, to remember
your flesh in a thousand ways. Inside
are the quiet places even the wind can't find.

That stone path you can see from the road,
its forks lead to nowhere you know
but everywhere you've been calling to
from your wild heart.

It forks until there are no forks
where your footfalls become as natural as rain,
in a country where fear has no name.

Appendix

Organizations for Education and Connection

American Teilhard Association

teilharddechardin.org

Explores and shares the insights and cosmic vision of Pierre Teilhard de Chardin through scholarship, artistic expression, and educational programming.

Animas Valley Institute

animas.org

Animas Valley Institute of guided immersions into the mysteries of nature and psyche, including Soulcraft intensives, contemporary vision fasts, and training programs for nature-based soul guides.

Center for Ecozoic Studies

ecozoicstudies.org

Mission is to advance ecology and culture as the organizing principles of societies.

Center for Humans and Nature

humansandnature.org

Mission is to explore and promote human responsibilities in relation to nature — the whole community of life.

Center for the Story of the Universe

storyoftheuniverse.org

A resource site for the work of Brian Thomas Swimme, the Center offers award-winning videos to expand collective consciousness and redirect the current self-destructive trajectory of society towards a vibrant community.

Creation Spirituality Communities

cscommunities.org
Mission is to build community with people who want to integrate sacred Earth and human existence. Based in the vision of theologian Matthew Fox.

DeepTime Network (DTN)

dtnetwork.org
Mission is to orient humanity to an evolving interconnected universe. DTN brings together science, ancient wisdom and the arts inside community to share learning, global conversation, celebration, and action.

The Human Energy Project

humanenergy.io
Explores and shares a new scientific story introducing the Noosphere and Third Story as a source of meaning for future generations in our globalizing world.

Journey of the Universe

journeyoftheuniverse.org
Resource site for the book and film by Mary Evelyn Tucker and Brian Thomas Swimme based in an integrated cosmology and new universe story for our time.

Mosaic Voices

mosaicvoices.org
Founded by storyteller Michael Meade, Mosaic offerings bring the medicine of myth and story in ways that inspire creative imagination

and genuine hope.

Project Regeneration
regeneration.org
Mission is to bring humanity into alignment with the living world in order to end the climate crisis in one generation. It is a response to the urgency of the climate crisis, a growing set of interlocking initiatives that unlock our collective agency.

The Embodied Present Process (TEPP)
embodiedpresent.com
Based on the work of Phillip Shepherd, TEPP provides resources and exercises for getting out of the head and into the present through the body.

The Institute for Educational Studies (TIES)
ties-edu.org
Offers an online Masters in Education in Integrative Learning (IL). IL begins from universal understanding that life on Earth is a derivative of an evolutionary cosmos.

The Work that Reconnects—Joanna Macy
workthatreconnects.org
Helps people around the world discover and experience their innate connections with each other and the self-healing powers of the web of life, transforming despair and overwhelm into inspired, collaborative action.

Yale Forum on Religion and Ecology
fore.yale.edu
Mission is to inform and inspire people to preserve, protect, and restore the Earth community.

Endnotes

1. Pierre Teilhard de Chardin, *The Human Phenomenon*, p. 184.

2. E. F. Schumacher, *Small is Beautiful*, (New York: Harper and Row, 1973), 82.

3. Henry Adams, *Mont-Saint-Michel and Chartres*, (England: The New American Library, 1961), 106.

4. K. Lauren de Boer, "Reinventing Education: An Interview with Matthew Fox," *EarthLight Magazine* Volume.11, No.4 (2001): 16-19.

5. Barry Lopez, *Resistance*, (New York: Alfred A. Knopf, 2004), 138.

6. ibid., 138-139.

7. K. Lauren de Boer, "Watering then Seeds of the Future: An Interview with Michael Meade," *EarthLight Magazine* Vol. 12 No 2 (2002): 5-13.

8. Thomas Berry, *The Great Work* (New York: Bell Tower Press, 1999) 173-174.

9. Mario Luis Rodriguez Cobos, *Silo: Collected Works* (San Diego: Latitude Press, 2003), 118.

10. Matthew Fox, *The Coming of the Cosmic Christ* (New York: Harper and Row Publishers, 1988), 202-203.

11. *The Healing of Trauma*, Gabor Mate. Citing the author Dr. Lewis Mehl-Madrona, a Lakota Sioux.

12. John O'Donohue, *Beauty: the Invisible Embrace*, (New York: Harper Collins, 2004), 33.

13. Carolyn Finney, *Black Faces, White Spaces: Reimagining the Relationship of African Americans to the Great Outdoors*, (Chapel Hill: The University of North Carolina Press, 2014), 55. Finney's book suggests ways in which our culture and the environmental community needs to rethink mistaken notions of race and ecology.

14. See joannamacy.net for more information on her deep ecology and deep time work.

15. Gabor Maté, Interview: "The Myth of Normal: Dr. Gabor Maté on Trauma, Illness, and Healing in a Toxic Culture," Democracy Now, 2022.

16. J. Krishnamurti, "Beauty, Pleasure, Sorrow, and Love," *Ojai Talks*, audiotape, Harper & Row (1989).

17. Robert Burton, *The World of the Hummingbird*, (Richmond Hill, Ontario: Firefly Books, Ltd., 2001).

18. Thomas Berry, *The Dream of the Earth*, (San Francisco: Sierra Club Books, 1988) 137.

19. Thomas Berry, *The Great Work*, p. 13.

20. Originally published in the anthology *Eco-Therapy* by Sierra Club Books (2009) as "Healing and the Great Work."

21. Thomas Berry, "Contemplation and the World Order," *Riverdale Papers*, V (1993), 2.

22. John Daniel, *Common Ground* (Lewiston, ID: Confluence Press, 1989).

23. Phillip Shepherd, "The Elevator and the Bond of Love," *The Embodied Present Process*, video meditation, tepp.life, 2020.

24. Philip Shepherd, "Deepen Into the Security of Your Being," talk at the Embodiment Festival 2024, Embodiment Unlimited, embodiment unlimited.com.

25. D.H. Lawrence, *Selected Poems*, (New York: Penguin Books, 1947), 116.

26. Rainer Maria Rilke, *Collected Poems*, edited and translated by Stephen Mitchell (New York: Vintage Books, 1989) 199, 201.

27. Emily Dickinson, *Collected Poems*, (Philadelphia: Courage Press, 1991) 218.

28. Thomas Berry, *The Great Work* (New York: Bell Tower Press, 1999) 169.

29. K. Lauren de Boer, "The Evolutionary Power of Play: An Interview with Gwen Gordon and Brian Thomas Swimme," *EarthLight Magazine,* Vol. 13 No. 3, Spring, 2003.

30. Derrick Jensen, "Indigenous Soul and the Repair of the World: An interview with Martín Prechtel," *EarthLight Magazine,* Vol. 13 No 1, April, 2001.

31. Suzi Gablik, "The Reenchantment of Art," *New Art Examiner,* December, 1987, 32.

32. The powers Swimme articulates are: Seamlessness, Centration, Allurement, Emergence, Homeostasis, Cataclysm, Synergy, Transmutation, Transformation, Interrelatedness, and Radiance.

33. Brian Thomas Swimme, *Powers of the Universe,* DVD, Center for the Story of the Universe, 2004.

34. Coleman Barks with John Moyne, *The Essential Rumi,* (San Francisco: Harper Collins, 1995) 36.

35. Ursula King, "Rediscovering Fire: Religion, Science, and Mysticism in Teilhard de Chardin," *EarthLight Magazine,* Fall, 2000, 12.

36. Henry David Thoreau, *Walden,* (Ann Arbor: Borders Classics, 2004), 95.

37. Thomas Berry discusses some of these insights into Teilhard's strengths and weaknesses in a videotaped interview, "Teilhard in the Ecological Age," with Jane Blewett in 1980.

38. Primordial flaring forth is a less militaristic reinvention of the term "Big Bang" by Brian Swimme and Thomas Berry in their book *The Universe Story.*

39. Teilhard de Chardin, *Writings in Time of War* (New York: Harper & Row, 1968), 262.

40. Marion Woodman, *Feminine Consciousness, Archetypes, and the Addiction to Perfection,* Better Listen Audiobook, 2021, 27:25.

41. Marion Woodman, ibid., 1:06:30

42. Marion Woodman, *Dreams: Language of the Soul,* Audiobook (Louisville, Colo.: Sound True, 2005).

43. Teilhard de Chardin, *The Heart of Matter,* (San Diego: NewYork: Harcourt Brace & Co., 1976), 51.

44. Teilhard de Chardin, ibid., 71.

45. Marion Woodman, *Dreams: Language of the Soul,* Audiobook (Louisville, Colo.: Sound True, 2005).

46. Matthew Fox, "The Return of the Black Madonna," matthewfox.org, 2006.

47. A version of this essay was published as "Toward a New Cultural Reverie" in *Minding Nature Journal,* Spring 2020.

48. Teilhard de Chardin, *The Human Phenomenon* (Brighton: Portland: Sussex Academic Press, 1999), 3.

49. Teilhard de Chardin, ibid., 3.

50. Silo (Mario Luis Rodriguez Cobos), *Collected Works,* (San Diego: Latitude Press, 2003), 227.

51. Henryk Skolimowski, *The Song of Light,* (Michigan: Creative Fire Press, 2013), 41.

52. Paul Shepard, *Nature and Madness,* (Athens, Georgia: The University of Georgia Press, 1982), 70. Brackets added.

53. Brian Thomas Swimme and Mary Evelyn Tucker, *Journey of the Universe* (New Haven & London: Yale University Press, 2011), 109.

54. Loren Eiseley, *The Unexpected Universe* (New York: Harcourt, Brace & World, Inc., 1964), 193.

55. Teilhard de Chardin, ibid, 195.

56. Teilhard de Chardin, ibid, 188.

57. ibid, 188.

58. Francis Heylighen, "The Third Story," talk given at the Human Energy Project N2 Conference in Berkeley, November, 2023.

59. Teilhard de Chardin, *The Human Phenomenon* (Brighton: Portland: Sussex Academic Press, 1999), 190.

60. Teilhard de Chardin, ibid.,189.

61. Rainer Maria Rilke, *Collected Poems* translation Stephen Mitchell (New York: Vintage International, 1989), 201-202.

62. Coleman Barks, (translated by), "The Dream that Must Be Interpreted," *The Essential Rumi* (Harper San Francisco: 1995), 113.

63. Brian Thomas Swimme and Mary Evelyn Tucker, *Journey of the Universe* (New Haven & London: Yale University Press, 2011), 10-11.

64. ibid., 118.

65. Thomas Berry, *The Great Work* (New York: Bell Tower Press, 1999), 196. The final chapter of Berry's book describes moments of grace in the evolutionary story.

66. Teilhard de Chardin, *The Human Phenomenon* (Brighton: Portland: Sussex Academic Press, 1999), 197.

About the author

K. Lauren de Boer is an essayist, poet, and com-poser with a special interest in landscape and the human imagination. As Executive Editor of *EarthLight* magazine in the 1990s and 2000s, he played a pioneering role in fostering dialogue on the interconnected themes of ecology, spirituality, and cosmology. His essays and poetry on Earth, creativity, and spirit have appeared in a number of magazines and book anthologies.

He has a published a *Pocket Guide to Northern California Oaks*, a collection of 95 poems, *Where It Comes From*, and has a new collection forthcoming in 2025, *Feather Wonder*, based on his love affair with birds.

Some of his writing and piano compositions reside at terravitabooks.net (TerraVita Media) and his music videos can be found at his YouTube channel. He currently lives in the Viera Creek watershed of the Shasta Bioregion, Turtle Island.